STORIES
OF THE
BUDDHA

STORIES
OF THE
BUDDHA

Being Selections from the Jātaka

Translated and Edited by
Caroline A. F. Rhys Davids

DOVER PUBLICATIONS, INC., New York

Published in Canada by General Publishing Company, Ltd., 30 Lesmill Road, Don Mills, Toronto, Ontario.

This Dover edition, first published in 1989, is an unabridged and unaltered republication of the work as published by the Frederick A. Stokes Company, New York, n.d. [1929]. (This was the first American edition of the work originally published by Chapman & Hall, Ltd., London, 1929, as Volume 3 in the series "The Treasure House of Eastern Story.")

Manufactured in the United States of America
Dover Publications, Inc., 31 East 2nd Street, Mineola, N.Y. 11501

Library of Congress Cataloging-in-Publication Data

Tipitaka. Suttapiṭaka. Khuddakanikāya. Jātaka. English. Selections.
    Stories of the Buddha : being selections from the Jataka / translated and edited by Caroline A.F. Rhys Davids.
        p.   cm.
    Reprint. Originally published: New York : F.A. Stokes Co., 1929.
    ISBN 0-486-26149-2
    1. Gautama Buddha—Pre-existence. I. Davids, Caroline A. F. Rhys (Caroline Augusta Foley Rhys), 1857–1942. II. Title.
BQ1462.E5D36 1989
294.3'823—dc20   89-35688
                                                                                        CIP

CONTENTS

Introduction   *page* xi
The Sandy Road Jataka (No. 2)   1
The Divine Nature Jataka (No. 6)   5
The Faggot-Bringer Jataka (No. 7)   11
The Banyan-Deer Jataka (No. 12)   14
The Dead Men's Food Jataka (No. 18)   23
The Cane-Drinking Jataka (No. 20)   26
The Antelope Jataka (No. 21)   29
The Bhoja-Thoroughbred Jataka (No. 23)   31
The Nestling Jataka (No. 31)   34
The Mosquito Jataka (No. 44)   43
The Park-Spoiling Jataka (No. 46)   45
The Unwise Folk Jataka (No. 50)   47
The Great Silava-King Jataka (No. 51)   50
The Bar of Gold Jataka (No. 56)   54
The Monkey-Lord Jataka (No. 57)   58
The Blindfold Jataka (No. 62)   61
The Hard-to-know Jataka (No. 64)   68
The Apronfull Jataka (No. 67)   71
The Saketa Jataka (Nos. 68 and 237)   73
The Gate of Weal Jataka (No. 84)   76
The King's Lesson Jataka (No. 151)   78
The Gagga Jataka (No. 155)   82
The Vulture Jataka (No. 164)   85
The Falcon Jataka (No. 168)   88

vii

CONTENTS

The Advantage in Morality Jataka (No. 190) *page* 90

The Gem-Thief Jataka (No. 194)   93

The Cloudhorse Jataka (No. 196)   97

The Shoes Jataka (No. 231)   101

The One-Course Jataka (No. 238)   103

The Tawny King Jataka (No. 240)   105

The Guttila Jataka (No. 243)   108

The Judas-Tree Parable Jataka (No. 248)   116

The Decayed Well Jataka (No. 256)   118

The Crab Jataka (No. 267)   121

The Hundred-Feathered Jataka (No. 279)   125

The Sujata Jataka (No. 306)   128

The Hare Jataka (No. 316)   131

The Kanavera and Indriya Jataka (Nos. 318 and 423)   136

The Sujata (well-born) Jataka (No. 352)   143

The Karandiya Jataka (No. 356)   146

The Great Ape Jataka (No. 407)   149

The Chanda-Fairy Jataka (No. 485)   154

The Ummadanti Jataka (No. 527)   159

The Six(-rayed) Tusker Jataka (No. 514)   167

The Kusa Jataka (No. 531)   181

The Sama Jataka (No. 540)   206

The Nimi Jataka (No. 541)   221

Index   241

NOTE ON THE FRONTISPIECE

THE photograph is of one of the many bas-reliefs still to be seen on the ruined Bharhut or Bharahat Stupa, some way south of Allahabad, and which have been identified, in fact are inscribed as, Jātaka scenes. It is the story, given in this volume, of the Banyan Deer. As is usual, three episodes in the story are crowded in: the deer being shot at by the king; the Bodhisat-deer sacrificing himself for the doe; the same deer preaching to the king, " sitting " while his disciple stands reverently. The bas-reliefs are ascribed to the third century B.C.

INTRODUCTION

THE collection of about 550 stories, entitled "Jătăkă," or "The Jatakas,"[1] is included in the second of the threefold Pali (Buddhist) Canon, known as the Pĭtăkăs. It was first published in roman character in the excellent critical edition compiled by the Danish scholar, Victor Fausböll: London, 1877-1896. "About 550" is not very precise, but whereas, in the collection, a few stories are just duplicates, a few others consist, under one title, of two, three or more stories, and hence "about 550" is near enough. The appeal of the stories being wide, and their specific framework also of great interest, a translation was felt to be a desideratum. The first two volumes were associated on their title-page with the name of my husband as translator, and in 1880 he produced *The Buddhist Birthstories*, Vol. I, published in Trübner's Oriental Series, London. In this there were only the first forty stories, but preceding these was a translation of the long introductory "talk," entitled Nidāna-kathā, "Talk on the Origin," or "on the Connected Basis." Thereafter he handed over the completion of his work, actually the entire collection, to the eminent Indologist, Edward Cowell, that it might be more quickly accomplished by a group of workers. Even so, and after many years' interval, it was a matter of ten years more, 1897-1907, that was needed for the publication, in six volumes, of the 550 stories, the translators being Messrs. (Robert, now Lord) Chalmers, Rouse, Francis and Neil, Cowell himself

[1] Literally, " born-thing," " happened-thing."

xi

also contributing a portion. This translation, exclusive of the Nidana-katha, was produced by the Cambridge University Press. My husband's translation of the Nidana-katha, with his critical discussion on the nature and history of the Jatakas as canonical material, and on the problem of the migration of some of them into or from other countries, has been reissued lately in the Broadway Translation Series (London: Routledge's).

To publish a selection from so great a whole, of materials so diversely attractive, has appealed to purveyors of books ere now. Two of such known to me are that from the Cambridge University Press (1916), of 114 stories, selected by Messrs. H. T. Francis and E. J. Thomas, and that in *Die Märchen der Weltliteratur*, compiled by Mrs. E. Lüders (E. Diederich: Jena, 1921), entitled " Buddhistiche Märchen," to the number of 70. Yet one more is a modest volume of selected stories by my friend, Miss Marie Shedlock, intended for telling to children: *Buddhist Birthstories*: Routledge, 1910. To this my husband wrote a preface, in which he shares, with those of us who have it not, his memory of the telling of the stories by the monks of Ceylon to the people on warm full-moon holy-day nights. The stories are naturally told in Singhalese, but the verses will be chanted in Pali, and then turned into Singhalese. I am not so fortunate as to have experienced the keeping up, down to the present, of this venerable custom many centuries old. But my students from that island are capable of intoning for me Jataka verses in a curious chant, strongly suggestive of responses or scripture as chanted in Catholic churches, *plus* a touch of Oriental querulousness in the cadences.

The present selection is not a reproduction of

any of the foregoing, either in choice of stories, or in its English. In choosing, I have been guided by a different motive. In translating, I have gone to the original Pali, and have kept closer to it. To do this, I have not been careful, in the verses, to secure scansion or rhyme, or to try to make, of what is seldom more than doggerel, poetic expression.[1] And even my prose at times limps uncouthly. But the reader may read with the assurance that what he reads is at least verbally in the Pali not less, and sometimes more, than in previous translations. The one liberty taken with the text has been here and there condensation, especially excision of repetitions. Pali compilations for the first three or four centuries took birth in oral shape, and repetitions and refrains were probably aids to memory. And they *went on growing, orally.* Thus the whole Jataka collection, as we now have it, is like a great petrified tree. Committed early in our era to writing, it became practically petrified. But till then, as it grew, year after year, in the memories and mouths of generations of story-tellers, it changed, as when that tree put forth new growth every spring. Had it not petrified somewhere about the beginning of our era it would by now be in many details a different collection.

The fact of these changes is betrayed in the collection as it has come down to us. Here and there it would seem a whole story may have dropped out; it is cited by name in the collection, but is no longer there. Here and there in the collection are stories occurring elsewhere in the scriptures—such

---

[1] Among the few cases of doggerel rising suddenly into poetry one is in the verses on p. 180 below, of the Chaddanta:
" This world-old faring, high and low,
This long procession of the nights
On which the sun doth not yet set," etc.

is the Kinsukôpămă Jataka[1]—on the other hand several Jatakas are in the older scriptures, which either never were, or it may be no longer are, in the Jataka Book.[2] And the changes in details and in diction which have " grown up in " and partly transformed the stories will be legion. In diction we no longer find certain stereotyped phrases, used, concerning everyday activities, in what are held to be the older corpus of the scriptures—that called Vinaya and Dhamma. In the details of narrative we find frequent reference to *writing of letters*, a procedure never met with in that older body of records. Countries, too, emerge in the stories for the first time, such as Ceylon and Kashmir, never met with in the older books.

And there has not only been " growth " of this sort going on; there have also been readjustments, editorial efforts to cobble stories with their " moral " in verses, where there had come lapses in memory. or wilful misplacements. The older of the two Ceylon " Chronicles," The Dīpavamsa, composed during the fifth century A.D., testifies that the important Mahā-sanghika school of Vesāli, in refusing to recognise certain accretions to the oral records, " rejecting some portions of the Jatakam, made (*sic*) different ones." This is said to have occurred as early as the first century after the founder's death. The other Ceylon " Chronicle," the Mahāvamsa, about a century younger, embellished the account by telling of a revision of the records carried out at Vesali to undo the changes. This is very possible; nevertheless neither the Dipavamsa, nor the yet older Vinaya record of the Mahāsanghika " schism " make any reference to such a work of revision. Both

[1] See *Kindred Sayings*, vol. iv, p. 24: P.T.S. ed., Mr. F. L. Woodward's translation.
[2] See Rhys Davids, *Buddhist India*, p. 194 f.

Chronicles, however, testify to the important revision undertaken at Patna, a century and a half
later, in the reign of the Emperor Asoka. It is very
possible that there, as part of the colossal labour of
reducing to orderly consistency, and what is more,
to the new orthodoxy of the majority of the editors,
the oral records of a bookless world, it was sought
to fit together verses with story in many jumbled
Jatakas. That the effort was not always successful
students of the Jataka know.[1]

There is no evidence that, amid these many
vicissitudes, the verse portions were partly lost, so
that we never get a story completely told in verse.
The Indian would appear to have liked his minstrel,
his ballad-monger, to present a story in mixed prose
and verse, much as the music drama of Europe has
approved of a presentation, in which after some
talk or some " recitative," with or without action,
an actor comes forward and sings an " aria." Such
arias are the Jataka verses, still chanted, as I have
said, when a monk is the teller, and chanted very
likely with accompanying lute[2] when a layman
narrated. The verses will have suffered less change
than the story, because of their metrical form. Their
verbal form is now and then archaic relatively to
that of the prose. But archaic forms are deliberately
chosen by poets, as e.g.

Yet now I charge thee, quickly go again,
As thou art lief and dear, and do the thing
I bad thee, watch, and lightly bring me word,[3]

[1] A detailed study of the problems of Jataka history may be
read in the new revised English translation of Dr. M. Winter-
nitz's *History of Indian Literature*, vol. ii, Calcutta, 1928.

[2] *Buddhistische Märchen.* Introduction by Dr. Lüders, p. xi.

[3] Tennyson, of the nineteenth century, using idioms of an
earlier English.

and hence we may not build history on that. But that the stories lead up to, and find a sort of seal and consummation in the verse is seen in the way they are introduced, often severally by the prose, thus: " Then the boy, asking . . . said the first verse . . . then the father telling him . . . said the second verse."[1]

Then with respect to my selection, and the motive determining it: my motive has not been, as in one of such compilations, the joy and growth of the child-mind, nor, as in another, to get together the stories most interesting as stories and as folk-lore material,[2] nor, as in another, the attempt to bring out such as appear to be relatively the older, simpler types of the *märchen* or fairy tale.[3] This has all been done and done excellently. To a limited extent the stories in this volume occur in the other selections, but for the most part they will not be found in any selection. My motive has been to show that, in the Jataka Book, " the man " is presented in a way in which he is not presented in any other compilation in the world, And he is so presented because the Jataka is not just Eastern or Indian, but is also Buddhist. Many of the stories, perhaps most, are, as Indian, older than the time when the Sakya, that is, the Buddhist movement, began. Some are very possibly imported into India. Some are very likely of Buddhist invention. But all have been adopted into the oldest known tradition of Buddhist teaching; all have been set in a specifically Buddhist frame; to all has been prefaced the Buddhist Talk of the Origin, and all still are taught, year in year out, as a mild popular religious, or at least moral,

[1] Below, p. 103.
[2] Jakata Tales, Francis and Thomas, p. 10.
[3] *Buddhistische Märchen*, p. 11.

xvi

propaganda by Buddhist officials. If, then, the stories are to be shown as not just Eastern or Indian folklore or fairylore, but as Buddhist popular propaganda it is necessary that they be presented to the reader in Buddhist guise, i.e., as Jatakas. On this account I have thought fit to give a few stories in full Jataka garb, rather than double the number shorn of that garb.

The full Jataka garb is this: the story itself, technically called " story of the past," is introduced by an account of some event alleged to have just happened in the little inner world of the " Order " (Sangha). This is technically called " story of the present." The teller of the " story of the past," who is always presented as the founder himself of the Sakya (i.e., Buddhism), is then made to remember some similar act or speech, in the dim past, of the chief person in the story of the present. This he tells. He then, in concluding, " assigns " this chief person, together it may be with one or two others, to the story of the past, as having had the recorded experience in a former life.

Sometimes the pair of stories are in so many words just repetitions the one of the other. Certain persons, X, Y, Z, appear in similar bodies, with similar minds, in similar circumstances. As to what we call " character "—what they do in a given situation—either they are no better, or they are better, or they are worse now than then. But the very persons are presented as practically identical: thus A was then X, B (whom you know now as she) was Y, but Z was just I myself (whom you now see). This is how the stories end.

That they do so is a feature of high significance. No student of the history of Buddhist ideas can afford to neglect it. I will try briefly to show why not.

In the introductory "Talk" to which allusion has been made, we are given, not such an unprogressive mixture of rebirths of the Founder, the "Teacher," or Blessed One, as in the Jatakas themselves, but a quite different legend, presenting the Bodhisat, or future "Buddha" in about a dozen rebirths, at long intervals of time, but always as a distinguished man, whether as king, of men, devas or snakes, or as warrior, or as anchorite, or as brahman. In these he is shown successively developing growth, not in bodily or mental attainments, but in specifically spiritual advance—an advance I should call, in the Indian sense of the word, in the "man," in man-growth. He is shown as graduating in ten "perfections" (*pāramitās*), constituting the perfect man. And in the earliest rebirth included in the legend, his definite point of departure in the long Wayfaring in the Better is told as an act of will, a resolve. There was in Indian tongues no word for "will"; the word used is the makeshift: he made *abhinīhāram*—that is, a "super-bringing-out," a self-projection, so to speak, a vow that one day he, "having become supremely wise (literally, awake), might build a Dhamma-ship (a ship of the Right), and so cause the multitude to cross over the ocean of Wayfaring, and then (himself) pass utterly away."

The talk in the opening sentences refers to all the Jatakas, naming the first, as told by "our Teacher and Leader" about himself during the long period in which he wayfares "desirous of crossing over the world as guide, after maturing in the infinite wisdom-complex." Taking then the Jatakas with their introduction, it is scarcely an overstatement to say that, for all the much foolishness we find in them, the oddities, the inconsistencies, the many distortions in ideals and in the quest of them, they are collectively the greatest epic, in literature, of the Ascent of Man, the greatest ballad-book on the theme that man willing the better becomes the better. In this book we are given—crudely, childishly though it be—the life history of the individual man; not as type of a tribe or race, but as a human unit, with a long life history of his own, within and distinct from the history of tribe or race. What he was passing through in those many lives is often referred to collectively as " becoming " (*bhava*). The stories show that the given stage of becoming is not always for the better. In some the Bodhisat is made to appear, as man, a very scoundrel—an impenitent thief, an adulterer, and worst of all, a king hiring a seducer—much worse as such a man than he usually appears as animal. It is strange that such stories— they are sampled in this volume—should have been ever included by compilers and retained by editors.

But it is possible that the compiler was keener in storymongering than in piety. (Love of truth, of course, has no say in the matter.) In the Nimi Jataka,[1] where the journey of the personally conducted visitor to purgatory and to paradise invites comparison with Christian and Mahommedan beliefs on the subject, specific forms of punishment for all those three crimes are mentioned. We have therefore no reason to judge that, even when perpetrated by a king, they were less heinous then than now. In one case of the Bodhisat as bandit, a curious apology for him has been inserted,[2] but not in the case of the other two wicked actions.

And as to the whole lot of stories of Bodhisat as monkey, deer or other beast, we are here, in my judgment, up against a popular method of giving moral powder in a dose of jam that is, as serious

[1] Page 221.   [2] Page 126, cf. 138.

religious teaching—of something that really ever happened—quite inconceivable in the faith, let alone knowledge of a man of the calibre of Gotama called the Buddha. Pythagoras and Empedokles may very possibly, one or both of them, have derived from the East the notion of metempsychosis as breaking down the barrier between animal and human rebirth, but our vague knowledge of both men does not warrant us in saying more than that they played with the notion, rather than taught it seriously. In Gotama we have a bigger proposition: a man inspired with a new and positive message for the many concerning man's life and destiny. It was not his business to play around the might-have-been, the may-be. His concern was with something which for the many was new and at the same time true. Had rebirth of man as animal been in that new and true message, he would have uttered it as that. It is true that, in a discourse here and there in the books of " Suttas," words concerning possible rebirth as animal are imputed to him. But they are discourses which bear, with practically all the rest, the stamp of ecclesiastical compilation; there is no good evidence that they were very words of the Founder or of his co-workers.

But, discounting the few stories of a stage in the Bodhisat's life-career for the worse, the vast majority show him as either choosing in his own actions the better way, or at least as onlooker commending the better way in others.

That the individual man, and not the race only, requires ages of life-spans in which to consummate is not, or is not yet, accepted by us. And as Indian tradition it is not a little wonderful that it should be accepted by Buddhists, who of all religionists might seem to be the last likely to do so. We might, in the light of their development in ecclesiastical dogma, have looked to see monks rejecting the Indian belief in rebirth, as being a vindication of the doctrine they came to condemn, of the persistence of the very, the individual man. On the contrary, they not only accepted it, but raised it in power to a uniformity of nature, a natural law. With them it was no longer a question of how rebirth might be won by the sacrifice, the word-ritual, the priest; it was man's natural, inevitable fate to be somewhere, somehow reborn, not once, but indefinitely often.

How they reconciled, or deemed they had reconciled, this with their coming to deny in plain words that the individual did transmigrate cannot be told here. But in a nutshell the problem in their position is this: For India, man as immortal was man as godlike, man as of God; or, as it was worded, " Thou art THAT : finest essence, world-soul, the Real, Atman.' But as a fact man, even the very man, was a changing fleeting weak creature, and so, ungodlike. So the Buddhists saw him. But here in the Jatakas we are shown one and the same man winning his slow, long-drawn-out toilsome way upward, yet in curve and zigzag, from beast to man, from man bad to man better, emerging finally as one, a mighty lover and helper of men, who was gradually deemed to have been not man only but very God-in-man. Here was a triumph over both the Indian ideal of the unchanging Divine who is the Real in man, and the Buddhist doctrine of the man as not-divine (*an-Atman*).

Here it may be said: " Yes, but the Jataka name of that man " Bodhisat " (Buddha-to-be) was but a label for an ever-changing complex. And the similes of the all-but-canonical book *Questions of*

King Milinda—late and medieval similes—will be trotted out: of the light transmitted from candle to new wick, the butter evolved from milk, the mangoes from seed. As if these merely physical similes afforded any safe analogies, any sure guide to that other unique world of the real, the spiritual man, whom we should valuate as contemplator, not to be identified with the contemplated; whom we should reckon as valuer, not to be merged in the thing valued. The earlier Pali books of the " Canon " have nothing to say in terms of these quibbles, saving only the equally clumsy one of the chariot as fit analogy to the man, *when* the man has come to be reckoned as merely body and mind. The earlier books make the Founder, the so-called Buddha, say of himself, when these birth stories are told as actual memories of his : " 'I ' was then X "; " I was then ' Y ' ". There is never a word from him— " all-knowing one ":—" the complex that you now call ' Me ' was then the different complex I tell you of: ' X ' or ' Y.' ' I ' . . . ' I ' . . . how emphatic he often was with his ' aham ' . . . ' aham '! "

The Jataka tradition of bygone stories told as real memories is probably entirely factitious, and belongs to the cult we call Buddhology. But it was expressed in stories told for their edification to a story-loving people. And in that it has ever maintained the continuity of the one very man through many " lives," it has in its teaching something that is far nearer to the original Sakya message than all the dogmatics of the Sangha. The Sangha or " Church " merged that message into its own changed and changing values. And these, in the matter of the very man's reality, we see at their worse in the Milinda, and at their worst in the works of Buddhaghosa. But in the Birthstories we have a treasury of teaching for the Many, for Everyman. And Everyman wants a religion about " the man," not about ideas in a wordy abstract way. He wants in his religion to hear about life, about the worlds, about man and the unseen. He does not usually suffer gladly the values of the learned, the mandate of the pundit.

Here perhaps we see the reason for the religious value, curious otherwise to us, which the Buddhist church or Sangha has ever attached to a constant flow of Jataka teaching. It would almost seem as if they found herein a compensating value for the shrunken artificial picture of the superman or arahan, as presented in the less popular, the monastic ideal.

If this be so, we may see some justification in the agelong and still persisting zest showed for Jataka teaching. When this is valued as just " stories with a moral," we can respect such zest as little as we should that of Christian teachers who concentrated mainly on recitations from the book of Proverbs. For apart from the really great theme, the ground-wave, the vital thread, which makes this *potpourri* into a unity, it wavers much in its standards of spiritual or ethical excellence. There is in it no very clear ideal of what constitutes " weal " in the worthiest sense. There is a great deal about wisdom considered as superior cunning, about wisdom as practical efficiency. There is a great deal about worldly success as layman or as ascetic—either may be so called in India. But the highest achievement in that " weal " or " well " (" good " is a stodgy word), which it is of the very nature of the real " man," the *ātman*, to seek, does not appear to be much in the thoughts of the compilers. Yet this highest aim (*artha, attha*) was a very present thing for the thoughtful in India from very early times.

It may be said this cannot be maintained in view
of the fact, that leaving the world is so frequent a
feature in the stories, both of the present and the
past. But then I am not prepared to concede that
to leave the world is for the most part either the
accomplishment of a man's weal, or a progress towards it. To believe this is one of the great delusions
of mankind in its efforts towards the better.

And herein, so interwoven is the monastic with
the saner human ideal—the ideal as I believe of the
original Sakya gospel—the stories by no means
always advocate monastic aspiration. For instance,
here and there constant love between man and
woman is told of, and is in no way belittled. This is
the guiding motive in the Kusa Jataka. Here it is
amusing to note the jar between the monkish story
of the present and the imported unmonkish story of
the past. Whereas in the former, woman is held up
as the very bane of man, in the latter woman is
shown, not only as sagacious manager and as regent,
but also as the very inspiration and incentive to the
man to overcome physical and professional impedi-
ments and to test and draw out his will and endurance,
finally as the woman's husband winning, not ruin
but success and happiness. Yet because the West as
yet sees in the original Sakya gospel a religion of
monks for monks—and this indeed is what it grew
to be—Professor Lüders, in his interesting introduction, finds it " somewhat strange " that a Bodhisat should figure as the constant lover.[1]

Woman in fact—albeit in the Hinayana Buddhism
of the Canon she may not be Bodhisat—plays in
the Jataka as many parts as does the man, and is
credited with both will and capacity in many forms
of activity. She appears as governing whether it be

[1] *Buddhistische Märchen*, p. xiii.

husband, son, daughter-in-law, or kingdom; she mothers the man as the weaker; he admits he is unable to understand her (so much the worse for his wisdom[1]); she saves his life;[2] she—"the false one" —by the power of a true word brings divine aid to his rescue; she chooses her mate;[3] and, in that same strangely jumbled Jataka, the Nestling, she persists in taking part in work for the public good. But to conclude:

When we shall come to grasp, in the Sakya gospel, the figure of the Way aright—the figure for man's will and man's life as a whole—in which the original message was first taught, we may still appreciate much in the Jatakas as just stories; but not unless we are mindful of the long wayfaring of the individual, to which they are made to point as necessary even for the best, shall we appreciate the religious purpose they were made to serve. Mindful in this way, it is not easy for us now to be. The swing in current thought is running strong on the race, on the whole, not on the individual, in whose worth alone the greater worth of the whole can be looked for. The history of what is specifically Indian thought lies in this—that it is the man, not men, that matters. No other people's ancient literature, I believe, has called the very " Me," the very " You," (not the body, not the mind) the " Man " (" purūsa," " puggāla "). We indeed are far from doing so. Man's body, we say, man's mind, and then, as if we had a third entity, we say " man's soul "— man's wraith! Thus the Indian point of view is not caught. In Buddhism the Indian point of view came to be rejected. But the Birthstories had at the heart of them the ejected " man," not just the complex of body and mind, but their owner and their user.

[1] Pages 67-69.   [2] Pages 72, 95, 121, and 158.   [3] P. 42.

And pulsing at the heart of them, not as just Eastern stories, but as " birthstories," is the message of not one, but countless, opportunities given to each man whereby he may grow and become in virtue of what and how he has willed and wrought.

This is what I meant above as to the high significance, in the history of Buddhist ideas, of the Jatakas being so presented as to show the *survival*, through many lives, *of the individual*, the while the scholastic teaching explicitly denies it. The orthodox explanation of this " jolt," from the days of the Commentators till now, is to say, " The Buddha had two ways of teaching—one for the many, with use of terms in a merely popular sense, and one for the more thoughtful, in which those same terms: the " man " (self, soul), the " woman," " I," " you," were rated, just like " house," " chariot," as merely labels for what did not as entity really exist. As to this maligning of that great Helper of men, the Founder of the Sakya gospel, I will here only draw attention to the interesting allusion in two of the stories in this selection, where it is said " No Bodhisat ever has the teacher-fist (now open, now closed); he teaches all he knows."[1] But this is just what he is recorded as saying of himself when not Bodhisat, but " Buddha "; and it is among his last earnest sayings: " I have taught with no inner, no outer: mine is not the teacher-fist."[2]

It may be that on these matters and unexpectedly we may in the Jatakas find something of " What India has to teach us." The man who in the last generation chose that wise title for a well-known discourse, found in them no such lesson.

[1] Pages 101, 110.

[2] *Buddhist Suttas*, S.B.E. xi, p. 36; *Dialogues of the Buddha*, ii, p. 107.

The man who first made English readers acquainted with the Birthstories also found it not.

Will the next writer on the subject see beneath the " motley " of the Jataka, which for a treasury of folklore is " the only wear," the theme which constitutes its real significance—its real significance not for one elect man alone, but for every human being?

I see, look you, myself:
E'en as I wished, so have I come to be.[1]

Hard is it now for readers of Buddhism to realize all that the central figure of ' life, as any one man's wayfaring through worlds to a Goal,' meant for the early followers of Gotama! That figure of the WAY has been much shoved aside as less than central, and weakened as to its main lesson, by ethical analysis. The more significant is its reverberating with its original force in Jatakas Nos. 1 and 2, these being, in Buddhist reckoning, the most important of the collection. Both are about wayfaring in the desert, and both show the Way as a great Adventure, calling for wise choice and dauntless will. And here we can understand how loyal followers came to call their great Founder " Lord of the Caravan."

C. A. F. RHYS DAVIDS.

[1] Page 53.

STORIES
OF THE
BUDDHA

THE SANDY ROAD JATAKA

(*Vannupatha-jātaka*)

"UNWEARIED digging . . ."—This lesson the Blessed One taught while living at Sāvatthi. About what? About a monk who gave up effort.

It is said that, the Tathâgata residing at Sāvatthi, a man of the Sāvatthi families went to the Jetavana and heard the Teacher teaching the Right.[1] Pleased in mind and seeing the danger of sense-desires, and being now a five-yearer since his ordination, and having learnt two Summaries and trained himself in method of insight, he received from the Teacher a subject of exercise which appealed to his mind, and entering the forest he passed the rainy season striving. But he was unable to bring forth either aura or after-image. Then this occurred to him: "Four (types of) men have been taught by the Teacher; among these I ought to become of the highest grade. There is, methinks, for me in this birth neither Way nor Fruit. What shall I make of forest-life? Going back to the Teacher I will live contemplating the supremely beautiful Buddha-body, listening to the honeyed teaching of the Dhamma." And he went back to the Jetavana.

His companions and messmates said: "Reverend, you took an exercise from the Teacher, saying 'I will work at recluseship.' Now you are back again and going about in the enjoyment of society. What then? Have you won the top of a religieux' duties; are you become a not-rebirth-er?"

"Reverends, I have got neither Way nor Fruit; I am to become one of the 'incapable men.' I

---

[1] Dhamma. Co-extensive in Buddhism with "religion," "that which ought to be."

am come back because I have given up effort."
" There is no reason, Reverend, in what you have
done, in giving up effort when you had left the
world in the religion of a Teacher mighty in effort.
Come, we will show you to the Tathâgata." And
taking him they went to the Teacher. Seeing them
he said : " Monks, you are come bringing a monk who
is unwilling. What has happened to him ?" "Reverend
sir, this monk, having left the world in such an away-
leading religion and working at recluseship, is returned
having given up effort." Then the Teacher said : " Is
it true, monk, that you have given up effort ?" " It is
true, Blessed One." " How comes it, monk, that when
you have left the world in such a religion you should
not be known as either of little desires, or contented,
or secluded, or of strenuous effort, but have given up
effort ? Was it not you who were full of effort in bygone
days ? Was it not on account of what you did alone,
that when five hundred carts were in a sand-desert,
men and oxen obtained water and were made well ?
Why have you given up effort now ? "

Thereat that monk was encouraged. But when they
heard that saying, the monks begged the Blessed One :
" Reverend sir, that this monk is now lost to effort is
clear to us, but what you say he did in the past is hidden
from us ; only to your all-knowing knowledge is it clear.
Tell us this matter." " Well then, monks, listen ! "
And the Blessed One, calling up in them mindfulness,
made clear what through rebirth[1] was hidden.

In the past, when Brahmadatta was reigning at
Benares, the Bodhisat, taking rebirth in the family
of the leader of a caravan, had come of age and went
about doing trade with five hundred carts. He one
day was passing through a sand-desert of sixty
leagues. In the desert the sand was so fine that when

---

[1] *Bhava*, lit. "becoming."

2

grasped with the fist it did not stay in the hand; from sunrise it became hot as a heaped-up fire—no man could walk on it. Hence they who passed through it took oil and wood and rice in their carts and travelled by night, placing at sunrise the carts in a circle and spreading an awning on top, and after a timely meal passed the day sitting in the shade. At sunset they ate supper and, when the ground was become cool, yoked the carts and went on. The going was like sea-going: it was necessary to get a " land-pilot "; he brought the caravan through by his knowledge of the stars.

On that occasion, too, the caravan-leader was travelling by this method through that desert. And when they had gone fifty-nine leagues he said: " Now in one night we shall pass out of the desert." So after supper he had all the wood thrown away, and with the carts harnessed he went forward. The land-pilot had spread a cushion on the leading cart, and lay down watching the stars in the sky and would be saying, " Go forward this way." But, having gone for a long time without sleep, he was weary and fell asleep, and was unaware that the oxen had turned round and were going the way they had come. The oxen went on all night. Towards dawn the land-pilot awaked and, looking at the stars, said: " Turn the carts, turn! " As they turned the carts and made up the line, the dawn rose up, the men saying, " This is just where we camped yesterday! We have lost wood and water; now we are lost! " Loosing the carts and placing them in a circle and making the awning above, they lay down grieving, each by his own cart.

The Bodhisat thinking " If I give up effort all will be lost," early while it was yet cool looked around, and seeing a patch of dabba grass he thought:

3

" These grasses will have come up because there is water oozing beneath." And, taking a spade, he made them dig in that spot. They dug for sixty cubits. Digging thus far a spade of the diggers struck a rock, and at its striking they gave up all effort. But the Bodhisat, thinking " Beneath this rock there must be water," got down, and standing on the rock, he bent his ear and listened for a sound, and he heard the sound of water flowing beneath. Hearing it, he came up and said to a boy-attendant: " Tāta, if you give up effort we shall all be lost. Do not you give up effort. Take this hammer, get down into the hole and strike on that rock." He obeyed, and though all stood by with effort given up, he not giving up went down and struck the rock. The rock split in the middle and fell below and remained no longer keeping down the stream. And a spout of water rose up as high as a palm tree. All drank and bathed. They chopped up their spare axles, cooked rice and ate, made the oxen eat, and when the sun set, they set up a flag by the waterhole and went whither they wished. They sold the goods at double and fourfold profit, and with wares returned to their homes. So living their life long they went according to their deeds. And the Bodhisat working merit in giving and the like went according to his deeds.

The Rightly Enlightened then said this verse:
"In sandy desert digging never tired,
  in thoroughfare 'twas there they water found.
  So the wise man with effort and with strength
  untiring (works till) he finds peace of heart."

The Teacher joined on the series and assigned the Jataka: "Then the boy-attendant who did not give up effort was this monk who has given up effort; the others were the Buddha-company, but the caravan-leader was just I."

THE DIVINE NATURE JATAKA

(*Deva-dhamma-jātaka*)

"THEY who are modest and discreet."—This the Blessed One told while living at the Jetavana about a monk of many goods. It is said that a land-owner living at Sāvatthi left the world on the death of his wife. So doing he had a hermitage made for his own use and a fire-room and a store-house. When ordained he had this filled with butter and rice and the like; he then as monk sent for his slaves and had what he liked prepared for his food. And in monk-requisites he was richly equipped, clothing himself one way by night, another by day. And he dwelt on the outskirts of the monastery.

One day, when he had taken out clothes and bedding and spread them in the hermitage to dry, monks from the country on more than a day's tour and seeking a lodging came to his hermitage, and seeing the clothes, asked: " Whose are these? " He said, " Mine, reverends." " Reverend, this upper robe and that one, this undercloth and that one and the bedding—is all just yours? " " Yes, mine." " Reverend, three cloths are allowed by the Blessed One; you who have entered the Order of so-little-wanting a Buddha have become so richly equipped! Come, we will lead you to the Ten-Powered." And they did so.

The Teacher, seeing them, said: " Why now, monks, are you bringing a monk against his will? " " Reverend sir, this monk is of many goods, much equipment." " Is it true, monk, what they say? " " It is true, Blessed One." " But why are you a man

5

of many goods? Am I not one who praises few wants and content and the rest, also seclusion and stirring up of energy?" He, hearing the Teacher's word and vexed, said: "Now will I go about stripped like this!" And, laying aside his cloak, he stood with but one garment. Then the Teacher, coming to his support, said: "Was it not you, monk, who of old were a seeker after modesty and discretion and, though you were a waterdemon, for twelve years you lived in that quest? Why do you who have now left the world in so reverent an Order as the Buddha's lay aside before the four companies your cloak and stand lost to modesty and discretion?" He, hearing the Teacher's word, was set up in modesty and discretion, donned his cloak, bowed before the Teacher and sat down. The monks begged the Teacher to make clear the matter. The Blessed One made manifest an affair hidden by intervening becoming.[1]

In the past Brahmadatta was king at Benares in the kingdom of Kāsi. Then the Bodhisat took birth as the child of the chief queen and was named Mahingsāsa. When he could get about, running to and fro, another son was born to the king, and they named him Chanda (Moon). But when he could get about, running to and fro, the Bodhisat's mother died. The king appointed another his chief queen. She was dear and charming to him. She living in love brought forth a son, and they named him Suriya (Sun). The king, seeing his son, was gratified, and said: "Lady dear, for the son I grant you a choice."[2] The queen put by the choice to be claimed when a wish would arise.

When her son was of age she said to the king: "By the lord at my son's birth a choice was given: give

---

[1] *Bhava*, i.e. rebirths.   [2] *Varo.* Cf. p. 42 *n.*

me for my son the kingdom." The king refused her, saying " I have two sons like flames of fire in their goings; I am not able to give the kingdom to your son." When he saw her begging for this again and again he thought " She may be devising evil against my sons," and sending for the sons he said: " Tātas, when Suriya was born I gave a choice, and now his mother begs for the kingdom for him. I am not willing to give it him. Woman is wicked; she might devise evil against you; do you go into the forest. When I am gone you may reign over the kingdom which belongs to our family." And, weeping and sobbing, he kissed their heads and let them go. They saluted their father and descended from the palace. Suriya saw them as he was playing in the courtyard, and learning the affair, " I will go with my brothers," he said, and went forth with them.

They entered the Himâlaya region. The Bodhisat, turning aside from the way, sat down beneath a tree and bade Suriya: " Tāta Suriya, go down to that lake, bathe and drink and fetch us some water in lotus-leaves." Now the lake had been got by a waterdemon from Vessăvănă, and Vessavana had said to him: " Excepting those who know what it is to be divine, you can take and eat all who come down to that lake; them you do not get." From that day that demon, asking them who came down to that lake about what is divine, ate those who did not know. Then Suriya, going to that lake and not scrutinising, the demon seized him and asked: " Do you know what is divine? " He said: " Chanda, Suriya are divine." Then he was told, " You don't know what is divine," and he was made to enter the water and placed in the demon's abode. The Bodhisat, seeing he was a long time, sent Chanda. The demon, seizing him too, asked him: "Know you what is divine?" "Yes, I know; the four quarters (of the firmament) are divine." And he, too, was taken and put there. He also tarrying, the Bodhisat thought "There will have been an accident," and himself going there, and seeing the track of feet descending, he thought "There will be a haunting of this lake by a demon," and he drew his sword and grasped his bow, and waited. The waterdemon, seeing he did not descend to the water, became like a forester, and said to the Bodhisat: "Sir man, you are weary with the way; why don't you descend to the lake, bathe and drink, eat lotus-stalks, deck yourself with lotuses and go where you will?" The Bodhisat saw and knew him for a sprite, and said: "You have seized my little brothers." "Yes, I have." "Why?" "I win those who descend to this lake." "What, do you win all?" "Not them who know what is divine: I get all the rest." "Have you but need of what is divine?" "Yes, I have." "If that is so I will tell you the divine things." "Well then, tell; I will listen what are divine things." The Bodhisat said: "I would tell about the divine ones but my limbs are weary." The sprite bathed the Bodhisat, made him eat and drink, decked him with flowers, anointed him with perfumes, spread a seat for him in an ornate pavilion. The Bodhisat, sitting down and making the sprite sit at his feet, said this verse:

"Those who are modest and discreet,
On things that are pure intent,
The holy men, the lovely men,
These the world calls divine."

The sprite, hearing this righteous teaching spoken, was pleased, and to the Bodhisat: "Wise man,

I am pleased with you; I give you one brother; which shall I bring?" "Bring the younger." "Wise man, you know thoroughly just what are divine things; but you do not act accordingly." "How is that?" "Putting the elder aside for some reason you bid me bring the younger, and do not carry out what is due to an elder." "I both know who are divine, sprite, and I act accordingly. It was on that boy's account that we entered this forest; it was for that boy's sake that his mother begged the kingdom of our father; now our father, not granting her choice, enjoined us for our safety's sake to live in the forest; that boy never turning back came with us; were it to be said ' he was devoured in the forest by a sprite ' no one would believe us; wherefore out of fear of blame I bid you bring that one." "Very good, very good, wise man, you both know what are divine things and you act accordingly." And, pleased in mind, the sprite, applauding the Bodhisat, gave him back both brothers.

Then the Bodhisat said to him: "My good man, through what you have done in the past that was evil you have been re-born as a sprite, eating flesh and blood of others. You are still doing evil. This evil-doing of yours will not grant you release from hell and the rest. Wherefore from henceforth put away evil and do well!" And he succeeded in taming him. Continuing there to dwell with the sprite as guardian, he one day reading the stars saw that his father had died. And taking the sprite he went to Benares, and seizing the kingdom, and making Chanda viceroy and Suriya general, and appointing a pleasant spot as abode for the sprite, so that he got the best garlands, best flowers and best food: these things he did. And ruling righteously, he went according to his deeds.

The Teacher . . . having told the double story, joined on the series, and assigned the Jataka: " Then the waterdemon was the monk of many goods, Suriya was Ānanda, Chanda was Sāriputta, the elder brother Mahingsāsa was just I."

THE FAGGOT-BRINGER JATAKA

(*Katthahāri-jātaka*)

"**Y**OUR son am I, your majesty."—This the Teacher told while living at the Jetavana about Vāsabhā the noble lady. The story is amplified in the twelfth Jataka book, the Lucky Hall Jataka. It is said she was the daughter of Mahānāma the Sakyan by a slave girl named Nāgamundā, and that she became the chief queen of the king of Kosala. She bore a son to the king. The king, having come to know that she was of a slave, degraded her position and degraded also the position of her son Vidū-dabha. Both kept always within the palace.

The Teacher, learning of the matter, came early with a retinue of five hundred monks to the palace and took his seat on the seat prepared. And he said: "Your majesty, where is Vāsabhā the princess?" The king told him of the matter. "Your majesty, whose daughter is Vāsabhā the princess?" "Ma-hānāma's, reverend sir." "Coming, to whom came she?" "To me, reverend sir." "Your majesty, she is a king's daughter, she is come to a king, because of the king she got a child; how comes it that this son is not as of the master in the kingdom owned by his father? Of old kings gave a kingdom to the son of a mere faggot-bringer, after the briefest intercourse (with her)." The king begged the Blessed One to make the matter clear. The Blessed One made manifest the affair hidden by intervening becoming (*i.e.* re-births).

In the past, Brahmadatta king, having gone in great state to his garden, was walking about in it with a lust for flower and fruit when he saw a woman, singing ever as she gathered up sticks in the thickets of the garden. Losing his heart to her, he dallied there with her. She conceived the Bodhisat, and when she came to know how it was with her, for she was heavy as with the bolt of Indra, she told the king. He gave her his signet ring, saying " If it be a daughter, let this go that you may maintain her; if it be a son, bring him to me with the ring." And she in due time brought forth the Bodhisat. When he was able to run to and fro at play in the play-ground, some (children) said: " No-daddyling has hit me! " When he heard them, he went to his mother and said: " Mother, who is my father? " " Tata, you are the son of the king of Benares." " Mother, is there any witness to that? " " Tata, the king gave me his signet ring . . ." and she told him the charge given her. " Mother, that being so, why don't you bring me to him? "

Seeing the child's inclination, she went to the king's gate and had herself sent for. And entering, she did homage to the king and said: " Sire, this is your son." The king, though he knew, out of shame at the surrounding assembly, said: " Not mine is the child." " This, sire, is your ring; you recognise that? " " Neither is mine this ring." " Sire, now have I no other witness save the Act of Truth: if it was through you this child was born let him remain in the air; if not let him fall down and die! " And taking the Bodhisat by the foot, she threw him into the air. The Bodhisat, with crossed legs, sat in the air telling his father with honeyed voice what was right, and saying this verse:

" Your son am I, your majesty!
'Tis yours to rear me, lord of folk!
Since the king doth others rear,
His very brood he'll not neglect."

The king, hearing the Bodhisat thus teaching him, stretched forth his hand, saying "Come, tāta, I alone shall rear, I alone shall rear!" A thousand hands were stretched out, but the Bodhisat descended into the hands of the king and sat on his hip. The king gave him the viceroyalty and made his mother chief queen. When the father died, he became the King "Faggot-bearer" and, ruling in righteousness, went according to his deeds.

The Teacher, having brought up this righteous teaching for the king of Kosala, joined on the series and assigned the Jataka: "Then the mother was Great Māyā, the father Suddhodana, the Faggot-bearer King was just I."

THE BANYAN-DEER JATAKA

(*Nigrodha-miga-jātaka*)

"THE Banyan 'tis you should frequent."—This the Teacher told while staying at the Jetavana about the mother of the Elder Kumāra-Kassapa. She, it is said, was the daughter of a wealthy leading merchant of Rājagaha; a well of virtue, neglectful of worldly things and in her last state. As a lamp within a jar, the conditions of saintship shone in her. From the hour when she came to know the "self"[1] she had no more joy in the home, and desiring to leave the world, she said to mother and father: "Dear ones! my heart takes no delight in houselife. I desire to leave the world in the Buddha-religion that leads onward. Have me ordained." "Dear, what are you talking about? This is a very wealthy family, and you are our only daughter! You cannot leave the world!" Though she begged many times she did not win their consent. Then she thought: "Be it so! Gone to another family, I will persuade my husband and then leave the world." And, coming of age, she went to another family and dwelt at home a devoted wife, virtuous and lovely. And in due time she conceived but knew it not.

Now in that city they proclaimed a festival. All the citizens kept holiday and the city was decorated like a deva-city. But she, even while the festival-sports were at their height, did not anoint or adorn her body, but went about in everyday attire. Then her husband said to her: "Lady dear, all the city is

[1] This is an interesting clause, rare in Buddhist writings, and more Brahmanic than Buddhist.

given up to the festival, yet you do not deck your body." " Sir, the body of me is filled with thirty-two corpses—what boots the adorning of it? Verily this body is neither deva-created nor Brahmā-created; it is not made of gold or jewels or yellow sandalwood; it is not sprung from a matrix of lotuses and lilies, nor is it filled with ambrosial balsam, but it is bred in corruption, the product of a mother and father; it is a thing of wearing and wasting away, of dissolution and destruction, a graveyard-sweller, derived from cravings, source of sorrows, basis of lamentation, abode of all diseases, receptacle of action-workings, foul within, without, ever dripping, dwelling of vermin and worm, farer to the charnel-house, ending in death, faring as all the world may see. Son of the house, what shall I be about adorning this frame? Is not the adorning of it like work of painting the outside of a muck-filled sink?" The merchant's son, hearing her word, said: " Lady dear, since you see such blemish in this body, why do you not leave the world?" " Son of the house, if I may leave the world I would do so to-day." The merchant said, " Very good, I will let you leave it," and giving a donation at great cost, he brought her with a great following to the nuns' quarters and let her be ordained with the nuns of Devadatta's party. She winning ordination was glad at the fulfilment of her intent.

Now when she was far gone with child the nuns noticed the changes in her, and asked her: " Madam, you appear as one with child; what does this mean?" " Ladies, I wist not of this matter; but my conduct has been moral." Then those nuns brought her to Devadatta and asked him: " Sir, this gentlewoman, having persuaded her husband, got ordained, but now she appears to be with child. We know not

STORIES OF THE BUDDHA

whether she became so when in her home or after
ordination. Now what are we to do?"

Devadatta, by his not-awakened[1] state and being
without forbearance, goodwill or kindness, thought
" Blame will arise of me that ' a nun of Devadatta's
party carries on with child, and Devadatta condones it.'
It behoves me to disordain her," and without any
inquiry and on impulse, as if brushing away pebbles,
he said: " Go you and disordain her." They, hearing his word, rose up, saluted and went to their
quarters.

Now that girl said to the nuns: " Ladies, Elder
Devadatta is not the Buddha, nor did I get ordination from him; my ordination was from the rightful
Buddha, the chief man of the world. Deprive me
not of that which I won with trouble. Come, take
me and go to the Teacher at Jetavana." They took
her, and when they had surmounted the five-and-
forty league-long way from Rājagaha, and come in
due course to the Jetavana, they did homage to the
Teacher and told him the matter.

The Teacher thought: " Though she became with
child in her home-life, yet will there be a chance for
other schools to say, ' The recluse Gotama goes
about having accepted one expelled by Devadatta.'[2]
Therefore to cut off such talk it behoves (us) to
come to a judgment on this matter in the presence
of the king and his ministers." On the next day he
sent for king Pasenadi the Kosalan, the elder and
the younger Anāthapindika, the lady Visākhā the
great lay-disciple, and other well-known heads of

---

[1] Or, " because he was not Buddha."
[2] It reflects little credit on the compilers of these stories of the
present (from it may well be a few legendary outlines) that they
make Gotama guided here as much by " what they say " as Devadatta.

families. And in the evening, when the fourfold congregation was assembled, he bade Elder Upāli: " Go, clear up the actions of this young nun in the presence of the congregation." " Very well, reverend sir," said the Elder, and seated in the assembly before the king, he summoned Visākhā and placed the matter in her hands: " Go, Visākhā, ascertain the month and day of this girl's ordination, and then judge if it was before or after that she conceived." The laywoman consented, and held a private examination of the nun, whereby it was shown that she was with child while living at home. She announced this to the Elder, and he declared the nun innocent in the assembly. She, thus cleared, did homage to the Order and the Teacher, and went with the nuns to their quarters.

In due time she brought forth a son, strong in spirit as she had wished in wishing at the feet of (the Buddha) Padumuttăra. And one day the king, going near the nuns' quarters, heard a child's voice and asked his attendants. They were informed and told him: " That young nun has had her child; it is his cry." " I'd say child-tending is a hindrance to nuns; we will tend him." And the king had the child brought up by his nautchwomen and reared as a young noble. On his naming-day they called him Kassapa, and he was known as Kumāra-Kassapa.[1] At seven years he was made a novice under the Teacher, and fully ordained when old enough. As time went on he became among religious preachers notable for varied eloquence. . . . Both he and his mother reached the topmost fruition. . . .

Now, one day after almsround and meal, the Teacher, exhorting the monks, retired to the Fra-

[1] On this disciple cf. esp. *Dialogues of the Buddha*, ii, Dial. xxiii; also *Further Dialogues*, i, Dial. xxiii.

17

grant Hut. The monks then spent the time in day or night quarters till evening when they met in their temple and sat together praising the Buddha-virtues —for instance, how the mother and son had found in him safety. The Teacher, with Buddha-grace entering the hall, asked them: " For what talk are you the while come together? " " Reverend sir, to talk of your virtues," and they told him all. " Monk, not now only did the Tathâgata become a basis and foothold to these two; he was so in the past." The monks begged the Blessed One to make the matter clear. The Blessed One made manifest that which had been hidden by intermediate rebirth.

Long ago, when Brahmadatta was reigning in Benares, the Bodhisat took rebirth as a deer. When his mother brought him forth he was of golden hue, his eyes were like round jewels, his horns were silver-coloured, his mouth was the colour of a bunch of red cloth, his hooves were like polished lac, his tail was like a yak's, and the body of him was as large as a colt's. He dwelt in the forest with a herd of five hundred deer, and was called Banyan Deer King. Not far away dwelt another also with a herd of five hundred deer called Branch Deer, and he too was golden of hue.

At that time the Benares king was much given to deer hunting, had no meal without flesh, and assembled town and countrymen for his daily hunt,[1] interrupting their work. Men thought: " This king interrupts our work; how would it be if we were to sow deer-food and supply water in his park, and driving a lot of deer into the park, were to fix a gate and hand it over to the king? " And they did so, and when food, water and gate were provided they

[1] Presumably as " beaters."

took the townsfolk and, with clubs and other weapons in hand, they entered the forest seeking deer. And saying " We will catch those living in the middle," they encircled a space of a league, so that the home of those two king deer was at the centre. When they saw the deer they set to striking trees, bushes and ground with their clubs, bringing them out of their haunts, making a great din by rattling their weapons: swords, javelins, bows. And, driving that deerherd into the park and shutting the gate, they went to the king and with these words, " Sire, we going continually deer-hunting, you harm our work. We have brought deer from the forest and filled your park. Henceforth eat their flesh," they took their leave and went away.

The king, hearing their word, went to the park, surveying the deer. And seeing two golden deer he made them immune. From that time sometimes he would go himself, kill a deer and bring it in; sometimes the food purveyor would go, kill and bring in. The deer, as soon as they saw the bow, frightened with deadly fear, ran away; after two or three shots they faltered and fainted and found death.

The herd told what was going on to the Bodhisat. He sent for Branch Deer and said: " Friend, many deer are perishing; needs be they die, but henceforth let them not be wounding deer with arrows; let deer go to a regular execution-block in turn; let the turn fall on my herd one day, on your herd one day; let the deer whose turn has come lie down with his head on the block. In this way the deer will not get wounded." He consented, and this was carried out, the purveyor catching and taking away the prostrate deer.

Now one day the turn fell on a doe of Branch's

herd who was with young. She went to Branch, saying " Master, I am with young; when I have brought forth my kid, we shall be going in our turn as two persons. Let the turn pass me by! " He said: " I am not able to make others take your turn. You admit the lot is yours. Go." Finding no favour with him, she went to the Bodhisat and told him the matter. He, hearing her word, said: " Be it so. Do you go, and I will make the turn pass you by." And he himself went and laid down with his head on the block. The food purveyor seeing him, thought " The deer-king who was made immune is lying down at the block—what's the reason for this? " and he swiftly went and told the king. The king got on his chariot and came with a great retinue till he saw the Bodhisat: " Friend deer-king, did I not give you immunity? Why are you lying here? " " Your majesty, a doe with young came and said: ' Let my turn fall on another.' It was impossible for me to place the deadly trouble of one upon another. I, giving her my own life and taking the death that belongs to her, have lain down here." The king said: " Friend deer-king of golden hue, never have I seen even among men one in whom was such forbearance, goodwill and kindness. Hereat am I pleased with you. To both you and her I give immunity." " Two have won immunity; what will the rest do, ruler of men? " " To the rest also I give immunity, master." " Your majesty, the deer in the park will have won immunity; what will the others do? " " To these also I give immunity, master." " Your majesty, the deer so far are to be immune; what will the remaining four-footed things do? " " To these also I give immunity, master." " Your majesty, four-footed things so far are to be immune what will the bird-flocks do? " " To these also I give it, master." " Your majesty, the birds so far are to be immune, the fish dwelling in the water, what will they do? " " To these, too, I give immunity, master."

Thus the Bodhisat, having begged immunity of the king for all beings, got up and established the king in the five precepts, taught the king his duty with the grace of a Buddha, saying " Carry out duty, your majesty! Carrying out your duty towards parents, sons and daughters, town and countryfolk, carrying out justice, you will go the happy way-faring to the bright world." For some days he stayed in the park admonishing the king, then, attended by his deer-herd, he entered the forest.

And that doe brought forth a kid like to a jasmine blossom. He used to play near the Branch deer. Then his mother, seeing him go near that deer, said: " Son, from now go not near him; you should go near the 'Banyan'"; and in admonition she spoke this verse:

> The Banyan 't is you should frequent
> You should not with the Branch consort.
> Beside the Banyan better dead
> Than with the Branch to be alive.

From that time the deer, with won immunity, used to devour men's crops. Knowing them immune, the men did not dare to strike or drive them away. They assembled in the king's courtyard and told him the matter. The king said: " Pleased I gave a boon to the excellent Banyan deer; I might give up my kingdom but not my plighted word. Go! Let no one in my kingdom hurt the deer." The Banyan deer, hearing what was going on, assembled his herd and forbidding them " Henceforth you are not allowed to eat the crops of others," he let the men know:

21

" Henceforth let corn-growers make no fence to ward their crops. Let them fix a tablet-mark round the fields." Thereupon a tablet-badge-sign[1] came to pass in the fields; nor ever was there a deer who trespassed against it, for so the Bodhisat had admonished them. So, admonishing, he stayed with them all his life and went according to his deeds. The king too, keeping his injunctions, wrought merit and went according to his deeds.

The Teacher then joined together the series, and assigned the Jataka: " Then the Branch deer was Devadatta, his men were Devadatta's men, the doe was the Therī,[2] her kid was prince Kassapa, the king was Ānanda, the Banyan deer was just I."

[1] Panna-bandhana-saññā.

[2] This is perhaps a late oversight. She was not yet an "Elder" nun.

THE DEAD MEN'S FOOD JATAKA

(*Matakabhatta-jātaka*)

"IF only men thus knew."—This the Teacher told while living at the Jetavana about " Dead men's food." At that time, namely, men put to death many goats, sheep and the like, and offered them as " Dead men's food " on behalf of deceased kinsmen. Monks, seeing men do this, asked the Teacher: " Reverend sir, is there any progress[1] in such a procedure as that? " The Teacher said, " No, monks, though life be taken in the idea that ' it is a giving of food for the dead,' there is no progress thereby whatever. In olden time wise men seated aloft and teaching the Right herein, telling of its danger, made all Jambudīpa renounce this work. But now it has broken out again because men have got confused through ' becoming ' ";[2] and he brought up the past.

In the past, when Brahmadatta was reigning at Benares, a brahman, master of the Three Vedas, and a leading teacher, took a goat to sacrifice it as dead men's food, and said to his pupils: " My sons, take this goat to the river, bathe it, throw a garland round its neck, sign it with the five-finger mark, groom it and bring it back." They did so and then set it on the river bank. The goat, ware of its own past karma, rejoiced, thinking " To-day I shall be released from all this ill! " And it laughed a great laugh like the smashing of a jar. But anon, thinking " This brahman having slain me will acquire ill through me! " and, feeling pity, it broke into loud

---

[1] *Vaddhi*, lit. " growth," " increase."   [2] Used for " rebirth."

weeping. Then those young brahmans asked it:
" Good goat, you laugh loudly and you weep loudly;
for what reason do you laugh? For what reason do
you weep? " " Do you ask me the reason before
my own master." They took it and told him. The
Teacher asked the goat as they had done. The goat,
remembering by knowledge of the memory of births,
told this: " I, brahman, in the past was a mantra-
reciting brahman like you. I killed a goat on behalf
of the dead. I, through the killing of that goat, have
had my head cut off in five hundred lives save one.
This is the five hundredth life, and I laughed to
think ' This is the last time, henceforth I shall be
released.' But I wept out of pity for you, who are
about to incur like reward hereafter." " Fear not,
goat, I will not kill you." " Brahman, what are you
talking about? Whether you kill me or not, you
cannot rid me of dying to-day." " Goat, fear not,
we will set a guard on you and go about with you."
" Brahman, your guard is of little avail, but the evil
I did is very strong." Nevertheless they all guarded
the goat, taking it with them. The goat, no sooner
free, stretched out its neck over a bush growing on a
rock and began to eat the leaves. At that very moment
a thunderbolt fell on the rock. A splinter, torn off,
fell on the goat's neck and cut off its head. A crowd
came together.

Then the Bodhisat, who had then been reborn
as the spirit of a tree, saw those people, and sitting
crosslegged in the air by his power as deva, thought
" These beings coming to know the fruit of evil
might desist from taking life," and he taught the
Right saying this verse:

" If only men thus knew: 'This birth-series is ill,'
  The liver would not liver slay; grief is the slayer's lot."

Thus did the Great Being, frightening with fear of hell, teach the Right, and men hearing him abstained from life-taking, being afeared of hell. And the Bodhisat, establishing the multitude in the moral code, went according to his works; the multitude working merit became fillers of deva-city.

The Teacher . . . assigned the Jataka: " I at that time was the tree-spirit."

THE CANE-DRINKING JATAKA

(Nala-pāna-jātaka)

"SINCE no upfaring track I saw."—This the
Teacher told when, on tour among the
Kosalese, he had reached Reedwater[1] village and
was staying in the Ketăka Wood by the Reedwater
Tank, about reed-stems. The monks, when they
had bathed in the tank, had reed-stems gotten for
them by the novices for needlecases. And finding
them hollow throughout, from base to tip, they
asked him how it came so to be. The Teacher, saying
" This, monks, was a mandate I gave of yore,"
brought up the past.

In the past 'tis said this forest was a dense jungle,
and whoever went down to the lake a waterdemon
ate him. The Bodhisat was then become a monkey-
king as big as a red deer's fawn, with a following of
eighty thousand apes, whom he led about dwelling
in that forest. He admonished his herd: " My dears,
in this forest are both poison-trees and non-humans-
infested lakes. If you will be eating any fruits you
have not eaten before, or drinking water you have
not drunk before, ask me about it." They hearkened,
saying " Very good." One day they came to a place
for the first time. There, going about for most of the
day, they sought water, and seeing a lake, they did
not drink but sat down watching till the Bodhisat
should come. When he came, he said: " Why, my
dears, don't you drink? " " We watched for your

[1] Nalakapāna.

coming." " Well done, my dears," said the Bodhisat, and scrutinising the lake and marking the downward tracks, he saw none upward going. He knew then, " Without doubt this is haunted by non-humans," and he said: " You have done well, my dears, in not drinking the water; this is a haunt of non-humans."

And the waterdemon, noting that they did not come down, became a blue-bellied, pale-faced, red-handed, red-footed fearsome sight, and cleaving the water, came out and said: " Why sit you? Come down and drink water." Then the Bodhisat asked him: " Are you the waterdemon here?" " Yes, I am." " Yours are they who go down to the lake? " " Yes, I get them. I never let anyone go who comes down here from even a little bird upwards. You, too, I shall eat." " We don't give ourselves to you to eat." " But you'll be drinking the water? " " Yes, we shall be drinking the water, but we shall not get into your power." " How, then, will you drink the water?" " Why! you are deeming:—'they will come down to drink,' while we, without going down, each of the eighty thousand of us, shall take a reed-stem and drink the water of your lake as if we were drinking water with a lotus-stem. So you won't be able to devour us."

When the Teacher had become very Buddha, he understood this matter and uttered the former half of this verse:

" Since no upfaring track I saw, seeing the track
    that downward fared,

.   .   .   .   .

We'll drink the water through a cane; me verily
    thou wilt not kill."[1]

[1] This line is missing in many MSS., but the word-commentary shows knowledge of it.

So saying, the Bodhisat had a reed-stem brought to him and, turning his mind to the Ten Perfections, and making the Truth-act, he blew with the mouth. The reed became quite hollow throughout with no knot left in it. By this method, having one brought after another, he blew and gave . . . but if this had been so he had never finished, therefore it must not be taken so. But the Bodhisat gave the mandate, including the whole lake: " Let all canes that grow be hollow throughout! "

Verily because mighty is the access of Bodhisats to welfare, the mandate succeeded. From that time all the canes that came up encompassing the lake grew hollow throughout.

In this aeon are four aeon-lasting wonders; which are they? The haremark of the moon[1] will persist through this aeon; the fire quenched by the quail will not burn in that spot during this aeon; on the place where the potter's dwelling stood no rain will fall this aeon; and the reeds will be hollow as described.

The Bodhisat, having given the mandate, took a reed and sat down, and so did the eighty thousand encompassing the lake. When the Bodhisat at drinking time sucked up the water through his cane, they all drank, also seated, on the bank. They thus drinking the water the waterdemon got nothing, and went dejected to his own habitation. The Bodhisat, with his following, entered the forest.

But the Teacher . . . joined up the series and assigned the Jataka: " Then the waterdemon was Devadatta, the eighty thousand apes were the Buddha-assembly, but the monkey king good in resource was just I."

[1] See p. 135. The other three wonders are told in Jatakas Nos. 316, 35, and in Book of Sayings translated as *Further Dialogues of the Buddha*, by Lord Chalmers, vol. ii, No. 81, respectively.

THE ANTELOPE JATAKA
(*Kurunga-jātaka*)

"**K**NOWN to the antelope it is."—This the Teacher told while living at the Bamboo Wood about Devadatta. For once, when the monks were assembled in the chapel,[1] they were seated talking in dispraise of Devadatta, saying " Venerable Devadatta sent forth archers to shoot the Tathâgata, hurled down a rock, let loose Wealthwarder (the elephant); in every way he went about to kill him-of-the-ten-powers." The Teacher came in and, taking the seat put ready, asked: " For what talk here and now are you seated? " And they telling him, he said " Not in the present only has Devadatta sought to kill me; he sought also in the past, but was not able to kill me," and he brought up the bygone time.

In bygone time, when Brahmadatta was reigning at Benares, the Bodhisat had become an antelope and dwelt in a forest region, feeding on fruits. At one time he was feeding on the fruit of a fruit-laden sepanni tree. Now a deerstalker of the village used to note the tracks of deer, and then fixed a platform up in the tree, so that by slaying such deer as came to the tree he might sell their meat and maintain himself. Seeing one day the track of the Bodhisat beneath that tree, he fixed a platform, and after early breakfast he took his javelin, entered the wood, climbed on the platform and sat down.

---

[1] *Dhamma-sabhā*, or -*sālā*, as distinct, in the early Viharas, from the refectory *bhatt'agga*. A difficult word to render justly, and used here unsacerdotally.

The Bodhisat, too, left his lair early, and, thinking
" I will eat sepanni fruit," came to that tree, but not
hastily, for, thought he, " Sometimes deerstalkers
fix a platform on the trees—can there be now that
danger here? " And he stood beyond reconnoitring.
And the hunter, perceiving that the deer did not
come on, sat in his platform, and threw *sepannis*
down so that they fell in front of him. The Bodhisat
thought, " These fruits have come falling in front
of me—is there now a hunter up there? " And he
looked and looked till he saw the hunter, but acting
as if he did not see him, he said: " My good tree,
you used to let your fruit fall straight down like a
pendant growth; but to-day you have cast off your
tree-nature. That being so, I will go and seek my
food at another tree," and he said this verse:

> " Known to the antelope it is
> What thou, *sepanni*, layest down.
> I'll get me to another one.
> Not fain am I to taste thy fruit."

Then the hunter in his platform threw his javelin,
saying, " Go! I've lost you this time! " The Bodhisat
turned and stood, saying, " My good man, this time
it's true you've lost me, but the eight main and the
sixteen special hells and the fivefold bondage and
torments—these you have not lost! " So saying he
ran away, going whither he desired. The hunter,
too, coming down, went whither he desired.

The Teacher, moreover, joined up the series and
assigned the Jataka: " Then the deerstalker was
Devadatta, but the antelope was just I."

THE BHOJA-THOROUGHBRED JATAKA
(*Bhojâjānīya-jātaka*)

"THOUGH lying on his side."—This the Teacher told while staying at the Jetavana about a monk who gave up effort. It was then that the Teacher spoke to that monk, and saying " Monks, of old the wise wrought with energy even when opening there was none; though smitten they did not give up," he brought up the past.

In the past, when Brahmadatta was reigning at Benares, the Bodhisat was born of Bhoja-thorough-bred horses of Sindh, and was made the king of Benares' state charger, and given every kind of decoration. He was fed on three-year-old rice of the finest flavour on a golden dish valued at a hundred thousand, and he stood on a stable-floor anointed with the four perfumes. His place was hung round with crimson curtains; above was a canopy painted with golden stars, and around went perfumed festoons and garlands, and a perpetual lamp was there of perfumed oil.

There were no kings who did not covet the kingdom of Benares. At one time seven kings surrounded Benares and sent a letter (*lit.* leaf) to its king, which said : " Either give us the kingdom or give us battle!" The king assembled his ministers and informed them, saying, " Now, tātas, what do we? " " Sire, you yourself must not at first go out to battle. Send out some cavalier to engage in battle; if he does not succeed we shall afterwards know what to do." The king sent for a cavalier: " Tāta, will you be able to give battle to seven kings?" " Sire, if I get the

Bhoja thoroughbred Scindhian I will war with all the kings of Jambudīpa, let alone those seven." " Tāta, be it the thoroughbred Scindhian or another, take what you want and set to." " Very good, sire," and he did homage, and coming down from the palace, he had that horse brought and clad in mail, and donning all his own armour, girding on his sword, and sallying forth from the city, charged like lightning, broke through the first entrenchment, taking one king alive, came back to the city and handed him to the guard; then going, broke through the second entrenchment, and also the third; thus taking five kings alive, he broke through the sixth entrenchment, and had taken the sixth king alive when the thoroughbred received a wound. Blood flowed and mighty pain was felt. The cavalier seeing his state, made him lie down at the king's gate and, easing the mail, set about arming another horse.

The Bodhisat, lying on his least painful side, opened his eyes and, seeing the cavalier, thought: " He is arming another horse, but that horse won't be able to break through the seventh entrenchment and catch the seventh king. My work done will be all lost; the cavalier, though peerless, will be destroyed; the king, too, will fall into the enemy's hands. Except me there is no horse who can do what remains to do." So lying he called the cavalier and said: " Good cavalier, no other horse can break through the seventh entrenchment and catch the seventh king but me. I will not have the work destroyed which I have done; help me up and arm me! " And he spoke this verse:

"Though lying on his side and wounded sore with darts,
Better than hack the Bhojjan! Rider, harness thou me!"

The cavalier helped up the Bodhisat, bound his wound, fastened on the mail, seated himself on his back, broke through the seventh entrenchment, took the seventh king alive and handed him over to the king. They brought the Bodhisat, too, to the king's gate. The king came out that he might see him. The Great Being said to the king: "Your majesty, slay not the seven kings. Make them take an oath and let them go. Let the renown due to me and the cavalier be given to the cavalier alone. It is not right to let a warrior who has taken seven kings come to naught. Do you give gifts and ward your morals and rule your kingdom with right and justice." From him, thus admonishing the king, they took off his mail. He, as piece by piece came free, passed away.

The king did what was meet to the body, gave great honour to the cavalier, made the seven kings take oath that they would not injure (him), sent them home and, reigning with right and justice, at his life's end fared according to his deeds.

The Teacher thus speaking, the monk, who had given up effort, was established in the fruit of saintship. The Teacher, having brought up this righteous discourse, joined on the series and assigned the Jataka: "Then the king was Ānanda, the cavalier was Sāriputta, but the Bhoja thoroughbred Scindhian was just I."

THE NESTLING JATAKA

(Kulāvaka-jātaka)

"LET the nestlings."—This the Teacher while staying at the Jetavana told about a monk who drank water without having strained it. They tell that from Sāvatthi two young monk-comrades went to the country, and after dwelling at a pleasant spot as long as they were minded, said: "Let's go to see the Very Buddha." So they left and set out for the Jetavana. One carried a strainer, the other had none; both used the strainer before drinking. One day they fell out. The owner of the strainer did not give it to the other, but strained and drank by himself. The other, not getting the strainer and being unable to bear his thirst, drank unstrained water. They both coming in due course to the Jetavana, did homage to the Teacher and took their seats. He greeted them with courteous speech and asked them: "Whence come you?" "Sir, we have been living in a little village in the Kosala country, and we have come thence for the sake of seeing you." "I trust you have come in harmony?" He of the no strainer said: "This man, sir, quarrelled with me on the way and did not give me his strainer." The other said: "This man, sir, using no strainer, has been knowingly drinking water with live things in it." "Is this, monk, that he says of you true?" "Yes, sir, I did drink unstrained water." The Teacher said: "Monk, in the past wise men governors of Deva-city, when beaten in battle and flying in rout along the deep, said 'We will not for (our) advantage kill creatures,' but sacrificed great renown

34

and turned back their chariot to save the life of a roc's young." And he brought up the past.

Long ago a king of Măgădhă was reigning in Rājagaha in the land of Magadha. And just as he who is now Sakka came to life in his preceding birth in the hamlet of Machala in the land of Magadha, even so it was in the selfsame hamlet that the Bodhisat came to life in those days as a nobleman's son. On the naming-day they called him Prince Magha. When he grew up he was known as the mānava Magha. His parents brought him a wife from a family of equal rank, and he increasing in sons and daughters became a lordly giver, a keeper of the five precepts.

In that village there were as many as thirty families, and one day those thirty family-men were standing in the middle of the village transacting village affairs. The Bodhisat pushed aside with his feet the loose soil at the place where he stood, making the place pleasant, but another man, coming up, stood in that place. The Bodhisat made another place pleasant, and there, too, another took his stand. The Bodhisat did this again and again, until he had made pleasant standing-place for all. On another occasion at the same place he made a pavilion; again, removing that, he had a hall made, distributing benches in it and placing a jar of water. On another occasion those thirty men became united in purpose by the Bodhisat. They being established by the Bodhisat in the five precepts, thenceforth he went about doing with them works of merit.

And they, so doing, with him used to rise early, go out with axes, billhooks and crowbars in hand, and set to work rolling away with the crowbar stones in the four highways and elsewhere, taking away trees obstructing the axles of vehicles, making rough places plain, broadening the causeway, digging tanks, making a hall, giving gifts, keeping the precepts. In this wise did the entire village abide in the Bodhisat's injunctions and keep the precepts.

Now their village headman thought: " I once used to gain much by fines, by taxes and pot-money, when they used to get drunk or take life, and so on. But now the mānava Magha, saying ' I will have the precepts kept,' lets no one break them. I'll make them keep their five precepts!" And in wrath he went to the king and said: " Sire, many robbers are going about sacking villages." The king listened and said: " Go, bring them up." And he went and bound those men and brought them up and told the king: " Sire, the robbers are brought up." The king, without examining their deeds, said: " Let an elephant trample them." Forthwith they made them all lie down in the courtyard and brought up an elephant.

The Bodhisat gave them injunction, saying, " Do you mind the precepts. Make goodwill arise towards slanderer, the king, the elephant and your own body all in one." And they did so. They led up the elephant for the trampling, but for all that he did not approach; he trumpeted loudly and ran away. One elephant after another they brought up. They also forthwith ran away. The king, thinking " They will have some drug in their hand," said " Search them." Searching and finding nothing they said: " There's none, sire." " Well, then, they will be reeling out a spell; ask them ' Is there among you a spell-reeler? ' " The king's men asked; the Bodhisat said: " There is." The king's men told him: " Sire, there is." The king sent for them all and said: " Tell me the spell you know." The Bodhisat said: " Sire, we have no other spell than this: we

36

thirty folk kill no living thing, we steal not, we don't act wrongly in sex, we tell no lies, we drink no strong drink, we practise goodwill, we give gifts, we make the way plain, we dig tanks, we make the hall; this is our spell and protection and growth." The king, well pleased with them, gave them all the house-wealth of the slanderer and him for their slave, and he gave them an elephant and the village.

Thenceforward doing works of merit to their heart's content, they said " We will make a great hall at the four highways," and sending for an architect they erected the hall. But, with desire for women lost, they suffered no access of women to the hall.

Now, at that time there were in the Bodhisat's house four women: Sudhammā, Chittā, Nandā and Sujātā. Of these Sudhammā, finding herself alone with the architect, gave him a bribe and said: " Little brother, make me a leading person in this hall." " Very well," he agreed, and before going further he had some pinnacle-wood dried, planed, bored and made into a finished pinnacle, wrapped in a cloth and put aside. Then when the hall was finished and the time had come for putting up the pinnacle, he said: "Dear me, my masters, one thing we haven't done." " What's that?" " We ought to get a pinnacle." " So be it; let's fetch one." " We cannot make it with a tree just cut; we ought to have got timber seasoned, planed, bored and laid by." " What's to be done now?" " If in anybody's house there's a pinnacle finished and put by for sale, that's what you must seek." They, looking and finding one in Sudhammā's house, did not get her to set a price for it; she said: " If you let me take part in the hall I will give it you." They replied: " We give no share to women." Then the architect said: " Masters,

what are you talking about? Save for the Brahmā-
world there is no place deprived of women! Accept
the pinnacle, and then our work will be completed."
" Very well," they said, and accepted the pinnacle
and completed the hall, distributing benches and
placing jars of water, and arranging for a supply of
rice-gruel. Surrounding the hall with a hedge they
fixed in that a gate, strewing sand within the
hedge, and without they planted an avenue of
fan-palms.

Chittā, too, made a garden in that spot, and there
was no fruit and flower-bearing tree that was not
there. Nandā, too, had a tank made, covered with
lotuses of five colours, lovely. Sujātā did nothing
whatever.

The Bodhisat fulfilling these seven duties: waiting on his mother, waiting on his father, paying
respect to elders, truth-speaking, not speaking
harshly, not slandering, suppressing niggardliness,
thus:

> That person who his parents doth support,
> Pays honour to the seniors of the clan,
> Is gentle, friendly-speaking, slandering not,
> The man unselfish, truthful, conquering wrath:
> Him e'en the Thirty-three devas call " good,"—

attained such a praiseworthy state that at life's end
he was born as Sakka, raja of (those) devas. And
there, too, his friends were born again.

At that time, in the realm of the Thirty-three,
Asuras were yet dwelling. Sakka deva-raja said:
" What to us is a kingdom held in common? " And,
letting nectar be given the Asuras to drink, when
they were drunk, he had them taken and thrown
down the precipices of Sineru. They got down to

the place called Asura-realm, on the lowest level of Sineru, equal in size to the world of the Thirty-three. There, like the Coral-tree of the devas, is the tree called the Pied Trumpet-flower, lasting for a kalpa. This tree being in blossom, they knew it was not the Coral-tree, and said: " This is not our deva-world, for there the Coral-tree blossoms." And they: " Old Sakka made us drunk, cast us into the great deep, and has taken our city." They saying " We will fight him and seize our deva-city," arose, swarming up Sineru like ants up a pillar.

When Sakka heard " The Asuras are up!" he sallied on to the great deep giving battle. Beaten by them, he began to run away along crest after crest of the southern deep in his Victory-chariot a hundred and fifty leagues in length. Now his chariot sped swiftly along the deep, passing Silk-cotton-tree Wood, and mowing down the trees in its way like palms, so that they fell into the deep. The young of the Garuda birds,[1] rolling over into the deep, uttered loud cries. Sakka asked Mātali (his charioteer): " Good Mātali, what noise is that? 'Tis a pitiful cry." " Sire, as the Silk-cotton-tree Wood falls, pounded by the swiftness of your chariot, the young of the Garudas, frightened by fear of death, are crying out together." The Great Being said, " Good Mātali, let there be no distress because of us. Let us not do murder for empire's sake. Let us rather for the sake of these give up our life to the Asuras," and he added the verse:

> " Let nestlings in Silk-cotton Wood
> Escape our pole's brunt, Mātali.
> Willing we yield our life to Asuras.
> Let not these birds unnested be!"

[1] A mythical bird, like the near-Eastern " roc."

Mātali, the driver, hearing his word, turned back the chariot, making for the deva-world by another way. But the Asuras, seeing him turning back, thought: " Surely Sakkas from other world-systems are coming; the chariot will be turned because of reinforcements." And, in fear of death, they ran away and entered their realm. And Sakka, entering the deva-city surrounded by deva-hosts, stood in the midst thereof. At that moment, through the riven earth, the palace of Victory rose up a thousand leagues in height—called Vejayanta because of its arising at " victory's end." Then, to prevent the Asuras coming, Sakka placed a guard in five places, anent which it is said:

Between two towns invincible
A five-fold ward stands firmly placed.
Of snakes and garudas and dwarfs
And ogres and the four great ones.[1]

Now, when Sakka, ruler of devas, had placed this warding in five places and was enjoying his deva-success, Sudhammā died and was reborn as his handmaiden. And as result of her gift of the pinnacle there appeared for her a jewelled hall named Sudhammā, where under a divine white canopy on a golden throne a league in width Sakka, ruler of devas, administered what was to be done for devas and men. Chittā also died and was reborn as his handmaiden. And as result of her making the garden, a garden appeared for her called Chittā Creeper Wood. Nandā also died, and was reborn as his handmaiden. And as result of her tank, a tank appeared for her. But since Sujātā had done no deed of good, she was reborn as a crane, by a pool in a certain forest.

Sakka, seeing and noticing " Sujātā does not

[1] Warders of the Four Quarters of the World. Cf. *Dialogues of the Buddha*, iii, Dial. xxxii.

appear. Now where has she been reborn? " went there and took her to the deva-world, showing her the lovely deva-city, Sudhammā the devas' hall, Chittā's Creeper Wood and Nandā's tank. " They," he admonished her, " having wrought good work have been reborn as my handmaidens, but you who wrought no good work have been reborn in the animal matrix. Henceforth ward your morals." So, establishing her in the five precepts, he took her back and left her. She from that time warded the moral code. And after some days Sakka, thinking " Has she been able to ward her morals? " went and lay prone before her in the shape of a fish. She, deeming it was a dead fish, seized it by the head. The fish flapped its tail, and she thinking " Why, it's alive? " left it.[1] " Well done, well done," said Sakka, " you will be able to ward your morals," and he went away. After her decease she was reborn at Benares in the house of a potter. Sakka thinking " Now where is she reborn? " discovered this, and causing a cart to be filled with gold cucumbers, he took the guise of an old man seated in the centre of the village, calling "Take cucumbers! Take cucumbers!" Men came and said: " Give, tāta! " " I give to those who ward their morals. Do you ward them? " " We don't know what you mean with your ' morals.' Give them for a price." " I want no price. I only give to those who ward their morals." The men said, " This is some wag," and went their way. Sujātā heard of what was going on and thinking " This will be something brought for me," went and said " Give, tāta! " " Do you ward your morals, good woman? " " Yes, I ward them." " This have I brought here for your sake," and placing them with the cart as well at her house-door, he went his way.

[1] That there is no reference to replacing in water is curious.

And she, warding her morals as long as she lived, was at her decease reborn as the daughter of Vepachitti, ruler of the Asuras. In consequence of her good morals she was very beautiful. When she was of age, he assembled the Asuras, saying " Let my daughter take a husband after her own heart."[1] Sakka, looking about, thinking " Now where is she reborn? " and, discovering this, assumed the look of an Asura and went there, with the idea: " Sujātā taking a husband after her own heart will take me." And they adorned Sujātā and brought her to the place of assembly, saying " Take a husband after your own heart! " She, looking about and seeing Sakka, because of her former love for him, said, " This is my husband," and took him. He, bringing her to the devas' city, made her chief of twenty-five hosts of nautchgirls. And persisting till his life's term, he went according to his deeds.

The Teacher, having cited this righteous discourse, rebuked the monk with the words: " Thus, monks, in the past wise men reigning in deva-kingdom did not murder, even giving up their life. You who have renounced the world in so away-leading a religion will be drinking water unstrained having life in it." And joining the sequence he assigned the Jataka, saying " Then the driver was Mātali, but Sakka was just I."

[1] The *svayam-vāra*, or maiden's " self-choice," occurs in Indian literature as far back as the Mahābhārata, I, and is permitted in Manu, and the other Law-books, where a girl's guardians neglect, within three years from puberty, to find her a husband. An interesting point here in language is that no word from *vāra* (choice) is used, but only " take," " *ganha*." The Indian concepts of the mind were very static; singularly poor in the vocabulary of " will."

THE MOSQUITO JATAKA
(*Makasa-jātaka*) [1]

"**BETTER** a foe."—This the Teacher told at a certain village while on tour among the Magadhese, about villagers who were fools. It is said that the Tathâgata, having once gone from Sāvatthi to the kingdom of Magadha and there making a tour, reached a certain hamlet. That hamlet was usually noted for the blind folly of its men. There such men had one day come together and taken counsel, saying " Masters, when we go and work in the forest, mosquitoes bite us, and on that account we have to knock off work. Let's take our bows and weapons and wage war on mosquitoes; hitting and chopping we shall have killed all the mosquitoes." They went into the forest, and saying "We shall hit the mosquitoes," they hit and struck each other, and much hurt they came back and laid down in the village and in the market-place and at the gate.

The Teacher, with his train of monks, entered that village for alms. The residue of wise men, when they saw him, made a pavilion at the gate, made many offerings, and saluting him took seats. The Teacher, seeing wounded men here and there, asked those laymen: " Many are the folk that ail; what have they done? " " Reverend sir, these men, saying ' We will wage war on the mosquitoes,' went and wounded each other. They've made themselves ill." The Teacher, saying " Not now alone have those blindly foolish men thinking to strike mos-

[1] The Rohinī Jātaka, No. 45, is a similar story told of a girl killing her mother with a pestle in the attempt to " swat " flies.

quitoes struck themselves; in the days gone by also there were men who, saying ' We'll strike the mosquito,' became strikers of another man "; and begged by the men he brought up the past.

In the past, when Brahmadatta was reigning at Benares, the Bodhisat was making his living by trade. Then, in a border village in the kingdom of Kāsi, many woodcraftsmen were living. And there a bald man was planing a tree. Now a mosquito alighted on his head, which shone like the back of a copperplate, and as if it had been a blow from a dart wounded him with its jaws. He said to his son seated by: " Tāta, a mosquito is wounding my head as if it were hitting me with a dart." " Tāta, hold steady, I'll kill it with a blow." And just then the Bodhisat, in quest of business, had arrived at that village and was seated in the woodcraftsman's workshop. Then the woodcraftsman said to his son: " Tāta, stop this mosquito! " He, saying " I'll stop it, Tāta," raised a sharp axe and, standing behind his father—" I'll hit the mosquito "—broke his father's head in two. The woodcraftsman there and then died.

The Bodhisat, seeing that action, thought, " Better is a wise foe for he will not kill from fear of men's vengeance," and he said this verse:

" Better an enemy who's won some sense,
  Than friend of any sense bereft.
The silly babbler says ' I'll slay the gnat! '
  And breaks his father's topmost limb."

Saying this verse, the Bodhisat arose and went according to his deeds, and the kinsmen of the woodcraftsmen did their duty by the body.

The Teacher . . . joined on the series and assigned the Jataka: " Then the wise trader who spoke and went away was just I."

THE PARK-SPOILING JATAKA
(*Ārāma-dūsaka-jātaka*) [1]

"WHEN for the better 'tis not fit."—This the Teacher told in a certain village of Kosala about a garden-spoiling. They say the Teacher, when on tour among the Kosalese, reached a certain village. There a landowner invited the Tathâgata to rest in his garden, and giving gifts to the Buddha-led company said: "Reverend sirs, walk at your pleasure in this garden." The monks arose and, taking the garden-warder, walked about in the garden. And seeing a barren space they asked him: "Lay-follower, in this garden there is elsewhere dense shade, but in this place no tree nor bush. What is the reason?" "Reverend sirs, when this garden was planted a village lad was watering; and in this spot he uprooted the young trees and watered according to the size of the roots. The young trees withered and died; this is why the spot has become bare." They told the Teacher, and he said: "Monks, the village lad was not only in the present a park-spoiler; he was that in the past also." And he brought up the past.

In past times, when Brahmadatta was reigning at Benares, they proclaimed a festival in the city. From the time when the sound of the festival drum was heard, all the citizens became absorbed in the festival. There were then many monkeys in the king's garden. The garden-warder thought: "In the town they're calling out the festival; if I tell

---

[1] The Ārāma-dūsa-jātaka, No. 268, is a very similar version of this story, the story of the present being located in Dakkhina-giri, the Deccan Hills, lit. Southern.

these monkeys to do my watering, I shall be able to amuse myself at the festival." And he went to the senior monkey and asked him: " Good senior monkey, this garden is of great use to you; you eat the flowers and fruit and young shoots. There's a festival being called in the city; I would take part in it; till I come back will you be able to water the young plants in the garden?" " Good, I will water." " Well then, be in earnest about it." And, giving them for the watering skins and buckets, he went off. The monkeys took these and watered. Then the senior said this: " My masters, save up the water. When you are watering the young plants, keep pulling up and look at the root of each. Where the roots have gone deep, give much water; where they haven't, give little. Later on it will be hard for us to get water." They consented, " Very well," and did so. At that time a wise man, seeing those monkeys do this in the royal garden, said: " Master monkeys, why are you rooting up each young plant and watering according to the size of the root? " They said: " So our senior monkey bade us." He, hearing their word, thought: " Alas! verily the fools, the stupid, saying we will make better, make worse! " And he said this verse:

" When for welfare it is not fit,
    Work for welfare no pleasure brings.
    The stupid man undoes the weal,
    As does the monkey in the park."

Thus the wise man, upbraiding in this verse the senior ape, left the garden with his own following.

The Teacher thereupon joined up the series and assigned the Jataka, saying, " Then the senior ape was the park-spoiling village lad, but the wise man was just I."

THE UNWISE FOLK JATAKA

(Dummedha-jātaka) [1]

"OF unwise folk."—This the Teacher told while living at the Jetavana about conduct for the world's welfare. This will be explained in the "Great Dark-One Jataka" of the Twelfth Book.[2]

In the past, when Brahmadatta was reigning at Benares, the Bodhisat took rebirth in the chief queen of that king. And on his name-day they called him Brahmadatta. When he was sixteen years old he studied at Taxilā, got beyond the Three Vedas and attained mastery of the eighteen stages of lore. Then his father gave him the viceroyalty. At that time the inhabitants of Benares were given to the cult of the unseen world,[3] honouring its denizens, and slaying many goats, sheep, poultry and swine, offered with flesh as well as with flowers and perfumes. The Bodhisat thought : " Men in these rites are now making great slaughter of life. The multitude for the most part are sunk in what is not right. When my father has gone and I get the kingdom, I by some innocuous plan will not permit the slaughter of life to be made." So one day, mounting his chariot

---

[1] The other Jataka bearing this title, No. 122, is entirely different in contents, and refers to Devadatta as being jealous of the Founder.

[2] In this story, by way of contrast with the gently beneficent methods of the Founder, the Bodhisat as Sakka is shown coercing men for their good by the threat of letting loose a terrible black hound to ravage the earth.

[3] *Devatā-mangalikā*, lit. " divine-luck-ers." *Mangāla* is a far-reaching word, including omens and all cult of the unseen.

and going out of the city, he saw a great votive tree, where the people were assembled, praying to the unseen being, reborn in that tree, for son, daughter, fame, wealth and the like, each one according to his wish. Descending from his chariot he went up to the tree, offering perfumes and flowers, sprinkling and pacing round the tree to the left. Thus following that cult he returned. And thenceforth he went time after time and repeated the rites.

Later on, when his father was gone and he was reigning righteously in every way, he thought: " My mind has now won to the summit; I am established in the kingdom; now will I cause to win to its summit that one weal which I had in mind." And, assembling the people, he said: " Know you, sirs, for what reason I have won the kingship? " " We do not know, sire." " Have you not seen me in the past worshipping at such and such a votive tree with perfumes and the like? " " Yes, sire." " I was then making a prayer, ' If I get the kingship I will make thee a sacrifice.' By the influence of that being I have got the kingship; now will I make her[1] the sacrifice; do you without delay swiftly prepare it." " What shall we take for it, lord? " " Sirs, when I was entreating the spirit (of the tree), I entreated that whoever should commit the five immoral acts, namely, taking of life and so on, and the ten ways of wrongdoing, I should make sacrifice with them, offering their entrails, flesh and blood. Do you thus proclaim with drum: ' So did our king pray while viceroy, and he now wills that all such be slain and their hearts be offered to that being. Let all citizens take note.' " So saying, he explained: " They who henceforth shall practise immoral acts, of them will

[1] *Devatā* (deity) is, in form, as abstract noun in *ā*, feminine, but may have been conceived as a masculine tree-spirit.

48

I sacrifice a thousand; offering them in sacrifice I shall be released from my promise in praying." And he said the verse:

" Of unwise folk to sacrifice a thousand once I vowed;
   Now will I sacrifice, for many are the unrighteous folk."

The officials, hearing the Bodhisat's word, said, " Very well, sire," and had the drum beat in twelve-leagued Benares city. And so, while he reigned, not one man showed immoral conduct, such was the result of the drum's behest. Thus the Bodhisat, without harming one person in the whole kingdom, warded morality, and himself, working merit with giving and the like, at the end of life went with his own following to fill the city of devas.

And the Teacher . . . assigned the Jataka: " Then the people were the Buddha's people, but the king of Benares was just I."

THE GREAT SILAVA-KING JATAKA
(*Mahāsīlava-jātaka*)

" MAN should just hope."—This the Teacher
told while living at the Jetavana about a monk
who had relinquished effort. Asking him about this,
the Teacher said, " Why have you, monk, in such an
away-going religion as this, relinquished effort? In
olden times wise men, even though they lost their kingdom, standing on their own effort, even though done
for, raised up fame," and he brought up the past.

In the past, when Brahmadatta was reigning at
Benares, the Bodhisat as the gifted son of the king,
his name Sīlavant (" Moral "), succeeded his father
at Benares, and was a righteous king of the Right.
At each of the four city gates he built a giving-hall
for giving alms to poor wayfarers,[1] one also in the
city's midst and one at his own doors. He warded
the moral code, kept holy days, and ever showed
patience, goodwill and kindness, cherishing all
beings like a father cherishing his child at his hip.

One of his courtiers had misbehaved in the harem,
and the king, coming to know it, said to him:
" Blind fool, you have done what is not seemly; you
deserve not to live in my country; take your property
and family and go elsewhere." Leaving the Kāsi
kingdom the man took service with the king of
Kosala, and grew to be in his confidence. One day
he made out that the Benares king was exceeding
soft, and that kingdom like an intact honeycomb,
needing scarcely an army to seize it. The Benares
kingdom was large, and the king feared the man

[1] Or " poor folk and wayfarers."

might be a traitor. The other advised him to send a raiding party into Kāsi, saying that, when caught there and brought to the king, they would be released and gifts given them in place of the goods they had wished to loot. This he did once and twice, and in truth the raiders got off as had been said, a third raid even entering Benares.

Then the king of Kosala, saying that the king was overmuch righteous, decided to seize his kingdom. Nor could the thousand peerless warriors of the Benares king persuade him to let them repel the invader. " Tātas," said he, " there is to be no work of injury done on others because of me. Let the king take the kingdom; do not go forth." And no entreaty would move him. When the king of Kosala entered the city he met with no resistance, and the doors of the royal dwelling stood open. Mounting to the great terrace where sat the blameless king Sīlavant in state with his ministers, he bade men seize them, bind them, take them to the cemetery, did them in up to their throats, and then " the jackals by night will do what should be done." And taken off they were. But even then king Sīlavant wrought no violence, nor did one of his men break the king's behest.

So they, buried and with the ground stamped solid around them, were left, the king exhorting his ministers not to be wrath with the bandit-king, but to practise goodwill. Then at midnight came the jackals. The king and his men all set up one shout and the beasts scattered. Gradually they ceased to fear, and came near each to seize his prey. The chief jackal made for the king. The king, skilful in stratagem, marked him coming, and raising his throat as if to give opportunity for the biting, he (himself) bit the beast by the throat, drawing its jawbone as if he had put it in a vice. The jackal, in mortal fear, raised a mighty howl, and the pack, scenting man's work, all fled. Held by the king's jaw, the jackal, plunging hither and thither, loosened the earth. When he saw it was loose, he let the jackal go, and using the strength of an elephant, he got his arms disengaged and drew up both himself and the others.

Now, two Yakkhas each had a range in the cemetery, and men had exposed a corpse so that it overlay the boundary between them. Quarrelling as to the dividing of it, they said: " This king Sīlavant is righteous, he will divide it for us." When they asked him he said: " Master Yakkhas, I will do so, but I am dirty, I will first bathe." The Yakkhas by their power fetched the water put ready for the king's bath; they also brought him the bandit-king's garments, with perfumes and flowers. Could they do anything else for him? Yes, he was hungry. They brought him choice viands prepared for the bandit-king's meal, water also to drink and wash mouth and hands withal, and betel to chew. Could they do anything else for him? Yes, he wanted the sword of state laid at the bandit-king's head. Then the king clove the corpse in twain, and gave half to each. They ate and were glad, and was there anything more they could do for him? " Yes, take me to the bandit-king's bedroom and each of my ministers to his home." This done the king went up to the bandit-king asleep on his own bed, and smote him on the stomach with the flat of the sword. Waking affrighted, he saw by the lamplight who was come, and rising up he summoned fortitude and said: " Majesty, at this hour of the night, when the guard is set, the door fastened and sentinels about the house, no chances taken, how is it that you adorned and armed have got here? " The king told him the whole story. Hearing this, the bandit-king was much moved in mind and said: " Majesty, though I am a man, I did not know your virtues, yet the fierce rough Yakkhas, eaters of flesh of those alien to them, knew your virtues. No more, lord of men, will I plot ill to one so good as you." And he swore an oath on his sword, and got the king's forgiveness, and made him lie down upon the royal bed, himself lying on a little one. At sunrise next day he had all the armies and populace assembled by beat of drum, and publicly spoke of the king's virtues, as if he was lifting up the full moon into the sky; publicly he apologised and restored the kingdom, saying, "Henceforth danger from bandits to yourself is my burden. You reign while I keep watch and ward." So saying, he gave orders concerning the man who had libelled, and betook himself with his army to his country.

Sīlavant, the great king, seated in state, bethought himself: " Such success as this and saving the lives of my thousand ministers had not been had I made no effort. But I by the strength of my effort regained my eclipsed fame and saved them. Verily without work of sword, one should put forth effort, for to one putting forth effort fruit follows." And inspired he uttered this verse:

" Man should just hope; falter the wise should not.
I see, look you, myself:
E'en as I wished so did I come to be."

And working merit the Bodhisat went according to his deeds.

. . . the hopeless monk thereupon became established in worthiness, and the Teacher assigned the Jataka: " Then the mischievous minister was Devadatta, the thousand ministers were the Buddhacompany, but the king Sīlavant was just I."

THE BAR OF GOLD JATAKA
(*Kancanakkhandha-jātaka*)

"HE who with gladsome heart."—This the Teacher while living at Sāvatthi told about a certain monk. It is said that a man of the Sāvatthi families, after hearing the righteous teaching of the Teacher, gave his bosom to the religion of the Jewels[1] and left the world. Then his teacher and his tutor declared to him the Moral Code thus:

"Reverend one, the Moral Code is manifold, to wit of one kind, two kinds, three kinds, and so on up to ten kinds; (further) this is the Minor Code, that the Middle Code, this the Great Code;[2] (further) this is the moral code of restraint according to Pātimokkha, that is the code of restraint of sense, this is the code of restraint by purity in life-maintenance." He thought: "Truly this Moral Code is too vast. Taking on me thus much I shall not be able to carry on. What's the use of my leaving the world unable to fulfil the Moral Code? I'll become a layman again and work merit in giving and the like and support wife and family." So thinking he said: "Reverend sirs, I shall not be able to keep the Moral Code; so what is the use of my leaving the world? I will turn me to the Low Thing.[3] Do you take my bowl and robe." Then they said: "This

---

[1] Ratana-sāsana, viz. of Buddha, Dhamma, Sangha: a late idiom.

[2] Cf. *Dialogues of the Buddha*, I, 1; three divisions on "Sīla." Pātimokkha: monastic rules.

[3] The usual way, in the scriptures, of alluding to life in the world.

being so, go hence, after saluting the Ten-powered One." And they took him before the Teacher in the temple. The Teacher, seeing, said: " Why, monks, are you come bringing a monk who has no use (for us)? " " Reverend sir, this monk is handing over his bowl and robe and saying he will not be able to keep the Moral Code, so we are come bringing him." " But why, monks, are you declaring to him (such) a lot of the Code? As far as he is able to keep, so far will he keep. Henceforth do you tell him in that way nothing whatever. I shall know what is here to be done."

" Come you, monk, what use have you for a mass of moral code? Will you be able to keep just three precepts? " " I shall be able, reverend sir." " Well, then, do you henceforth ward the three gates: the gate of the act, the gate of the word, the gate of the thought; do no evil action in act, word or thought. Go; turn not to the Lower Thing; just ward these three precepts." Thereupon the monk, glad at heart, said, " Very well, reverend sir, I will ward those three precepts," and saluting the Teacher, he went with teacher and repeater. He fulfilling those three precepts came to know this: " Though the Moral Code was declared to me by teacher and repeater, they because of their own unenlightened state were not able to make me enlightened. The Very Enlightened, by his own enlightened enlightenment, by supreme dominion in the Right, made me grasp so much moral code in just three gates. Ah! the very bed-rock that the Teacher has become for me! " And making insight to grow, after some days he graduated in saintship. The monks, learning this, were, while assembled in the temple, praising the Buddha-virtues when the Teacher came in and learnt of their talk. " Monks," he said, " a burden though heavy may, when analysed piecemeal, become as if it were light. And wise men in the olden time when they had gotten a mighty nugget of gold, which they couldn't lift, lifted it and went when it was divided." And he brought up the past.

In the past, when Brahmadatta was reigning at Benares, the Bodhisat was born in a hamlet as a farmer. He one day was ploughing a field where was a buried hamlet. And in times of old a very rich merchant of that village had hoarded up a gold nugget as big round as the thigh, four cubits long. On this the Bodhisat's plough caught and stood fast. Thinking it was a long spread root, he cleared away the soil, then seeing what it was, he covered it up again with earth and did the day's ploughing. At sunset, laying aside yoke, plough and all, he thought " I'll go and take the gold nugget," but was not able to lift it. Unable he sat down (and thought): " So much will be for stomach-maintenance, so much I'll put aside and save up, so much I'll use in business, so much will be for working merit in giving and the like," making four portions. To him, when dividing it so, the gold nugget seemed to become very light. He lifted it up, brought it to his house, divided it into four, and working merit went according to his deeds.[1]

The Exalted One, in adducing this righteous lesson, being the Very Enlightened, said this verse:

[1] In the Cambridge translation Lord Chalmers, by a freer rendering, has made this story end more plausibly, since no subjective division can well have worked such a miracle on the man's thews and sinews. In that rendering the *actual* division precedes the removal piecemeal; my translation is as is the literal Pali.

" He of thrilled heart, the man who's thrilled in mind,
He makes the good thing come to be, to win
The goal he seeks; he in due course may win
The bringing ev'ry hindrance to an end."

Thus completing the lesson with the pinnacle of
saintship, the Teacher joined on the series and
assigned the Jataka: " Then the gold nugget-win-
ning man was just I."

THE MONKEY-LORD JATAKA

(*Vanarinda-jātaka*)

" IN whom are these four things."—This the Teacher told while living at the Bamboo Wood about Devadatta's going about to kill him. " Not only now, monks," said he, " does he do so; he did so in the olden days also, but he was not able to destroy me." And he brought up the past.

In the past, when Brahmadatta was reigning at Benares, the Bodhisat, reborn in the monkey world, and in course of growth become as big as a colt and very strong, dwelt on the bank of a river. In the middle of the river was a little island, fertile in divers fruit trees such as mangoes, bread fruit and the like. The Bodhisat, being as strong as an elephant, would leap from his bank and alight on a flat rock, lying midway between his bank and the islet, and thence leap over to the isle. There he would eat his fill of fruit and then return in the evening, and on another day do the same. By this method he kept himself alive.

Now at this time there was a crocodile and his consort living in that river. And the wife, seeing that Bodhisat go by time after time, lusted after his heart's flesh, and told her mate of her craving. The crocodile said, " Very good, you shall get it," and thinking, " To-day as he comes back at evening from the island I'll catch him," he went and lay down on the flat rock. The Bodhisat, having spent the day on the island, stood there in the evening and looked over to the rock, and he thought: " That

rock appears higher to-day, what's the reason?"
For he used to determine the height of the water
and of the rock, and thus it occurred to him: "To-
day there is neither fall nor rise in the height of the
water, yet the rock has become bigger; I wonder
now whether there's a crocodile lying on the rock
to catch me? I'll first test him." And standing there
as if talking with him, he said: "Master rock!"
After three calls, getting no reply, he said: "Rock!"
The rock showed no response. Then the monkey
said: "Why, master rock, is it that to-day you make
no reply?" The crocodile thought, "Why sure,
on other days this rock has been giving answer to
the monkey; I'll now answer him," and he said:
"What is it, master monkey?" "Who are you?"
"I'm a crocodile." "What are you lying there for?"
"Hoping I'll get your heart's flesh." The Bodhisat
thought: "There's no other way for me to go; to-
day I'll have to get round that crocodile." And he
said to him: "Good crocodile, I'll give myself up
to you; open your mouth and catch me as I come."
Now crocodiles, when their mouths are open, shut
their eyes. This is what happened with this crocodile, he not seeing the plan. And so he lay. The
Bodhisat, seeing how he was, mouth open, eyes
shut, sprang from the island on to the crocodile's
head, and thence, like a flash of lightning, leapt
again and alighted on the river bank. The crocodile,
seeing the feat, thought, "It's a marvel this monkey
has done," and saying, "Master monkey, a man in
this world who has four things overcomes his enemies;
all four are inside you, I reckon," spoke this verse:

"In whom are these four things, lord monkey, as in
    you,
    Truth, right, resolve, surrender, he outruns the foe."

Thus praising the Bodhisat, the crocodile went to his own place.

The Teacher then assigned the Jataka: " Then the crocodile was Devadatta, his wife was the young Brahminee Chinchā, but the monkey-lord was just I."

THE BLINDFOLD JATAKA

(Andhabhūta-jātaka)

"THAT which while Brahman played."—This the Teacher told while living at the Jetavana about a monk who was a-hankering. The Teacher asked him if this were true, and when he said it was, he said, "Monk, women are not to be warded. In the past wise men, warding a woman from her birth, were not able to ward her," and he brought up the past.

In the past, when Brahmadatta was reigning at Benares, the Bodhisat, born to his chief queen and become perfected in all the sciences, at his father's death was established in the kingdom and ruled righteously. He used to play dice with his chaplain, and while he played he would, as he threw the dice on a silver table, sing this dicing song:

"Every river crooked runs and every wood is made of sticks;
And every woman may work ill, gin she but find a shelter fit."

Thus singing the king always won and the chaplain always lost, and he, when in due course house and fortune were coming to naught, thought thus: "Things being so, all the wealth in this house will be destroyed. I will look around and get a female in the house who has never been with a man." Then it occurred to him: "I shall not be able to ward a woman whom another man has seen. I will ward a female from her birth, and keep her under control

61

when grown up, and make her a ' one-man-ster,' and set a strong ward over her; so shall I draw in wealth from the court."

Now he was skilled in omen-lore. And seeing a poor woman about to be a mother, and discerning she would have a daughter, he sent for her and gave her money to be confined in his house, and when this had taken place he gave her money and sent her away. Not suffering other men to see the child, he gave her into the hands of women, reared her and kept her when grown up under his control.

While she was growing up, he did not play dice with the king, but when he had placed her under control, he said to the king: " Your majesty, let us play dice." " Good," said the king, and played as he used to do. When the king sang, as he threw the dice, the chaplain said: " Excepting my girl." From the time the chaplain won, the king lost. Considering this, the Bodhisat thought, " There will be in that house some woman who is a ' one-man-ster ' only," and understanding the state of things, he thought, " I will have her morals broken," and he sent for a knave and said: " Are you able to break the morals of the chaplain's woman? " " I can, sire." Then the king gave him money and dismissed him saying, " Well, then, get it done quickly."

Taking the king's money he procured a lot of perfumes, incense, and toilet powders and opened a perfume shop not far from the chaplain's house. And the chaplain's house was of seven floors and seven entrances, and at each entrance there was a guard of women; except the brahman, no man got leave to enter, and only after inspection could they let the dust and rubbish basket pass in. The chaplain was permitted to see the girl, and she had one attendant. Then the attendant, taking from her

money for perfumes and flowers, went past the
knave's shop. He, knowing well that this was her
attendant, saw her coming one day, and going out
of his shop he went and fell at her feet, gripping her
feet with both hands and sobbing, " Mother, where
have you been all this time? " Then the knave's
accomplices standing by said: " Hand, foot, face,
and figure and the way of them—the mother and
son are just alike! " The woman as they kept on
talking lost faith in herself, and thinking " This will
be my son! " herself began to weep. They both
stood sobbing and weeping and embracing each
other. Then said the knave: " Mother, where do
you live? " " My dear, I live doing service to the
chaplain's young woman, graceful as a fairy, and of
tiptop beauty." " Where are you going now, mother?"
" To get her perfumes and wreaths." " Mother,
why should you go elsewhere? Henceforth get them
from me." And refusing payment he gave her betel,
bdellium, and divers flowers.

The lady, seeing all these, said: " Why, mother,
how pleased the brahman is with us to-day? " " Why
do you say that? " " When he saw the quantity there
is." " It was not the brahman giving me much money,
but my getting them from my son." From that time
she took herself the money given her by the brahman
and fetched the perfumes and flowers from the man.

The knave after some days took to a sick bed.
The woman went to the shop and, not seeing him,
asked: " Where is my son? " " Your son is taken
bad." She went to his bed, sat down and stroked
his back, asking, " What ails you, tāta? " He was
silent. " Why don't you speak, son? " " Mother, I
could not tell you even were I dying." " If you don't
tell me, whom are you to tell, tāta? " " Mother,
there's nothing else wrong with me, but hearing the

praise of your lady, I've gone and fallen in love with her; if I get her I shall live, if not I shall just die." " Tāta, mine be this burden; don't you take thought about it." And comforting him she took many perfumes and flowers, and going to the lady said: " My son, dear, having heard your praises, has gone and fallen in love with you—what is to be done? " " If you're able to bring him we give him opportunity." She, hearing her word, from that time, sweeping together much rubbish from the corners of the house and placing it in a flower-basket, went with it at inspection time and emptied it over the woman-warder who, disgusted at that, went away. By the same method she emptied a basket over each of the other women if they said anything to her. From that time no one ventured to inspect whatever she fetched or took. Then she made the knave lie down in a flower-basket and brought him past to her lady. The knave broke the lady's morals and was in the mansion one or two days. When the chaplain went out they took their pleasure; when he came in the knave lay low.

Then after one or two days she said: " My master, you must be going now." " I am willing to go after I've hit the brahman." " So be it." And she hid him when the brahman came and said: " My lord, I would dance while you play the lute." " Very good, lady, dance," and he played the lute. " I shall be ashamed if you are looking. When I have fixed a cloth over your handsome face I will dance." " If you are ashamed, do so." The lady, taking one strip of cloth so as to shut off his eyes, bound his face. The brahman, with his face bandaged, played the lute. When she had danced for a little while she said: " My lord, I would like to give you just once a slap on the head." The brahman, doting on the woman and ignorant of the reason, said: " Hit."

The lady made a sign to the knave. He came softly up to the brahman and, standing behind him, hit him a bad blow on the head. His eyes were like to fall out and a lump rose on his head. Sore hurt, he said: " Where's your hand? " The lady placed her hand in his and he said: " The hand is soft, but the blow was tough." The knave, his blow given, lay low. The lady, he lying low, took off the cloth from the brahman's face and, taking oil, smeared the bruise on the head. When the brahman had gone out that woman made the knave lie down in the basket and carried him away. Going to the king he told him all that had happened.

The king said to the brahman when in waiting: " Let us play dice, brahman." " Very good, your majesty." The king had the dicing-board placed, and as before sang the play-song as he threw the dice. The brahman, ignorant of the broken state of the lady's fast, said " Except my lady," but though he said so he was beaten. The king knowing said: " Brahman, what are you excepting? Your lady's fast is broken. You ward a female from birth setting a guard at seven places, and you deem you will be able to ward her. You might stow a female in your belly and walk about and yet you wouldn't be able to ward her. There is no such thing as a ' one-man ' woman. Your lady saying ' I would dance ' to your playing the lute, and binding your face with a cloth, lets her lover give you a bad blow on the head and got him away—now why are you excepting? " And he said this verse:

" That which, while brahman played the lute face-
    bound,
  (She did) the wife reared from the very egg!—
  On them, good sooth! what man may place his faith?"

Thus the Bodhisat taught the right to the brahman. The brahman, hearing his teaching, went home and said to the lady: " By you I'm told such wicked deeds have been done! " " My lord, who has said so? I have not so done. 'Twas I struck, not anyone else. If you do not believe, I will do the Act of Truth, saying, ' Except you I know not the touch of any man's hand,' and I will pass through the fire and make you believe." " Be it so," said the brahman, and he had a bonfire made and, setting it on fire, sent for her and said: " If you yourself believe, pass through the fire."

Now the lady had trained her attendant beforehand: " Mother, make your son be there, and when I am entering the fire, tell him to catch hold of my hand." She went and told him thus. The knave came and stood among them. The lady, willing to deceive the brahman, stood amid the crowd and said, " Brahman, except you I know not the touch of another man's hand. By this true thing let this fire not burn me! " and she began to pass through the fire. At that moment the knave (crying), " See what the chaplain-brahman has done! He makes such a woman pass through the fire! " went and seized her hand. She, loosing her hand, said to the chaplain: " My lord, my Act of Truth is broken. I cannot enter the fire." " Why? " " My lord, I said to-day in my Act of Truth, except you no other man had touched me, and now my hand has been seized by this man." The brahman, seeing he had been deceived, had her taken away and beaten.

So, as they say, are these women full of unrighteousness. However great a wicked act they've done to deceive their own husbands, they will, even by day, swear " I have not done such a thing! " Manyminded are they, wherefore it is said:

Of these she-bandits and their many wits
Amongst them hard it is to find the true.
The nature of the woman's hard to know,
'Tis like the ways in water of the fish.
Lies are to them as truth and truth as lies.
Better, ay, better are to me the kine
Eating their fill of grass; but women sure
She-bandits are they, cruel and malign,
And hard and fickle; there is naught that men
Be saying and they'll not be ware of it.

The Teacher, showing in this righteous teaching how unwardable is the female, . . . joined on the series and assigned the Jataka: " Then the king of Benares was just I."

THE HARD-TO-KNOW JATAKA

(Durājāna-jātaka)

"**B**E thou not glad."—This the Teacher told while staying at the Jetavana about a lay-disciple. 'Tis said a certain lay-disciple of Sāvatthi, one established in the three Gems and the five Precepts, devoted to Buddha, Dhamma, Sangha, had a wife who was immoral and wicked. The days she did wrong she was as a slave bought for a hundred; on days she did not do wrong she became the mistress fierce and abusive. He was not able to understand her nature. And worried through her he did not go to wait on the Buddha. But one day he went to him, taking perfumes and flowers; and to him, after his salute and seated, the Teacher said: " Why have you not been, layman, these seven eight days to wait on the Buddha? " " My house-lady, reverend sir, is one day like a slave bought for a hundred, one day a mistress fierce and abusive; I'm not able to understand her nature; it's because I was worried through her that I did not come to wait on the Buddha." Then, hearing his word, the Teacher said: " Layman, woman's nature is hard to know— so have wise men declared in the past! And saying ' One is not able to distinguish that, because one is confused by life's becomings,' "[1] he brought up the past.

In the past, when Brahmadatta was reigning at Benares, the Bodhisat, becoming a world-leading teacher, was teaching science to five hundred young

[1] *i.e.* rebirths.

brahmans. Now a young brahman from beyond the kingdom, learning science under him, fell in love with a woman and, making her his wife, dwelling in the city of Benares itself, he did not wait on his teacher for two or three terms. Now that woman was immoral and wicked; on days when she practised wrong she was as a slave; on days when she did not she was the mistress fierce and abusive. He was not able to understand her nature, and worried and confused by her, he did not wait on his teacher. When seven eight days had passed and he did go to the teacher the teacher asked him: " Why, man, have you not put in an appearance? " And he: " My wife, teacher, on one day asks, entreats me, is as meek as a slave; one day, like the mistress, she is obstinate, fierce, abusive. I'm not able to understand her nature, and worried and confused by her I did not come to you." The teacher said: " Just so, just so, man, women on days when their conduct is amiss are compliant to their husband, are meek as a slave; on days when their conduct is not amiss they become proud and obstinate and the husband is of no account. In this way women are wrongdoers, immoral; their nature is hard to know; between them desiring and not desiring a middle state is to be observed." And as admonition he said this verse:

"Be thou not glad at thought: 'she's fain for me!'
Be thou not sad at thought: ' she is not fain.'
Of women hard the nature is to know,
As in the water is the way of fish."

Such was the Bodhisat's admonition to the pupil. Thenceforth he became middle-stated, above her. And she, thinking " methinks my immoral nature is known by the Teacher," thenceforth did not behave amiss.

So it happened with the layman's woman. And the Teacher . . . joining up the series assigned the Jataka: " The couple then were the couple now, but the teacher was just I."

THE APRONFULL JATAKA
(*Ucchanga-jātaka*)

" A SON to me, sire,'s but an apronfull."—This
the Teacher told while living at the Jetavana about a certain countrywoman. For at one time
in the kingdom of Kosala three persons were ploughing by the edge of the jungle. At that time thieves
plundered men in the jungle and made off. Men,
looking for the thieves and not finding them,
came to the field. " You plundered in the jungle
and now you would be ploughmen! " they said.
" These are the thieves," and they bound them and
led them to the king of Kosala. Now a certain woman
frequented the king's house again and again with
the wail, " Give me covering! Give me covering! "
The king, hearing her cry, said, " Give her covering,"
and taking a cloak they went to her. She seeing
them said: " I'm not asking for this covering."
The men went and reported to the king: " She says
she is not talking about this covering; she means a
husband as covering." Then the king sent for her
and said: " They say it's a husband as covering
you're begging for." " Yes, sire, for a woman a
husband is a covering; when there's none, though she
be clad in a robe worth a thousand, she goes in debt."
To settle this matter this saying should be cited:

Naked the waterless river; naked the kingless realm;
And woman that's widow is naked, though brothers
    ten be hers.

The king was pleased with her and asked her:
" Those three men, what are they to you? " " One,

sire, is my husband, one is my brother, one is my son." The king: " I am content with you; of these three I give one; which would you have? " She said: " I, sire, if I live, shall get a husband; I shall also get a son; but in that my parents are dead I shall find it hard to get a brother; give me the brother, sire." The king was gratified and had all three released. Thus by the one woman were three persons freed from trouble.

The affair became known in the Sangha, and when one day the monks were praising the woman for this as they sat in the temple, the Teacher came among them and said: " Not now only, monks, has this woman freed those three persons from trouble, she freed them also of yore," and he brought up the past.

The story is the same as that told of the present. The woman asked: " Can you not give me the three, sire? " " Nay, I cannot." " If you are not able to give the three, give me the brother." " Take your boy or your husband; what matters the brother to you? " She, saying " These, sire, are easy to get, but a brother is hard to get," added this verse:

" A son to me, sire, 's but an apronfull,
    And husband if I scour the road (I'll find),
    But I'll not see the land whence I
    Could from the home-brood fetch one more."

The king's heart was gratified and, saying " She speaks the truth," he had the three men brought from the prison and gave them (to her).

And the Teacher . . . joining on the series assigned the Jataka: "The four in the past are the present four, but the king was I at that time."[1]

[1] *Sic*, differing a little from the usual wording.

THE SAKETA JATAKA

" THE man in whom mind makes its home."—
This the Teacher told, while living in the
Anjana Wood near Saketa, about a brahman. Namely,
when the Blessed One was entering Saketa, attended
by the company of monks, an aged brahman of
Saketa going forth from the city saw the Ten-Powered in the gate. And he fell at his feet clasping him
by the ankles and saying, " Dear one, should not
parents in their old age be cherished by their children? Why have you not shown yourself to us for so
long? Now that I have seen you, come to see your
mother," and taking the Teacher he went to his
home. The Teacher, going there, sat down on the
prepared seat together with the monks. And the brahman's wife came and fell at the Teacher's feet,
lamenting, " My dear, where have you been gone
so long? Should not parents when grown be minis-
tered to? " And she made her sons and daughters
also salute him, saying, " Come, salute your brother! "
Both with joyful mind gave many things. The
Teacher, when the meal was over, told them the
Old Age Sutta. At the end both were established in
the stage of Non-returner's Fruition, and the Teacher,
rising from his seat, went to the Anjana Wood. The
monks seated in the temple started the talk: " The
brahman knows that the Tathâgata's father is Suddhodana, his mother Maya. Yet knowing this both
he and his wife called him ' our son,' and the Teacher
suffered it. What can be the reason? " The Teacher
hearing the talk said, " Monks, both of them spoke

73

of me as their own son," and he brought up the past.

That brahman, monks, for 500 births in immediate succession was my father, for 500 births he was my uncle, for 500 births he was my grandfather; this brahmanee also was for 500 births in immediate succession my mother, for 500 births my aunt, for 500 births my grandmother. Thus I for 1,500 births grew up in the hands of the brahman, grew up for 1,500 births in the hands of the brahmanee. So having told of 3,000 births, he having become the Very Enlightened, said this verse:

" The man in whom mind makes its home and heart
        finds rest,
    Though never seen before in him one willingly feels
        trust."

Thus the Teacher, having brought up this righteous teaching, joined the series and assigned the Jataka: " Then the brahman and his wife were those two and the son was just I."

THE SAKETA JATAKA

"WHAT, Blessed Lord, is now the cause?"— This the Teacher told while living near Saketa about a brahman. But the story here both past and present has been already told in the First Book. Now when the Tathâgata had gone to the Vihara, a monk asked: "That affection, reverend sir, how was it set up?" And he said the first verse:

"What, Blessed Lord, may be the cause as here
  That for some man the heart is wholly quenched,
  For some the mind rests in his pleasant charm?"

Then the Teacher, showing the reason for affection in those (two), said the second verse:

"By former life in company, or by goodwill shown
    here,
  Thus may affection breed as lotus in the water
  (blooms)."

The Jataka is then assigned as in the foregoing.

THE GATE OF WEAL JATAKA
(*Atthassa dvāra-jātaka*)

"HEALTH let him seek (as being) gain supreme."—This the Teacher told while living at the Jetavana about a son good at welfare.[1] There was, namely, at Sāvatthi a wealthy leading merchant's son who when (only) seven years old was wise, and good at welfare. He one day came to his father and asked him about the " gate of welfare." He did not know (the answer), and he thought: " This question is very subtle; except the all-knowing Buddha, no one, from the upper height of life to Avīchi below in the limits of the habitable world, is able to answer it." And, making his son take many garlands and sweet perfumes, he brought him to the Jetavana, greeted with offerings the Teacher, and, seated beside him, said: " This boy, reverend sir, wise, good at welfare, has asked me the question about the ' gate of welfare.' I, ignorant about it, have come to you. It were well if the Blessed One would talk to me about it." The Teacher said: " In bygone times I, layman, was asked that question by this little youth, and I talked to him about it. Then he knew, but now, incurring confusion through coming to be, he does not discern." The man begging (to hear), he brought up the past.

In the past, when Brahmadatta was reigning at Benares, the Bodhisat became a very wealthy leading merchant. And being asked by his son, as you

[1] *Attha-kusalo.* See Introduction, p. xxiii.

have been, he, the father, talking about it, said this verse:

" Health let him seek (as being) gain supreme,
   The moral code, to elders deference,
   Learning, and to the Right conformity,
   And non-adhesion: these the six gates are
   That open up the welfare (which is growth)."

Thus did the Bodhisat talk about the question of the gate of weal to the son. From that time he persevered in those six things. And the Bodhisat, working merit in giving and the like, went according to his deeds.

The Teacher then assigned the Jataka: " Then the son was the present son, but the merchant was just I."

THE KING'S LESSON JATAKA
(Rājôvāda-jātaka)

"HARD to the hard he throws."—This the Teacher told while staying at the Jetavana about a king's lesson. It will be expanded in the Jataka of the Three Dogs.

One day the king of Kosala had passed judgment on a case in court where judgment had been hard to arrive at. After he had breakfasted and washed his hands, he mounted his decorated chariot and went to the Teacher, saluting the feet that were beautiful as lotus-blossoms, and sat down at his side. Then the Teacher said to him: "Well, your majesty, why come you here at this hour?" "Reverend sir, I have been prevented from coming by having to pass judgment on a case in court where judgment was hard to arrive at; now that I have investigated it, eaten and washed my hands, I am come to wait upon you." The Teacher: "Your majesty, good is it to judge in court rightly and justly. It is the way to the Bright World. It is not wonderful that they who can get admonished by one all-wise like me should judge a case rightly and justly. It is wonderful that kings in the past, hearing the word of men who were not all-wise, should judge a case rightly and justly, should have avoided the four wrong ways, should not have upset the ten kingly things, and having ruled the kingdom righteously have gone to swell the Bright World." The king requesting him, he brought up the past.

In the past, when Brahmadatta was reigning at

Benares, the Bodhisat was born to his chief queen by a safe delivery, due requisites being paid him. On the naming-day they called him just Brahmadatta. Coming in due time of age, at sixteen years he went to Takkasilā and attained expertness in every art. At his father's death he ascended the throne and reigned rightly and justly, administering justice without respect to desire and the like. He acting thus the ministers also practised justice. Practice being by way of righteous judgments there were no fraudulent cases. There being none of these, the bustle of litigators in the king's court ceased. Ministers, though they sat all day to judge, seeing no one coming went away. The law courts became a negligible circumstance.

The Bodhisat thought: "I reigning righteously there is no coming up for judgment; bustle is no more; the law courts have become a negligible circumstance; it now behoves me to search whether there be any fault in me, so that learning ' such and such is a fault of mine' I having got rid of it shall progress in virtues." Thenceforth inquiring, " Is there anyone who will tell me of a fault? " and finding none among those within the court precincts, hearing only tell of his virtues, he thought, " These maybe from fear have not mentioned any fault in me, but tell of my virtues," and he inquired among those without the precincts, and finding none he inquired within the city, and without the city, at the four gates, in the gate-suburb. There also finding no fault-finder and hearing only his virtues, he thought, " I will inquire in the countryside," and handing over the kingdom to ministers, he mounted his chariot and, taking just the driver, left the city in disguise. Inquiring about the country he went to the marches, and seeing none to find fault, hearing only his virtues, he turned back from the marches towards the city by the high road.

Now just at that time Mallika, king of Kosala, reigning righteously, had become a seeker of (his own) shortcomings, and finding none to tell among those within the precincts and the rest, but hearing only his virtues, had inquired about the countryside and came to that district. They both came face to face where was a sunken (defile) in the carriage-road. There was no room for a chariot to pass.

Then the charioteer of king Mallika said to the charioteer of the Benares king: " Make your chariot give way." He too: " My good charioteer, make your chariot give way; in this chariot is seated the lord of the kingdom of Benares, the king Brahma-datta! " The other: " My good charioteer, in this chariot is seated the lord of the kingdom of Kosala, the king Mallika! Make your chariot give way to our king, give room for the chariot! " The char-ioteer of the Benares king thought: " This, too, then, must be a king! What's now to be done? . . . Here's a plan! Asking his age I'll make the chariot of the younger give place to that of the older." So deciding, he asked the charioteer the age of the king of Kosala. Finding out they were both of the same age, next the size of his kingdom, his power, his wealth, his fame, his caste, clan, family—all this he asked, and he found that both were lords of a kingdom of three hundred leagues, and were equal in power, wealth, fame, caste, clan, family. Then thinking " I will give way to one who is the more moral," that char-ioteer asked, " What is your king's moral conduct like? " He said: " This and this is the moral conduct of our king." And setting forth his own king's fault as virtue he said the first verse:

" Hard to the hard he flings—Mallika—soft with soft,
   Good by the good he conquers, bad by bad:
   Such is this king! ' Driver, out of the way.' "

Then to him the charioteer of the Benares king:
" What, good man? Have you been telling of your
own king's virtues? " " Yes," was the reply. " If
these be his virtues what are his faults like? " was
the reply, and (he added), " Listen, then! " saying
the second verse:

" By notanger anger would he conquer, notgood by
   good would he conquer,
   He would conquer meanness with a gift, with the
   true him who speaks false.
   Such is this king! Driver, out of the way! "

It being thus said, king Mallika and his charioteer
got down from the chariot, unharnessed the horses,
moved the chariot aside and gave way to the king of
Benares. The king of Benares exhorted king Mallika
saying, " Thus and thus is it meet to do," and going
to Benares, worked merit in giving and the like,
and at the end of life swelled the Bright World. And
king Mallika, taking to himself that lesson, inquired
in the country, and meeting no fault-finder of himself, went to his own city, working merit in giving
and the like, and at the end of life swelled the Bright
World.

The Teacher, having brought up this teaching
that he might admonish, assigned the Jataka: "Then
king Mallika's charioteer was Moggallāna, the king
was Ānanda, the charioteer of the Benares king was
Sāriputta, but the king was just I."

THE GAGGA JATAKA

" MAY you live a hundred years, Gagga! "— This the Teacher told, while living at the Royal Park built by Pasenadi the king, about a sneeze. One day namely, as the Teacher was seated in the midst of the fourfold congregation in that Park, teaching the Right, he sneezed. The monks, in saying in a loud voice " May the reverend, the Blessed One live: may the Well-Farer live! " made a great noise. By that noise the religious talk was disturbed. Then the Blessed One said to the monks: " Is it supposed that when one has sneezed and ' May you live! ' is said, because of that one may either live or die? " " That is not so, reverend sir." " It should not be said at a sneeze, monks; who should say that acts amiss."

Now at that time men used to say when a monk sneezed: " May you live, reverend sir! " The monks (now) scrupled to make response. Men were offended and said: " How is it that the Sakya recluses don't respond? " They told this to the Blessed One, and he said: " Men of the world, monks, are given to the wish-cult. I grant you, when it is said ' May you live, reverend sir,' to say, ' May you live long!' " They asked him: " Reverend sir, when did that wish and its response first arise? " " Monks, that wish and its response arose in days of old," and he brought up the past.

In the past, when Brahmadatta was reigning at Benares, the Bodhisat was reborn in the Kāsi king-

dom in a brahman family. His father was by calling
a general trader. When he was about sixteen years
of age the father handed over to him a consignment
of jewellery, and they going around to village and
town arrived at Benares. Finding nowhere to stay,
they had a meal prepared at the gatekeeper's house
and asked: " Where do incomers arriving at a wrong
hour stay? " Then men told them: " Outside the
city there's a building but it's haunted, but if you
wish you may stay there." The Bodhisat said: " Come,
tāta, let's go; don't be afraid of Yakkha. I will tame
him and make him fall at your feet." And taking his
father he went there. Then the father lay down on a
plank and the son sat down and chafed his feet.

There the Yakkha inmate, after waiting on Vessavana twelve years, getting the building, got it thus:
if of men entering the building one should sneeze,
he might eat all the rest save only those who said
" May you live! " and he who responded with " May
you live! " or " Same to you! " He lived on the top
rafters. He, thinking " I will make the Bodhisat
sneeze," set free fine powder, which entered their
noses and made him on the plank sneeze. The
Bodhisat did not say " May you live! " The Yakkha
came down the ridge-pole to eat him. The Bodhisat
saw him and thought: " It's by him my father was
made to sneeze. He will be a cannibal-Yakkha of
anyone not saying ' May you live! ' " And to his
father he said the first verse:

" May you live a hundred years, Gagga, and twenty
after that!
Me[1] may no goblins eat! Live you a hundred summers yet! "

[1] *Mam.* The translator has " you," *tam,* and it is possibly a
misprint in the Fausböll text.

The Yakkha, hearing that, thought: " I'm not able to eat this youth because he said ' May you live,' but I'll eat his father." The father saw him coming and thought: "This will be a cannibal-Yakkha of those who don't say 'Same to you!' I will make response," and he said to his son the second verse:

" May you too live a hundred years and twenty after that!
　Poison be goblins' fare! Live you a hundred summers yet! "

The Yakkha gave it up and turned back. Then the Bodhisat asked him: " Master Yakkha, why do you eat men who come into this building? " " Because I got permission from Vessavana after twelve years of service." " But did you get permission to eat everybody? " " Everyone save those who make no response and counter-response when anyone sneezes." " Yakkha, in the past, too, you did something wrong, and were thus reborn harsh, cruel, and a hurter of others. Now again, having done the same sort of actions, you will be a farer from dark to dark. From this time give up finding pleasure in taking life." And, having tamed him and frightened him with hell-fear, and established him in the five sīlas, he made the Yakkha like an errand-boy. On the next day men going past, seeing the Yakkha and learning of his taming, told the king. The king sent for the Bodhisat and placed him at the head of his guilds, paying also much honour to his father, and making the Yakkha a tax-gatherer. Persevering in the Bodhisat's advice he worked merit and went to fill a place in the Bright World.

The Teacher . . . then assigned the Jataka: " Then the king was Ānanda, the father was Kassăpa, but the son was just I."

THE VULTURE JATAKA

(Gijjha-jātaka)

"WHY when a vulture sees."—This the Teacher told while living at the Jetavana about a monk who supported his mother. The story will be expanded in the Sāma Jataka.[1] The Teacher asked that monk: " Is it true that you, monk, support a person leading a domestic life ? " Told it was true, he asked: " But what are they to you? " Told " It is my parents, reverend sir," he expressed approval, " Well done, well done," and said: " Do not, monks, be vexed with this monk; wise men of old by their virtue have rendered service even to those not related to them, but this one takes on the charge of parents." And he brought up the past.

In the past, when Brahmadatta was reigning at Benares, the Bodhisat was born as a vulture and supported his parents. Now there befell a mighty wind and rain. The vultures, unable to withstand the tempest, in peril from cold, went to Benares and, shivering with cold, alighted near a wall and a dyke. Then a leading merchant of Benares, coming out from the city and going to bathe, saw those weary vultures, got them into a dry place, had a fire lit, sent to the charnelfield of the cattle and had cattle-flesh brought and given them, and set a guard over them.

When the tempest abated the vultures, whole in body, went away to the hills. Assembled there they

[1] See below, p. 206.

took counsel thus: " Aid has been given us by the Benares merchant, and it is said ' To aid rendered aid in return is due.' Henceforth, therefore, he who gets a cloth or ornament is to drop it in the open court of that merchant's house." From that day, when the vultures saw people drying clothes and ornaments in the sun and not heeding, they seized these, like a hawk swiftly seizes flesh, and dropped them in the open courtyard of the Benares merchant's house. He, whenever he noticed them doing this, had each piece put by.

They told the king: "Vultures are plundering the city! " The king said: " Catch just one vulture; I will make it bring all back." And he had traps and nets laid here and there. The mother-supporting (*sic*) vulture was caught in a trap. Seizing him they said: " We will show the king." The Benares merchant, going to wait upon the king, saw the men taking the caught vulture, and saying " Don't hurt that vulture! " went along with them.

They showed the vulture to the king. And the king asked: " Is it your folk who plunder the city, taking clothes and the like? " " Yes, sire." " To whom have the things been given? " " To the leading merchant of Benares." " Why? " " He gave us life; we were bound to render him service for service, therefore we gave." Then the king, saying "Vultures, we know, though they be a hundred leagues away, perceive a corpse; why did you not see a trap set for yourself? " and spoke the first verse:

" Why when a vulture spies a corpse a hundred
  leagues away,
  Did you not heed or net or trap, though you
  alighted there? "

86

The vulture, hearing his word, said the second verse:

" When other-becoming is at hand at end of life the man
　Is heeding neither net nor trap, though he alighteth there."

The king, hearing the vulture's word, asked the merchant: " Is it true, sir merchant, that clothes and the like have been brought to your house by vultures? " " It is true, sire." " Where are those things? " " Sire, each thing has been put aside by me. I will give to each whatever is his property. Let the vulture go." And the vulture being let go, the merchant restored to each his property.

The Teacher . . . assigned the Jataka: " Then the king was Ānanda, the Benares merchant was Sāriputta, the mother-supporting vulture was just I."

THE FALCON JATAKA

(Sakunagghi-jātaka)

"THE falcon mightily dropping."—This the Teacher told when living at the Jetavana about the Bird-Saying as having reference to himself. One day namely the Teacher, having exhorted the monks "Go a-faring, monks, within bounds, in your own paternal range!" spoke to them this Suttanta collected in the Great Section,[1] and saying " Do you keep thus far. In the days of old, although, as animals, men abandoned their own paternal range and, faring beyond their beat, got into the claws of enemies, yet were they, by the efficiency of their own wisdom, by their excellence in resource, released from the claws of enemies," he brought up the past.

In the past, when Brahmadatta was reigning at Benares, the Bodhisat, being born in the bird kingdom as a quail, maintained himself among the clods produced by the plough. He, one day abandoning the hunting limits in his own range with the idea " I will seek food in another's range," went to the borders of a jungle. Then, seeing him seeking food there, a falcon, coming up swiftly, seized him. He haled by the falcon thus lamented: "O unlucky that we are! The little merit that is ours! We have fared beyond our bounds in another's range! If this day we had fared within bounds, in our own paternal range, it had not availed this falcon to have come in war!" " What, then, are your bounds, your own

[1] The Mahā-vagga of the Samyutta-Nikāya, P.T.S. ed. v, p. 146: the " Hawk " Sutta.

paternal range, my little quail?" "The place of clods where has been ploughing." Then the falcon, relaxing his own strength, released him: "Go then, you quail! Though you go there you will not escape!" Going there, the quail climbed on to a big clod and stood calling him: "Come along now, falcon!" The falcon, stiffening his strength, spreading both wings, swiftly accosted the little quail. But when the quail marked him—"My word! the falcon's upon me!"—he turned round and got within the clod. The falcon, unable to contain his speed, hurled his breast against it, and so, his heart broken, his eyes protruding, met with life's end.

The Teacher, then showing the monks that to fare beyond bounds, that is, to indulge the desires of the senses, was to give access to Mara, being very enlightened spoke the first verse:

"The falcon mightily dropping—the quail not in his
    (own) bounds—
Swiftly came on to (the victim); thereby the falcon
    met death."

But he having met his death, the quail, coming out, stood on his heart and uttering his emotion, "Aha! I have seen the back of the foe!" said the second verse:

"I sooth found out a way, loving the father-bounds.
Gone is the foe and I rejoice, watching my own
    welfare."

The Teacher . . . then assigned the Jataka: "Then the falcon was Devadatta, but the quail was just I."

THE ADVANTAGE IN MORALITY JATAKA

(*Sīlànisamsa-jātaka*)

"BEHOLD of faith."—This the Teacher told when living at the Jetavana about a believing layman. This elect disciple, a convinced believer, was going, they say, one day to the Jetavana, and coming by eventide to the banks of the Achiravatī, the ferrymen having beached their boat that they might go to the service, and he seeing no boat at the landing-stage, grasped the thought of Buddha as ecstasy and was crossing the river. His feet did not sink in the water. Going as if on land, when he got to midstream he saw waves, whereupon his ecstatic Buddha-thought grew weak, and his feet began to sink. But, strengthening the ecstasy, he went on the water's surface, and entering the Jetavana saluted the Teacher and sat down at his side. The Teacher making him welcome asked him: " Layman, did you come along your way without much trouble? " And he saying " Reverend sir, grasping the Buddha-thought as ecstasy, I won footing on the water's surface, as if I were pressing the earth, and so came," he said: " Layman, it is not only you who remembering the Buddha-virtues won footing, in bygone days, too, laymen, ship-wrecked in open sea, remembering Buddha-virtues, won footing." And being asked about it he brought up the past.

In the past, in the day of the Very Buddha Kassapa, a converted worthy disciple embarked on a ship, together with a land-owning barber. The barber's wife had committed him to the layman's hands, saying, " Sir, his welfare and ill is your burden." In a week that ship was wrecked in mid-ocean. And those two lying on a plank reached a little island. There the barber killing birds cooked them and eating gave to the layman. The layman, saying " Enough! (not) for me! " did not eat; but he was thinking, " In this place there is no other foothold save the three refuges," and recollected the virtues of the three gems. Then, as he recollected and recollected, a Nāga (cobra) king, born in that little island, transformed his own body into a great ship. A sea-deva became the pilot. The ship was filled with the seven kinds of gems. The three masts were of sapphire, the sail was of gold, the ropes were silver, the planks were golden. The sea-deva, standing on board, called out: " Anyone for Jam-budīpa? " The layman said: " We are." " Well, then, come aboard! " He went on board and sum-moned the barber. The sea-deva said: " You are allowed, not he." " Why? " " There's no moral quality or conduct in him; that's why. I brought the ship for you, not for him." " Let be; I, in my own gifts given, moral code warded, practices practised, give accomplishment to him."[1] The barber said: " Master, I thank you! " The deva, saying " Now I'm going," made him come aboard, and bringing them both from off the sea, and going by river to Benares, by his power deposited money in the house of each. Commending associating with the wise, he said, " One should keep company with the wise. If this barber had not kept company with this lay-man, he had been destroyed in mid-ocean," and he said the verse:

[1] This belief in vicarious merit is a valuation which grew up, but is not in the earliest features of the religion.

" Behold of faith, of morals and of generosity this
    fruit:
A serpent in ship's form bears home the pious lay-
    man.
With the good consort, make yourselves intimate
    with the good.
By the company of the good it was, the barber was
    saved."

Thus the sea-deva standing in the air admonished,
teaching the right, then catching hold of the serpent
went to his own mansion.

The Teacher . . . assigned the Jataka: " Then
the converted layman was one who passed beyond
life; the Nāga king was Sāriputta, the sea-deva was
just I."

THE GEM-THIEF JATAKA

(*Manichora-jātaka*)

"THERE are no gods! Surely they dwell afar."—
This the Teacher told while living at the
Bamboo Wood about Devadatta's efforts (to kill
him). Hearing of these he said, " Not now only,
monks, but in days of old also, Devadatta went about
to do so, but though he strove he could not," and
he brought up the past.

In the past, when Brahmadatta was reigning at
Benares, the Bodhisat was born in a householder's
family in a village not far from Benares. When he
was of age they brought him a daughter from a
family of Benares. She was lovely, fair and beautiful
as a divine nymph, graceful as a flowering creeper,
like a winsome fairy; her name was Sujātā; she
was a devoted wife, virtuous and dutiful, at all times
doing her duty by husband, mother-in-law and
father-in-law, and she was dear and charming to
the Bodhisat. And so they both dwelt in joy, of
one mind and in unity.

Then one day Sujātā announced to the Bodhisat:
" I would fain see my parents." He: " 'Tis well, lady
dear, prepare food sufficient for the journey." And
they cooked various foods and placed them in a
waggon; he driving the waggon sat in front and she
behind. Going near Benares they unharnessed the
waggon and bathed. Then the Bodhisat harnessed
the waggon again and sat in front; Sujātā, who had
changed her garment and adorned herself, sat behind. When the waggon was entering the city, the

93

king of Benares, on the back of his best elephant, was making a tour of the city and came to that quarter. Sujātā had got down from the waggon and was going behind on foot. The king seeing her his eyes were drawn by her beauty, and he lost his heart to her. He sent a courtier, saying " Go, find out whether she is married or not." He went and ascertained and told, saying, " They say she is married, sire; the man seated in the waggon is her husband."

The king, unable to master his passion, became viciously sick and thought: " I'll have him killed by some device and take her." And he bade a man, saying " Go, master, as if going along the street, and drop this jewelled crest in the man's waggon and come," and gave him a jewelled crest. He agreed and did so, came back and said: " I've placed it, sire." The king said: " I've lost my jewelled crest! " The people were all in an uproar. The king said: " Shut all the gates! Cut off all passages! Seek the thief! " His men did so. The city was all in commotion. That man taking people with him went up to the Bodhisat and said: " Master, stop the waggon; the king's jewelled crest is lost; we will examine the waggon." They did so and he, taking the jewel placed by himself, seized the Bodhisat, struck him with hands and feet, bound his arms behind and led and showed him to the king: " This is the thief! " The king ordered: " Cut off his head! " Then the king's men, beating him with whips at the crossways, dragged him out of the city by the southern gate.

And Sujātā had left the waggon and gone after him, her arms stretched out, and wailing, "Husband, for my sake are you come to this woe! " The king's men said, " We shall cut off his head," and they made the Bodhisat lie down. Seeing this, Sujātā,

94

mindful of their own virtue, wailed out, "Alas! there is methinks in this world no deity capable of restraining wicked violent men working scathe to the virtuous!" and she said the first verse:

"There are no gods! Surely they dwell afar!
There can be surely no world-warders here!
Those men who hurriedly work lawless deeds,
Are there indeed none here to bid them stop?"

She, virtuous one, thus lamenting, the seat of Sakka, ruler of devas, showed heat. Sakka minded: "Who now is desirous of making me decease from Sakkaship?" And discerning what was going on he thought: "The Benares king is acting over harshly; it behoves me now to go; he is making the virtuous Sujātā miserable." And descending from deva-world, by his own might he sat down on the back of the elephant, dismounted the wicked king from the elephant and laid him on his back on the execution block. But the Bodhisat he lifted up, adorned him with every ornament, caused him to take the king's garb and be seated on the elephant. When the axe was lifted and a head was cut off, it was the king's head they cut off, and when it was done, they found it was the head of the king.

Sakka, ruler of devas, in a visible body came to the Bodhisat and anointed him king, giving to Sujātā the position of chief queen. When the courtiers and brahmans and householders saw Sakka they rejoiced, saying, "The unrighteous king is killed! Now have we got a Sakka-given righteous king!" And Sakka, standing in the air, admonished them saying, "This is your king, Sakka's gift. Henceforth he will rule righteously. Verily if the king be unrighteous, the deva rains out of season, in season he rains not; fear of famine, fear of pestilence, fear of the sword: these three fears come upon (the earth)," and he said the second verse:

" For him rain out of season falls,
In season falls for him no rain.
From the bright world he falls away,
Surely thus far a ruined man."

Sakka, thus admonishing the multitude, went straight to deva-realm, and the Bodhisat ruling righteously fulfilled his course to the Bright World.

The Teacher . . . joined on the series and assigned the Jataka: " Then the unrighteous king was Devadatta, Sakka was Anuruddha, Sujātā was Rāhula's mother, but the Sakka-given king was just I."

THE CLOUDHORSE JATAKA

(*Valāh'assa-jātaka*)

"MEN who will not follow in the bidding."— This the Teacher told while living at the Jetavana about a hankering monk. When asked by the Teacher, " Is it true what they say that you are hankering after (something)? " the monk said, " It is true," and when asked, " How is that? " he said, " Because of passion, since I saw a woman decked in brave array." Then the Teacher said: " Women like that, monk, cause men to lust both through their own senses and, by woman-ways and dalliance, get them into their power, and when they see this is so, ruin them in both morals and money. Such are called ' ogresses ' (*Yakkhinī's*). In olden time, too, yakkhinīs looking like women approached a caravan of men, tempted the traders, got them into their power, and then, when they saw other men, they murdered the former lot and devoured them crunching as the blood flowed down their cheeks." And he brought up the past.

In the past there was a " Yakkha " city called Sirīsavatthu. There Yakkhinīs dwelt. When a ship was wrecked and men were come ashore, they dressed and adorned themselves and, having food roast and stewed brought, they with a following of slaves and bearing children on their hip approached the traders. To make them imagine, " We are come to human dwellings," they showed them here and there men ploughing and keeping cattle, herds of cattle and dogs and the like. And coming among the traders they would invite them to drink the gruel, eat the rice and the roast, and the traders, not being aware, would partake of what was given. Then, after the meal, at rest-time, they would make them welcome, asking, " You, where do you live? Whence are you come? Whither do you go? For what business did you come here? " And they saying, " We are shipwrecked and that's how we've come here," they would say, " Very well, sirs, 'tis three years and more since our husbands also took ship; they will be dead; you too are traders; we will be yours to attend on you." They having tempted those traders by their women's ways and wiles brought them into the ogre-city; if there were men who had been taken earlier, they would bind these with deva-fetters and cast them into a house of torture. And when they have gotten no shipwrecked men in their houses, they will scour the shore on the further side to Kalyāni¹ and on this side to Nāga (Serpent) Island.² This is their rule.

Now at one time five hundred shipwrecked traders came to land near their city. They going to meet them tempted them, brought them to the ogre city, imprisoned the men they had earlier taken, and then the chief ogress made the chief trader her husband, and the remainder did likewise, five hundred with five hundred. Then the chief ogress, at night when the traders were asleep, rose, went to the house of durance, killed men, ate them and returned. And the others did the same. When the chief ogress, after eating human flesh, returned, her body was cool. The chief trader, embracing her, discerned her ogre-nature, and thought: " These five hundred will also be ogresses; we must run away!" And

¹ A river in Ceylon, now Kaelani-gangā. *Dīpavamsa*, ii, 42, 53.
² Near, or a part of Ceylon. *Mahāvamsa*, i, ver. 47.

early the next morning, going to wash his face, he passed the word to the other traders: " These are yakkhinīs, not humans; when other shipwrecked ones are come, they will make them their husbands and will eat us. Come, let's run away! " Two hundred and fifty of them said: " We cannot leave them. Go you; we will not run away." The chief trader, taking the two hundred and fifty who did his bidding, ran away in fear of those (creatures).

Now at that time the Bodhisat was born as a cloud-horse, white all over, the head of a crow, the mane like muñja grass, of magic power moving through the sky. He flew up into the sky from Himâlaya and came to Ceylon. There, passing over the Ceylon lakes and tanks, he ate the wild rice. So going, he uttered in human voice (the call) full of pity thrice: " Are there any wanting to go to their country? Are there any wanting to go to their country? " They, hearing his word, went towards him with outstretched hands, saying, " Master, we would go to our country! " " Well, then, climb on to my back." Then some climbed up, some seized his tail, some just saluted with outstretched hands. The Bodhisat took them all up, all the two hundred and fifty traders, even those who just stood still saluting, and by his wondrous power he brought them to their country, settled them in their homes and went to his own abode. And the Yakkhinīs, when others came, murdered the two hundred and fifty left behind and devoured them.

The Teacher, addressing the monks, said: " Monks, just as all this happened to those traders, even so those monks and nuns and laymen and lay-women, who will not do the bidding of the Buddhas, arrive at great tribulation in the Four Catastrophes, in places of the fivefold bondage and durance, while they who do their bidding both arrive at these successes: the three kinds of families, the six bright worlds of sense-pleasures, the twenty Brahmaworlds, and also having realised the Great Nirvana of No Death enjoy vast happiness. And, becoming the very enlightened, he spoke these verses:

" Men who will not follow in the bidding by the
     Buddha taught,
  Will to their ruin go, e'en as befell the traders
     with the sprites.

  But men who will perform the bidding by the
     Buddha taught,
  Will to salvation yonder go e'en as the traders by
     the cloud."

So the Teacher . . . assigned the Jataka: " Then the two hundred and fifty obedient traders of the Cloudhorse-king were the assembly of a Buddha, but the Cloudhorse King was just I."

THE SHOES JATAKA

(Upāhana-jātaka)

" JUST as (the shoes a 'man) has bought."—
This the Teacher told while staying at the
Bamboo Wood about Devadatta. In the temple,
namely, the monks started a talk of Devadatta's
repudiating and opposing the Teacher and coming
into great disaster thereby. To which the Teacher,
saying he had also done so long ago, brought up
the past.

In the past, when Brahmadatta was reigning at
Benares, the Bodhisat, having been born in an
elephant trainer's family and grown up, reached
perfection in his art. Then a young man from a
farm hamlet came and learnt the art from him. Now
Bodhisats, when they explain a training, do not
make the fist of a teacher,[1] they train in their own
method of coming to know without any reservation. Hence the young man, having caught up the
Bodhisat's theory of his art without reservation,
said to him: " Teacher, I will wait upon the king."
The king offered the half salary . . . (as in the
case of Guttila and Mūsila),[2] and required test by
a public competition before consenting to give full
pay. This was arranged.

The Teacher thought, " The pupil does not
know my skill in stratagem," and taking one elephant
he taught him in one night to reverse (the com-

---

[1] This simile was used, it is recorded, of himself by the
Founder just before his death. See pp. xxvi.

[2] See p. 108 f. The narrative I here condense.

mand, in action). He trained him, when " go " was said, to retreat; when " come back " was said, to go; when " halt " was said, to lie down; when " lie down " was said, to stand still; when " take up " was said, to lay down; when " lay down " was said, to take up. And on the day following he mounted that elephant and went to the king's courtyard. The pupil also mounted a docile elephant, and a multitude assembled.

Both showed equality in their art. Next, the Bodhisat made his own elephant reverse, and what he had taught, it carried out. The multitude (crying): " Hi! you duffer of a pupil, do not you contend with your teacher! You don't know your own measure. *You* to think yourself his equal! " And they attacked and slew him. The Bodhisat, descending from the elephant, went up to the king: "Majesty, (men) learn an art for the sake of their own happiness; but to some the learnt art bears with it disaster, like ill-made shoes," and he said this pair of verses:

" Just as the shoes a man has bought
    For sake of pleasure bring but ill,
His soles oppressed with heat are chafed,
    The feet of just that man are worn;

E'en so the ill-bred worthless man,
    Learning and taking hence your lore,
Himself he there by learning doth destroy;
    Worthless he's called, like to the ill-made shoes."

The king being pleased gave great glory to the Bodhisat.[1]

The Teacher . . . assigned the Jataka: " Then the pupil was Devadatta, but the teacher was just I."

[1] With this story compare the much higher ethical level of the Guttila Jataka.

THE ONE-COURSE JATAKA

(Ekapada-jātaka)

" COME now! a ' one-course,' tāta."—This the
Teacher told while living at the Jetavana about
a landowner. They say that a landowner of Sāvatthi
had a son who one day, seated on his father's hip,
asked him about the " gate of welfare" . . . (The
father's procedure is told somewhat as in " The Gate
of Weal Jataka "¹) . . . The Teacher said: " Not
now only, layman, is this boy a seeker after weal;
he became so also in the days of old and asked wise
men about it and they talked to him, but incurring
confusion through coming to be he does not discern. And he brought up the past.

. . . ² seated on his father's lap the boy asked:
" Tāta, tell me of a ' one-course ' on which are
depending many (kinds of) welfare, a ' one-cause.' "
He said the first verse:

" Come now! a ' one-course,' tāta, tell (to me),
Based on the many ways there be to weal;
Something including these, whereby we may
In weal (in growth) bring what we seek to pass."³

Then the father, telling him, said the second verse:

" Aptitude,⁴ tāta, is the course-as-one,
Based on the many ways there be to weal;

---

¹ Above, p. 76. " Weal " and "Welfare " = attha. Cf. p. xxiii.
² Repeat from the foregoing " story of the present."
³ From the Commentary: " attha, reckoned as growth (vaddhi)."
⁴ Dakkheyya: a rare word, commented on as " effort linked
with knowledge."

And this with morals joined, by patience brought
  about,
Enough it is to gladden friends, and sadden foes."

Thus did the Bodhisat talk of the question to the
son. And he, by the method the father told him,
having accomplished his own weal, went according
to his deeds.

The Teacher . . . assigned the Jataka: " Then
the son was this (son), but the Benares merchant
was just I."[1]

---

[1] " One course "—eka-pada—has been rendered (C.U.P. ed.)
" one word." *Pada* always presents difficulties to the translator,
since the Pali is ambiguous, e.g. Nirvana is called santi-pada
accanta-pada, where " word " is obviously unfit. Dhamma-pada,
again, has been rendered " path," " way," of Dhamma (Neu-
mann, Sīlachāra). The Commentary leaves either rendering open:
" pada = kārana" (also an ambiguous word = case or cause, affair or
reason!) " *or* the word meaning or implying this." The connection
in the story with " The Gate of Weal Jātaka " makes it fairly
clear that a weightier meaning than " word " is meant.

THE TAWNY KING JATAKA

(Mahāpingala-jātaka)

"ALL the people."—This the Teacher told while living at the Jetavana about Devadatta. When Devadatta had for nine months pursued after the murdering of the Teacher, and had sunk into the earth at the portals of Jetavana, the inmates of Jetavana and the whole population were pleased and content, saying, "Devadatta, the chronic Buddhathorn, has been swallowed by the earth; now is the Very Enlightened One become one whose enemy is destroyed!" Hearing them as the rumour was handed on, the whole of Jambudīpa and the companies of Yakkhas, fairies, and devas were also pleased and content. One day the monks assembled in the temple were commenting on this, and the Teacher arriving and asking what they were talking about, and being told, said: "Not now only, monks, have people been pleased and merry at Devadatta's death; they were so in bygone times." And he brought up the past.

In the past there was at Benares a king named Great Tawny, who reigned unjustly and unrighteously. Working evil deeds according to his desire and the like, by penalties and taxes, by force and confiscations, he oppressed the people like sugarcane in sugarmill, hard, rough, violent, showing no kindness to others; unaffectionate, disagreeable also was he to the women in his house, to sons and daughters, to ministers, brahmans and citizens, like dust thrown into the eyes, like stones in almsfood, like a thorn piercing the hand. It was then that the Bodhisat was reborn as his son.

Great Tawny died after a long reign. At his death the entire population of Benares, pleased and contented, were merry with a mighty mirth; they cremated him with a thousand cartloads of logs, they extinguished the pyre with a hundred jars of water, they anointed the Bodhisat king, saying with pleased content, " We have gotten a righteous king!" and sending round a festival drum, decorating the city with erected flags and banners, making a pavilion at every gate, with dried and fresh flowers scattered on the floors: and seated in the decorated pavilions they ate and drank. The Bodhisat, too, sat on a decorated divan, in the centre of a fine white-canopied daïs, enjoying great glory, and his courtiers, brahmans, citizens, officials, and gatewardens were gathered about him.

But one gate-warden stood not far off, crying with every breath. The Bodhisat saw him and asked: " Good gate-warden, at my father's death all are busy keeping holiday in pleased content; you stand crying; how now? was my father to you dear and pleasant? " and he said the first verse:

" All folk were hurt by Tawny king;
Him dead they make their good cheer known.
Was dear the ' Not-black-eyed ' to you?
Why is't, gate-ward, that you shed tears? "

He hearing his word (replied) : "I am not shedding tears for grief that Great Tawny is dead. Maybe the skull of me is happy now. For king Tawny, coming down from the palace and going up again, gave me blows by the eight on the head, as with a smith's hammer. And now that he's gone to the other world, he'll be giving his blows on Yama's head (and) to the hell-warders as he did on mine; and they'll be saying, ' Too much are we bothered!' and they'll bring him back and let him loose over here again, and then he'll be giving me more blows on the head: it's from fear I'm shedding tears." And declaring this matter he said the second verse:

" Not dear to me was ' Not-black-eyed.'[1]
I fear he may come back again.
Gone hence he'll hurt the king of death.
He, hurt, may bring him here again."

Then the Bodhisat, comforting him thus, " The king has been burnt with a thousand loads of logs; the site of the pyre has been drenched with a hundred jars of water and entirely dug (over). Moreover, they who, gone to another world, have come under the influence of an otherwise-going, do not return again with just that body," and said this verse:

" Burnt with a thousand loads (of logs)
Is he, wetted with hundred jars,
That site is wholly dug about:
Fear not, he will not come again."

From that time the gate-warden was comforted. The Bodhisat reigned righteously, and working merit and the like went according to his deeds.

The Teacher, having brought up this lesson, assigned the Jataka: " Then Tawny was Devadatta, but his son was just I."

[1] Comy : " eyes like a cat."

THE GUTTILA JATAKA

"THE seven-stringed lute, the passing sweet."—
This the Teacher told while living at the Bamboo
Wood about Devadatta. On that occasion the monks
were saying to Devadatta: " Your reverence, the
Very Enlightened One is your teacher. It is through
him that you have learnt the three Pitakas,[1] have
made the fourfold musing arise; it is not fit to become the opponent of your teacher." Devadatta
repudiated the Teacher, saying, " How now? Is the
recluse Gotama my teacher? Have I not by my own
strength learnt and wrought these? " The monks
discussed this in the temple, saying, " He has attained
to great disaster in so repudiating." The Teacher,
coming and hearing the subject of their talk, said:
" Not now only has he repudiated me, become my
opponent, attained to great disaster; he attained it
also in days of old." And he brought up the past.

In the past, when Brahmadatta was reigning at
Benares, the Bodhisat was born in a family of
musicians, and they called him Guttila. Come of
age and attaining mastery in the musician's art, he
became senior musician in the whole of Jambudīpa.
Without making a wifely ornament[2] he maintained
his parents. It happened that when traders of Benares
had gone for trade to Ujjeni, a holiday was announced
there, and they, pooling what they wished, took

[1] This is not the only reference to the canonical sayings fancied
as then in existence.
[2] Without marrying.

many garlands and perfumes and divers foods, and meeting in the sports grounds, said: " Pay the fee and bring us a musician." At that time the chief musician at Ujjeni was named Mūsīla. They sent for him and made him their musician. And Musila was a lute-player, and stiffened up his lute (strings) to the highest pitch. To them accustomed to the art of Guttila, his art appeared like rubbing a rush mat, and not one of them applauded. Musila thereupon thought, " I play too sharp, methinks," and tuned the lute to middle stiffening and so played. There, too, they were indifferent. Then thinking, " These know nothing whatever, methinks," he played with the strings slack. They there, too, said nothing. Then Musila: " Good masters, why do I playing the lute not please you?" " But why? Were you playing the lute? We understood you were tuning it." " What then? know you of a better expert, or are you not pleased because of your own ignorance?" The traders said: " To those who have already heard the lute-tones of Guttila the musician, your lute tones are like the tones of women lulling their children." " Well, then, take back the fee you gave; I don't want it; but when you go to Benares let me go with you." They agreed and, taking him to Benares, showed him where Guttila lived.

Musila, entering the Bodhisat's house, saw his high-class lute hung up, took it and played on it. Then the Bodhisat's parents, being blind and not seeing him, said: " Methinks the mice are eating the lute! shoo, shoo! Rats are eating the lute." Then Musila, putting aside the lute and saluting the parents, answered their " Where do you come from? " with " I am come from Ujjeni to learn his art from the teacher." They assented, and being asked where he was, said: " He has gone out, tāta;

he will come back to-day." So he sat down till he came and then, after courtesies, told him the reason of his coming. The Bodhisat was a diviner in feature-omens, and discerning that he was not a good man, refused: " Go, tāta, there is no course for you." He clasped the feet of the parents, and making them his advocates, began to beg: " Make him give me the course! " The Bodhisat, being spoken to again and again by his parents, was unable to get out of it and gave instruction.

With just the Bodhisat he went one day to the king's dwelling. The king, seeing him, said: " Who is this, teacher? " " My pupil, your majesty." Mu-sila became in time the confidant of the king. The Bodhisat, not making the teacher's fist,[1] and training him in the whole art by the method of his own coming to know, said: " Tāta, your course is com-pleted." He thought: " My training is now excellent, and this city of Benares is the chief city in all Jam-budīpa; the teacher, too, is old; here is where I ought to live." And he said: " Teacher, I will wait upon the king." The Teacher, saying " Very good, tāta, I will inform the king," went and let the king be informed: " Our pupil wishes to wait upon the king; make us know the fee." The king replied: " He will get the half of what would be given to you." When Musila heard he said: " I will wait on him for the same as you would get, else I will not wait upon him." " For what reason? " " Do not I know all the training that you know? " " Yes, you know." " This being so why does he give me a half? " The Bodhisat informed the king. The king said: " If he is able to show a training equal to yours he will get the same as you." The Bodhisat informing him of the king's word and he saying

[1] See above, p. 101.

" Very good; I will show," the king being informed, said: " Very good. Let him show. What day is the competition? " He said: " Let the day be the seventh from this, your majesty." The king sent for Musila and said: " Is this true that you will compete with your teacher? " " It is true, sire." " Contest with the teacher is not seemly; don't do it." " Enough, sire, let the competition take place; we shall come to know which it is that knows." The king consented and sent round the drum inviting all to meet to hear teacher and pupil compete at the king's gate.

The Bodhisat thought: " This Musila is young and tender; I am old and wasted in strength; the performance of an old man does not succeed. With the pupil defeated there comes no honour to me; if the pupil win, 'twere better to go into the forest and die than win shame." And going into the forest he turned back in fear of death, and forth in fear of shame. While he thus came and went, six days elapsed. Grass died where he made a footway. Just then Sakka's seat showed heat. Noticing it and discerning the reason, Sakka thinking " Guttila the musician because of his pupil is suffering much ill in the forest; it behoves me to become a help to him," and swiftly going he stood before the Bodhisat and declared who he was. Then the Bodhisat said: " I, deva-king, have entered the forest in fear of defeat from a pupil." And he said the first verse:

" The seven-stringed lute, the passing sweet, the
    lovely thing I taught to him.
He to the arena summons me: be thou my refuge,
    Kosiya."

Sakka, hearing his word, said, " Fear not; I am your shelter and hiding-place," and said the second verse:

" I am your refuge, friend, the honourer of teachers I;
Your learner will not conquer you; 'tis you,
teacher, will conquer him."

" Now do you, playing the lute, break one string
and play on six. On the lute there will be your usual
tones. Musila may break a string, but in his lute
there will not be the tone: at that moment he will
incur defeat. Then, seeing he is defeated, you break
one after another all the other five strings, then you
should play on the bare body itself, and with the
string-ends broken, the voice of it will go forth and
persist, covering the twelve leagues of Benares city."
So saying, Sakka gave the Bodhisat three dice and
said: " When the sound of the lute is covering the
whole city, then you should throw one dice into the
air, then before you three hundred nymphs will
descend and dance. When these are dancing you
should throw the second, then another three hundred
will descend and dance before your lute; then you
should throw the third and other three hundred
will descend and dance in the arena. I will come
near them. Go and fear not."

Early next day the Bodhisat returned to his house.
At the king's gate they made a pavilion and prepared the king's seat. The king came down from
the terrace and sat on a divan in the midst, in the
decorated pavilion. Ten thousand adorned women,
courtiers, brahmans and men of the country surrounded the king. All the citizens were met. In the
royal courtyard they had fixed tier above tier, seat above
seat. And the Bodhisat, bathed and anointed, having
eaten food of divers choice flavours, and taken his
lute, sat down on his prepared seat, and Musila on
his. Sakka came with unseen body and stood in the
air. Only the Bodhisat saw him. Musila also came

and took his place, and a multitude was around. At
first the two played the same piece. At their play the
multitude sent forth a thousand plaudits. Sakka,
standing in the air, made just the Bodhisat hear:
" Break one string." The Bodhisat broke the bee-
string; though broken, from its broken tip it let out
tone, went on like deva-music. Musila, too, broke
his string, but no sound came forth. The teacher
broke the strings from the second to the seventh,
the sound of him playing on the bare body persisted,
covering the city; men waved a thousand handker-
chiefs, sent forth a thousand plaudits. Then the Bodhisat threw the dice and the dancers came as promised.
Just then the king made sign to the multitude, and they
rose (crying): " You were in error striving with the
teacher:—' I am equal to him!' You don't know your
own measure," and threatening him, they seized
sticks and stones and belaboured him till he was
dead, and they dragged him on to a rubbish heap.
The king, with pleased mind, gave much wealth, as
in a solid shower, to the Bodhisat, so did the citizens.

Sakka, exchanging courtesies with him, said:
" Wise one, I will after this send Mātali to take you
in the thousand-yoked chariot of thoroughbreds,
the elect chariot of Victory, that you may come to
deva-world." Him, gone back and enthroned, the
deva-daughters asked of his journey, and he told
them, praising the qualities of the Bodhisat. The
deva-daughters said: " Majesty, we are indeed
desirous of seeing the teacher; bring him here."
Sakka informed Mātali that the Bodhisat should be
brought (as described above), and he brought him.
Sakka, welcoming him, said: " The deva-maidens,
Teacher, are desirous of hearing you." " Majesty,
we musicians live by means of our art; we may play

where a fee is given." " Play; I will give you a fee."
" I have no need of other fee than that the deva-
daughters would talk to me of their own good deeds;
so will I play." Then the deva-daughters said to
him: " Afterwards when (you have) pleased us we
will talk to you of the good deeds we did; make
music, teacher." For seven days the Bodhisat made
music for the devas, surpassing in its flow the devas'
music; thenceforth he asked the deva-daughters
about their good deeds. And they told him one after
the other of deeds done on earth in the days of Kassapa Buddha: of a cloak given to a monk, of flowers
given to another; of garlands, fruits, essences presented to shrines; of hospitality to wayfaring monks
and nuns; of water given, when in the water, to a
monk; of duty done with good temper to husband's
parents; of things received being shared; of gentle-
ness and generosity as a slave; thirty-and-seven
deva-daughters told him thus, and in verse too, of
their karma (acts) and rebirth, as has been told in
the Vimānavatthu collection.[1]

Hearing this, the Bodhisat said: " A win in sooth
to me! a good win in sooth to me! I coming here
have heard of the rewards won even for trifling
action. Henceforth going to world of men I will do
good deeds in giving and the like." And he breathed
out this inspired verse:

" O welcome thing to me this day hath come!
Well in the setting forth, well the return!
That I have seen the deva-maidens, comely nymphs.
Now that among them I have heard the Right,
Much worthy (deeds) will it be mine to do:
In gifts, in justice, self-control, restraint;
There shall I go where gone we do not grieve."

[1] A book in the Buddhist (Pali) Canon.

Then the seven days being over the deva-king ordered Mātali the driver to let him be seated in the chariot and sent him back to Benares. He, having gone to Benares, declared to men the reason of the things he had seen in deva-world. From that time men full of energy gave their mind to work merit.

The Teacher . . . assigned the Jataka: "Then Musila was Devadatta, Sakka was Anuruddha, the king was Ananda, but Guttila the musician was just I."

THE JUDAS-TREE PARABLE JATAKA

(*Kimsuk'ôpama-jātaka*)

"BY everyone the judas-tree was seen."—This the Teacher told while living at the Jetavana about the Sutta of the Judas-tree parable.[1] It was thus. Four monks came to the Tathâgata and asked him for an exercise. The Teacher gave them one. They, taking it, went each to his own day and night residences. Among them one having learnt the six spheres of contact attained the state of arahan; the others, having severally learnt the five aggregates (body and mind), the four elements, the eighteen conditions, did likewise. They told the Teacher their several modes of access (to saintship). Then in one monk arose reflection, and he asked the Teacher: "To these (different) exercises there is one and the same Nirvana; how is it that saintship has been won by all?" The Teacher, saying "Why, monk, is it not the variety (in the case of) the little brothers who saw the judas-tree?" and the monks asking him, he brought up the past.

In the past, when Brahmadatta was reigning at Benares, he had four sons. One day they sent for the charioteer and said: "We, good charioteer, are wishing to see a judas-tree; show us one." The charioteer, saying "Very well, I will show you," did not show it to the four on one and the same occasion. He first placed the eldest son in the chariot, took him to the forest and, saying "That's a judas-tree," showed it at the time when it was bare boughs

[1] See *Kindred Sayings* (P.T.S. ed.), iv, p. 124 f.

and buds; to another at the time of young verdure; to another at (its crimson) blossom time; to another at the time of fruition. When later the four brothers were sitting together, they raised a discussion as to what is the judas-tree like? And one said, " Like a scorched pillar "; the second, " Like a banyan tree"; the third, " Like a mass of flesh "; the fourth, " Like an acacia." Dissatisfied with each other's remarks, they went to their father and asked him: " Sire, what sort of tree is the judas-tree? " When he said, " What did you yourselves say (about it)? " they told the king the manner in which they themselves had described it. The king said: " By each of you four the judas-tree was seen; but not one of you, when the charioteer showed it you, cross-questioned him and asked: ' Is it at this season that the judas-tree's like that? Is it at this season that the judas-tree's like that? ' In that way you've got into doubt over it." And he said the first verse:

" By everyone the judas-tree was seen;
Then why are you perplexed about it now?
Because you never asked the charioteer
Concerning what 'twas like at different times."

The Teacher, making this matter clear, said, " Just as the four little brothers, monks, by not having asked with discrimination, got into doubt about the judas-tree, so you too have got into doubt about this Dhamma," and being fully enlightened he said the second verse:

" So in all knowledges where aspects are not known;
They doubt anent them as the boys o'er judas-tree."

The Teacher, having brought up this teaching on the Right, assigned the Jataka: " Then the Benares king was just I."

THE DECAYED WELL JATAKA

(*Jar'udapāna-jātaka*)

"DIGGING a worn-out well."—This the Teacher told while living at the Jetavana about traders resident at Sāvatthi. They, it was said, collecting wares at Sāvatthi and filling carts with them, for purposes of business, before they went, invited the Tathâgata and gave a rich gift, embraced the Refuges, were established in the moral code, saluted the Teacher, saying " We, reverend sir, shall be going a long way for the sake of our custom; when we have got rid of our wares and have accomplished our business and have safely returned we shall again salute you," and went a-wayfaring. Where the road went through the jungle they saw an ancient well, and said: " In this well there's no water and we are thirsty; let's dig down in it." In course of digging they came upon much (treasure), from iron to beryls. Contented with this they filled their carts with the stones and returned safely to Sāvatthi. Collecting the wealth they had brought, and saying " We are in luck; we will give a feast," they invited the Tathâgata, gave a gift with salutation and, seated, told the Teacher how they had come by it. The Teacher: " You, laymen, are content with that wealth; in knowing moderation you won both wealth and your lives. But men of old, not content and immoderate, and not heeding the word of wise men, came by their death." And begged by them he brought up the past.

In the past, when Brahmadatta was reigning at

Benares, the Bodhisat was born in a trader's family and became a caravan leader. Having collected wares at Benares and filled carts, he took many traders, and on going through the jungle he saw a well. There those traders, saying " We will drink the water," dug about the well, and in their work got much iron and the like. Though they had gotten much treasure they were not content and went on digging, saying, " There will be other (stuff) here more beautiful than this." Then the Bodhisat said: " Traders my masters! greed is the root of ruin; much wealth have we gained; be content thus far and dig no further." They, though checked, went on digging.

But that well was haunted by Nāgas (cobras). The king of it dwelling below, his mansion being broken by falling clods and sand, was angry and smote them all except the Bodhisat with the wind of his nostrils and slew them. Coming forth from the Nāga[1] realm he had carts harnessed and filled with gems, and placing the Bodhisat on a lucky waggon and bidding young Nāgas propel the carts, he brought the Bodhisat to Benares, sent him home, collected there the wealth, and went to his own Nāga realm. The Bodhisat spent the wealth making the whole of India his furrow, gave gifts, observed the moral code, kept holy day, and at the end of life swelled the Bright World.

The Teacher, having brought up this past, and being very enlightened, spoke these three verses:

" Digging a worn-out well traders in need of water
  Came upon iron and copper and tin and lead—
      those traders—

---

[1] The Nāga was a serpent, with cobra-hood, who could assume human shape.

Silver and gold and pearls and cat's eyes—lots of
them.
They therewith not contented yet more, yet more
went on digging.

Them the serpent there, fearsome and fiery, with
fire slew.
Hence let him who digs dig not too much; over-
dug is of evil,
And the wealth, that is won by digging, by over-
digging is ruined."

The Teacher, having brought up this teaching,
assigned the Jataka: " Then the Nāga king was Sāriputta, but the chief caravaneer was just I."

THE CRAB JATAKA

(*Kakkata-jātaka*)

"CREATURE of golden horns."—This the Teacher told while living at the Jetavana about a certain woman. It was said that at Sāvatthi a landowner, taking his wife, went into the country to collect outstanding dues, and having collected them and returning, was on the way seized by bandits. Now, his wife was very beautiful and attractive. The chief bandit, lusting for her, set about to kill the landowner. But that woman, who was a moral, virtuous, and devoted wife, fell at the feet of the chief bandit, imploring him, "Master, if out of your fancy for me you kill my husband I shall kill myself, for either I shall take poison or I shall stop my breathing; with you I will not go; kill not my husband to no purpose!" And he let him go. They both reaching Sāvatthi in safety, and passing by the Jetavana monastery, they thought: "We will first enter the monastery and salute the Teacher." And, going to the pavilion of the " Scented(-wood) Cell," they saluted and sat down at his side. They being asked by the Teacher " Where have you been? " " In order to collect dues," and asked also " Did you come through the journey well? " the landowner said: " On the journey, reverend sir, bandits seized us, and then she, begging the bandit chief who was killing me, had me released. Through her my life was saved! " The Teacher, " Layman, now it is to you she has given your life; in the days of old she gave it also to wise men "; and begged by him, he brought up the past.

In the past, when Brahmadatta was reigning at Benares, there was in Himâlaya a pool of water, and in it a great golden crab, and by his living there it was known as the Crab-pool. The crab was big, the size of a threshing-floor; it would catch and slay elephants and eat them. From fear of it elephants were not able to go down there and get their food. At that time the Bodhisat had taken rebirth in an elephant, mate of the leader of a herd which dwelt near the lake. Now his mother, to ward her young, went to another region of the hills and so brought forth a son. He in due course waxed wise and was big, strong, and handsome as a mount of collyrium. He, mating with a young she-elephant, thought, " I will catch the crab," and he took wife and mother, and going to the herd, saw his father and said, " Tāta, I will catch the crab." The father forbade him and said, " Tāta, you won't be able to "; when he declared repeatedly he would, he said: " You will learn."

He collected all the elephants dwelling near the Crab Pool, and went with them down to the lake and asked them: " When does the crab seize: when you go down, or when you are feeding, or when you are coming up? " They said: " When you are coming up." " Well, then, do you go down and feed as long as you want, then you come up first and I will come away after you." The elephants did so. The crab gripped the retiring Bodhisat with his claw as a smith grips a slab of iron with his great pincers. His mate did not leave the Bodhisat but remained by him. The Bodhisat, dragging the crab, was unable to shake him off. But the crab was dragging and bringing him near himself. He in fear of death cried the cry of the captive, and ran, leaving droppings as he went. The mate, too, unable to

bear it, began to run. Then to let her know he was
fast and to stop her running, he said the first verse:

> " Creature of golden horn and outpushed eyes,
> With skin of bone and water-born and bald:
> Conquered by him I weep my wretched state.
> Oh leave not me whom you hold dear as life!"

Then the mate turned back and, comforting him,
said the second verse:

> " My lord, I will not thee forsake.
> Bull-elephant, worn by thy years
> Threescore, o'er all the earth foursquare,
> Thou hast been very dear to me."

Then supporting him she said, " My lord, now
will I awhile talk with the crab and make him let
you go," and begging the crab, she said the third
verse:

> " Whatever crabs be in the sea,
> In Ganges and in Nammadā,
> Son of the waters you are chief!
> Set free the lord to me who weep! "

The crab, while she spoke, got seized by the spell
of the woman's voice, withdrew his claw from the
foot, knowing nothing of what his prey when loose
would do. Then the elephant, lifting his foot, came
down on the crab's back and therewith broke his
bones. The elephant gave a cry of pleasure, and all
the elephants coming together drew off the crab
and, putting him on the ground, crushed him to
powder. His two claws broken from his body lay
beside him.

And this Crab Pool, being connected with the Ganges when Ganges was in flood, was filled with Ganges water; when the water subsided water went down from the lake to Ganges. And so those two claws were lifted and borne along in Ganges. One of them entered the sea; one the king's ten brothers got as they were sporting in the water, and made of it the drum called Anaka. The Asuras caught that which reached the sea, and made of it the drum called Alambara. When later on they were defeated in battle by Sakka, they laid down the drum and ran away. But Sakka had the drum kept for his own use, and this is the drum of which it is said: " Thundering like the Alambara-cloud."

The Teacher . . . assigned the Jataka: " Then the she-elephant was this laywoman, but the elephant was just I."

THE HUNDRED-FEATHERED JATAKA

(Satapatta-jātaka)

" AS the lad in lonely way."—This the Teacher told when living at the Jetavana about Panduka and Lohita. Of the six intransigent monks (called the Six-setter monks[1]), two, Mettiya and Bhummajaka, lived near Rājagaha, two, Punabbasuka and Assaji, lived near Kīta Crag, and the two, Panduka and Lohita, lived near Sāvatthi at the Jetavana. They raised disputes on matters laid down by the religion; they would back up co-cenobites saying, "You are no worse than such and such by birth or clan or morals; if you abandon your opinion, they will conclude they are better than you." In such ways they made an opinion persist, and quarrelling and controversies went on. The monks told this to the Blessed One. Concerning this the Blessed One held a meeting of the monks and sent for the two last named. They admitted that of which they were accused, and he said: " That being so, monks, your action is like that of the hundred-feather and the youth." And he brought up the past.

In the past, when Brahmadatta was reigning at Benares, the Bodhisat was reborn in a certain family in a village of Kāsi. And when he was of age, he did not earn his living at farming or trade or the like, but taking bandits to the number of five hundred he, as their chief, earned a living in highway robbery and burglary. At the time at Benares a landowner had died without reclaiming a debt from a man of the country

---

[1] *Cha-bbaggiya*. Frequently in the Vinaya.

of one thousand kahāpanas. Later on his wife, ill and on her deathbed, informed her son: " Tāta, your father died with that debt not cleared; if I too die, the man will not give it to you. Go to him while I yet live and claim and bring it." He went and got repayment. The mother meanwhile died, but out of love for her son she was reborn as a suddenly full-grown jackal on the way by which he would return. The bandit-chief and his men were just then staying by that road to plunder wayfarers. Then the jackal, when her son was entering the jungle, cut into the way again and again to check him, saying, " Tāta, don't go up into the jungle; robbers are there; they will kill and rob you." But he not understanding what she meant, and saying " This jackal of bad luck keeps cutting into my path," took clods and sticks and drove her away. Then a " hundred-feather " bird, flying towards the bandits, cried out: " That man has got one thousand kahāpanas in his hand; kill him and take them! " The youth did not understand what the bird meant, and thought " This is a bird of good luck; now I shall go in safety," and he lifted hands in salute, saying, " Crow on, master! Crow on, master! "

The Bodhisat, who had the lore of wild things' cries, saw the acts of the two, and rightly interpreted what they were meant to convey, and as to the youth he thought: " He is driving away his mother who desires his welfare and salutes the bird as the one who is desiring it. Lord! What a fool! "

Verily in Bodhisats, though they are supermen, the seizing of others' property comes to pass by way of a jolt in taking rebirth. Some say it is by a flaw in their stars.[1]

The youth, coming along, got into the midst of

[1] Cf. p. 138.

the bandits. The Bodhisat had him seized, and asked him where he lived and for what he was wayfaring. " Did you get the money? " " Yes, I got it." . . . " Do you know what has befallen your mother now?" " I do not know, master." " Your mother died after you left, and out of love for you she became a jackal and tried to warn you. You drove her away, but the ' hundred-feather ' was your enemy, and bade us kill you and take the money. In your folly you judged quite wrongly. He was of no good to you, but your mother was very good to you. Take your money and go." And he let him loose.

Then the Teacher spoke these verses:

" As the lad in lonely way, the jackal prowling in
    the wood,
Showing her will for 's welfare, held she willed him
    ill,
And held it was th' ill-willing bird which willed
    him well;

E'en such a man as this we meet, who 'with his left
Accepts '[1] the word that they who wish him well
    have spoke.
And when men praise him (for his views), inflat-
    ing risk,
He sooth would deem them friends as this youth
    deemed the bird."

The Teacher, having enlarged upon this lesson, assigned the Jataka: " Then the bandit-chief was just I."

---

[1] " As not weal-bringing." Comy.

THE SUJATA JATAKA

"WHAT egg-like things."—This the Teacher told while living at the Jetavana about the lady Mallikā. One day it is said there was between her and the king a state-chamber quarrel—it is spoken of as the couch-squabble. The king, being angry with her, would not recognise her existence. Mallikā thought: " I don't believe the Teacher knows of the king being angry with me." But the Teacher did know, and he thought, " I will make concord between these two," and, rising early, he went with bowl and robe and attendant monks to Sāvatthi and entered the king's door. The king took his bowl, made him enter and be seated, gave him and his men water of oblation, and brought soup and meats. The Teacher, closing his bowl with his hand, said: " Majesty, where is the lady? " " What is she, reverend sir, to you? She is mad with her high position." " Majesty, you yourself gave her that high position. That you should throw her over for an offence is not meet, not fit." So the king sent for her. She waited on the Teacher. He, saying " It behoves you to become at one with each other," spoke in praise of the essence of concord and departed. The monks speaking in the chapel of what he had done, he came and said: " Not now only, but long ago also I brought them to concord with one talk." And he brought up the past.

In the past, when Brahmadatta was reigning at Benares, the Bodhisat became his adviser of what was good and right. Then one day the king, having opened a great window, stood looking down on the courtyard. At that moment a fruiterer's daughter, a beautiful girl in the prime of youth, with a basket of jujube fruit on her head, went through the courtyard saying, " Take jujubes! Take jujubes! " The king, hearing her voice, fell in love with her, and ascertaining that she was not married, sent for her and raised her to the highest position, making her his chief queen. She was very dear and delightful to him. One day he was seated eating jujubes in a golden platter. Sujātā, seeing this, asked him what he was eating, saying the first verse:

" What egg-like things are those, sire,
    Heaped on the copper dish?
Of blood-red hue and lovely—
    I ask you; tell me now."

The king was angered. " You little jujube fruit-pedlar, you daughter of a greengrocer, you not to know jujubes, the goods of your own family!" and he said two verses:

" The goods which you, my lady, once in ragged garb,
    Apron in hand, did pluck, that fruit 's to you well known.
As scorched, your joy is o'er, your wealth abandons you,
    Back get you now where you will jujubes pick."

The Bodhisat, thinking " Save me, there is no one able to bring them to concord. I will appease the king, nor let him drag her forth," said the fourth verse:

" These surely, sire, are ways of woman raised to
    sudden power.
Forgive Sujātā, majesty. Let wrath cease, chariot-
    lord."

At his word the king condoned the lady's offence
and restored her to her place. From that time they
both dwelt in concord.

The Teacher assigned the Jataka: " Then the
Benares king was the king of Kosala, Sujātā was
Mallikā,[1] the minister was just I."

[1] Mallikā's story is also told in Jataka No. 415: " Lump of
Porridge." She is there carrying this, not selling fruit. The king
is Gotama's well-known protector and disciple, the Pasenādi of
Kosālă.

THE HARE JATAKA

(*Sasa-jātaka*)

"SEVEN red fish."—This the Teacher told while living at the Jetavana about giving all the requisites. They said that a landowner of Sāvatthi provided the Sangha, with the Buddha at its head, with a gift of all the requisites, invited them to a pavilion which he had set up at the door of his house, caused them to be seated on excellent prepared seats, dispensed various and choice foods, invited them for a week, saying always "Again tomorrow!" and on the seventh day gave to each of five hundred monks a set of requisites. The Teacher, at the end of the meal returning thanks, said: "Layman, it is meet that you give joy and gladness, for this is a tradition of wise men of old, who, laying down their lives for suppliants they met, even gave them their own flesh." And being begged he brought up the past.

In the past, when Brahmadatta was reigning at Benares, the Bodhisat, reborn of a hare, lived in the forest. Now on one side of this forest was the foot of the mountains, on the other side a border-hamlet. Later on he came to have three companions: a monkey, a jackal, and an otter. And those four wise folk, dwelling together, hunted their food each in his own beat, meeting together in the evening. The hare-pundit as a lesson to the three taught them the right, saying, "There should be giving of gifts, warding of morals, observing the holy day." They accepted his lesson, then entered each his own lair, and there abode. Now, as time went on, the Bodhisat one day, looking at the sky and seeing the moon, saw that " to-morrow is holy day," and said to the other three: " To-morrow is holy day; do you three people carrying out the moral code be keepers of the day; established in that code whatever you give becomes very fruitful; hence if a beggar arrive feed him with food you were going to eat yourselves." " Very good," they assented, and abiding each in his own place, on the following day the otter, going out early to seek his food, went to the bank of the Ganges. Now an angler having drawn out seven red fish, strung them on a withy, buried them in the sand on the bank, and to catch fish strolled down the Ganges. The otter, smelling a fish-smell, dug up the sand, saw the fish, brought them out and, thinking " Is there, I wonder, anyone who owns these? ", called three times. Seeing no owner, he bit hold of the withy and placed the catch in his lair, thinking " In due time I'll eat them." So warding his morals (by the fast) he laid down. The jackal, too, going out for his food, saw in the hut of a field-warder two spits of meat, a lizard, and a pot of milk. He did as the otter had done, and seeing no owner, he put the cord-handle of the milkpot round his neck, gripped spits and lizard with his teeth, brought them to his own lair, put them aside, thinking " In due time I'll eat them," and warding his morals lay down. The monkey, too, entering the jungle, fetched a bunch of mangoes, and placing them in his lair, and thinking " In due time I'll eat them," warding his morals, lay down.

Now the Bodhisat, going out betimes, thinking " I will eat dabba grass," thought as he lay in his form: " I cannot give grasses to beggars who may come to me, and I haven't got any rice and oil. If a beggar come to me I will give him my own body's flesh." By the moral splendour of that the bright cloth stone seat of Sakka showed heat. Mindful of it he saw the reason and thought: " I will examine the king of hares." And first he went to the otter's abode and stood in the garb of a brahman. When it was asked, " Brahman, needing what are you standing here? " " Wise man, if I could get food after observing holy day I could do my religious duty," he, saying " Good, I will give you food," conversed with him in the first verse:

> " Seven red fish have I here
> From water drawn to land.
> Brahman, I've these (to give):
> Eat and in wood abide! "

The brahman, saying " Let be till to-morrow; later on I shall know," went to the jackal, and when asked what he wanted, he said the same. The jackal said, " Good, I will give," and in conversing with him said the second verse:

> " Supper of field-ward brought
> Is mine and 'twill not keep:
> Two flesh-spits, lizard one,
> And eke a pot of milk:
> Brahman, I've these (to give):
> Eat and in wood abide."

The brahman, saying " Let be till to-morrow; later on I shall know," went to the monkey, and when asked what he wanted, he said the same. The monkey said, " Good, I will give," and in conversing with him said the third verse:

> " A mango-bunch, cool water,
> Cool and delightful shade:
> Brahman, I've these (to give):
> Eat and in wood abide."

The brahman, saying " Let be till to-morrow; later on I shall know," went to the hare-pundit, and when asked what he wanted said the same. Hearing that the Bodhisat was glad: " Brahman, you did well in that you came to me to find food. To-day I will give a gift never before given by me, but you, as being moral, will not be taking life. Go, tāta, drag sticks together and make a fire, and let me know. I giving up my own life will leap into the heart of the fire, and when my body is roasted, you having eaten my flesh will carry out your religious duties." And in conversing with him he said the fourth verse:

> " To hare belongs no oil,
> Nor any beans, nor rice.
> Me roasted on this fire
> Eat and in wood abide."

Sakka, hearing what he said, by his mighty power caused a heaped fire to appear and let the Bodhisat know. He, rising from his couch of dabba-grass and going to it, said, " If there be little beasts in my fur let them not die! " and he shook his whole body thrice and, giving his free gift, sprang up with joyful mind and like a royal swan fell on to the heaped-up fire. But the fire was not able to heat even the fur-pores on his body, and he became as if he had entered a cave of snow. Then he said to Sakka: " Brahman, the fire you have made is too cold; it isn't able to heat even the fur-pores on my body. How is this? "

" Wise man, I am not a brahman. I am Sakka come to examine you." " Sakka, leave it at that! If all the denizens of the world as well were to examine me in giving, they would not see in me reluctance to give! "—so the Bodhisat roared his challenge. Then said Sakka, " Wise hare, be your virtue manifest throughout this age! " and squeezing the hillside he took hill-essence and on the disc of the moon he scratched the mark of a hare.[1] And he told (this to) the Bodhisat, and laid him to rest on a soft couch of dabba-grass in that same thicket in that jungle and went to his own abode. And those four wise folk, in mutual concord and happiness keeping the holy day and fulfilling the moral code, went according to their deeds.

The Teacher . . . assigned the Jataka: " Then the otter was Ānanda, the jackal was Moggallāna, the monkey was Sāriputta, the hare-pundit[2] was just I."

---

[1] Cf. p. 28.　　　[2] *Sasa-pandito*, lit. " hare-wise-man."

THE KANAVERA AND INDRIYA JATAKAS

THIS the Teacher told while living at the Jetavana about a (monk) who lusted after her who had been his wife. The story will be made clear in the Indriya Jataka. . . .

(*Here follows the Indriya* (senses) *Jataka's episode of "the present!"*)

It is said that at Sāvatthi the head of a family, on hearing the Teacher preaching righteousness, thought: "I am unable while living amid domestic things to lead the God-life[1] in absolute perfection and purity. Leaving the world in the religion of the life apart, I shall make an end of ill." And handing over house and wealth to wife and children, he begged the Teacher for ordination, and the Teacher let him be ordained. Because of his being a novice and the great numbers of the monks when he went with his teachers and repeaters for alms, he got no seat either in the houses or in the refectory. As last of the novices, he got a bench or stool, the food was tossed over on a ladle, he got gruel of broken lumps, food sour or stale, sprouts dry or burnt; not enough to maintain him. Taking what he had got, he went to his ex-wife, and she taking his bowl with a salute, cleared it out and gave him well-cooked rice and curry. The old man, bound by cravings of taste, was unable to leave her.

She thought: "I will examine whether he is

---

[1] Brahma-charïya. This word suffered depreciation, coming in a monastic world to mean celibacy.

bound or not." One day, having got a man from the country to wash himself with white soap-powder, and take a seat in her house, she bade a few others of his folk come in, and gave them food and drink. The meal went on. At the house-door she had oxen harnessed to wheels and a cart put on there. But she herself sat in an inner room and baked cakes. The old man came and stood at the door. Seeing him, an old serving-man said: " Mistress, an Elder is standing at the door." " Salute him and send him on." But when, saying repeatedly " Pass on, reverend sir," he saw the monk would not go, he said: " Mistress, the Elder doesn't go." She came and, lifting the curtain, looked and said: " Why! this is the father of my children." And going out she saluted him, took his bowl, made him come in, gave him to eat, and afterwards, saluting him, said: " Reverend sir, you are here in the final training. We have meanwhile not taken up with another family. House-life where no master is cannot go on. We will go to a distant country. Do you become zealous. If I offend, forgive."

To the old man it was as if his heart would split. And he said: " I am not able to leave you. Do not go. I shall recant. Send a layman's gear to such and such a place; I will lay aside bowl and robes and come back." She assented: " Very well." The man went to the monastery and handed over bowl and robes to teacher and preceptor, answered the inquiry " Why are you doing thus? " with " I cannot leave her who was my wife. I shall recant."

They brought him unwilling to the Teacher, and on its being said " Why, monks, do you bring one who is unwilling? " they declared: " Reverend sir, this one has hankerings and wishes to recant." Then when the Teacher said " Is this true? " and

was answered " It is," " Who gives you to hanker?"
" She who was my wife," the Teacher said, " Monk,
that woman has been doer of ill to you . . . [*here
the Kanavera Jataka is resumed*]. In the past you
on account of her had your head cut off with a
sword." And he brought up the past.

In the past, when Brahmadatta was reigning at
Benares, the Bodhisat, born in a hamlet of Kāsi,
in the house of a householder under a robber-con-
stellation, and come of age, earned his living by
brigandage. And he became a notorious bully, strong
as an elephant, and no one was able to catch him.
One day he broke into the house of a leading merchant and carried off much wealth. The citizens
went to the king and declared: " Sire, a great bandit
is plundering the city. Have him caught! " The
king ordered the city warder to catch him. He,
setting men here and there in detachments, caught
him with his booty, and sent word to the king. The
king ordered the city warder: " Cut off his head! "
The city warder had his arms bound behind with
strong ropes, a wreath of kanavera flowers hung
round his neck, his head powdered with brick dust,
and letting him be flogged at each cross-road, brought
him to the place of execution, to the sound of a
harsh-toned drum. At the rumour " In the city a
plunder-devouring bandit is caught! " the entire
city was in a turmoil.

There was then at Benares a courtesan named
Sāmā, earning her thousand (piece) fee, the king's
favourite, with a following of five hundred beautiful
slaves. She, opening the window in an upper storey,
saw him being led by. Now he was very handsome
and attractive, of supreme beauty, like a god, a head
above everyone else. At sight of him she lost her

heart to him, and thinking " By what device can I make this man my husband?—there's this device! " she sent by the hand of her own servant a thousand pieces to the city warder (and the message): " That bandit is the brother of Sāmā. He has no one to depend on save Sāmā. Do you take this sum and let him go." The servant did so. The city warder said: " This is a notorious bandit. I cannot let him go like that. But were I to get another man I could have this one put into a closed car and sent." Now there was then a leading merchant enamoured of Sāmā, who gave her daily a thousand (pieces), and on that day, too, he came to her house at sunset with his thousand. And Sāmā taking the money laid it on her lap and sat weeping. And when he said " What is it? " she replied: " Master, that bandit is my brother; he has never come near me, because he says I practise a low calling. My messenger going to the city warder, word was sent me that if he got a thousand he will let him go. Now I have no one to go with this thousand to the city warder." He, out of fondness for her, said: " I will go." " Why, then, take what you brought me and go." He took it and went to the house of the city warder. He, placing the merchant in a closed place, set the bandit in a closed car and sent him to Sāmā. And he thought: " This bandit is a notorious fellow. It must first have got quite dark; when everyone has retired I will have him executed." And making some excuse he waited awhile till every one had retired, then brought the merchant with a large guard to the slaughter place and had his head cut off with a sword, his body mounted on a spike and sent to the city.

From that time Sāmā accepted nothing from the hand of any man, but in love with the bandit was

occupied with him alone. He bethought him:
" Should she lose her heart to anyone else she will
have me killed, and find pleasure with him; she is
infinitely treacherous to her friends; I must get
out of this and run away." Now leaving he
thought : " I'll not go empty-handed, I'll take
her jewels with me." One day he said : " Lady
dear, we are everlastingly in the house like a tame
cockatoo in a cage. Let's go one day to enjoy the
park." She consented and prepared various foods,
decked herself in fine array, and, seated with him in
a closed car, went to the park. He, after amusing
himself with her, thought: " Now will be the time
to run ! " And as if with a show of passion for her
he entered a thicket of kanavera, embraced her and
squeezed her out of her senses. Throwing her down,
he took off all her ornaments, tied them up in her
upper robe, slung the bundle on his back, leapt
over the park-hedge and made off.

When she came to her senses she got up and
going to her attendants asked: " Where is the
master? " " We don't know, mistress." " He must
have thought me dead, got frightened and has run
away." And in distress she went home and laid
down on the floor, saying " Only when I have seen
my dear master will I rest on a pukka couch." And
from that time she wore no charming dress, ate
never two meals a day, and cared naught for perfumes and garlands. And saying " By one way or
another I will seek and fetch back my lord " she
had dancers fetched and gave a thousand, saying,
" Let there be no place you do not go to; go to
village, township, and royal residence, collect a
crowd, and in the crowded circle sing first this song,"
and she taught them the first verse. " And if when
you have sung it my master comes into the crowd,

he will speak with you, and you will tell him I am well, and take him and go. If he comes not send me a message." And giving them provisions she sent them away.

They leaving Benares and performing here and there came to a border hamlet. There the bandit, after his flight, was living. They performing there sang the first song:

> " That day of spring when 'mid the kanaveras red
> Sāmā you crushed within your arm:
> She tells you now she is in health again."

The bandit, hearing that, approached and, conversing with them, said, " You say that Sāmā lives, but I don't believe it," and he said the second verse:

> " Good sir, I'd no more credit you were you to say
> The wind may sweep away the hill, yea, the whole earth,
> Than Sāmā dead tells me herself that she is well!"

Hearing his word, the dancer said the third verse:

> " Nor is she dead nor other doth she want,
> Fasting is Sāmā, thus she longs for thee."

Hearing that, the bandit with the words " Be she alive or be she not, I have no need of her," said the fourth verse:

> " Me she knew not well for one she long had known
> Sāmā exchanged, the untried for the tried.
> Me too would Sāmā for another change,
> So I further afield from her have gone."

The dancers went and told her how he had acted. She repented her, and occupied herself with that she was wont to do.

The Teacher . . . assigned the Jataka: " Then the merchant was this monk, but the bandit was just I."

THE SUJATA (WELL-BORN) JATAKA

(*Sujāta-jātaka*)[1]

"WHY in a hurry."—This the Teacher told while living at the Jetavana about a landowner bereaved of his father. It was said he went about lamenting his dead father, unable to suppress his sorrow. The Teacher, seeing in him the conditions for the fruition of stream-winning,[2] went for his alms to Sāvatthi and, with a monk in attendance, entered his house, sat down on the seat prepared, and saluting him as he sat, said: "Why, layman, are you sorrowing?" To the reply, "Yes, reverend sir," he said, "Sir, wise men of old, hearing the word of wise men, did not sorrow when their father died," and being begged to tell, he brought up the past.

In the past, when Brahmadatta was reigning at Benares, the Bodhisat was born in the house of a landowner, and was called Sujāta. When he was come of age his grandfather died. Then his father, from the day of his father's death, steeped in grief, brought the bones from the burning ghat, and making a clay sthupa in his own park, laid them there, and from time to time did honour to the sthupa with flowers, contemplating and lamenting, and he lived without bathing or anointing or taking meals or minding his business.

Seeing this, the Bodhisat thought: "My father,

---

[1] Distinguish from the two Jatakas also so called referring to two women, Sujātā by name.

[2] The first stage in a man's life who sees this as a Way in the Worlds.

from the time grandfather died, lives overwhelmed with sorrow. There's none but I can make him understand this. There's one plan by which I will make him lose his sorrow." And going out of the city he saw a dead ox; and he fetched grass and water and laying them before it called: " Eat, eat! Drink, drink!" Passers-by said: "My good Sujāta, are you crazy that you give grass and water to a dead ox?" He answered nothing. Then they went up to his father and said: " Your son has gone crazy; he is giving grass and food to a dead ox." Hearing that, the father-griever gave way, the son-griever prevailing. He went apace and said: " Are you not a wise man, dear Sujāta? For what reason are you giving grass and drink to a dead ox?" And he uttered two verses:

> " Why in a hurry cut
> Green grass and say ' Eat! Eat! '
> To creatures that are gone,
> To aged worn-out cow.
>
> Not verily by food,
> Nor drink will you raise up
> An ox that is no more.
> Vainly you call on him,
> Showing you're slow of wit."

Thereupon the Bodhisat uttered two verses:

> " The head's yet there, the feet,
> Front, hind, and eke the tail
> Are still the same—methinks
> The ox may yet rise up.
>
> But of the grandsire's head,
> Hands, feet, are nothing seen.
> Weeping beside clay tomb
> You only, slow of wit! "

THE SUJATA (WELL-BORN) JATAKA

Hearing that, the Bodhisat's father thought: "My son is wise. He knows what should be done as to this world and the next. He has done this deed in order to make me understand." And saying "Dear wise Sujāta, I know the saying 'All things are transient'; henceforth I will not grieve; this will come about because I have such a father-grief-dispelling son," he said these verses in praise of his son:

" Ah verily! as butter-whetted flame
By water sprinkled on 't, of me who was
On fire hath he extinguished all the woe.
Ah verily! pulled out hath he the dart
That lay nestled within my heart, who hath
Dispelled of me grief-smitten grief for my sire.

Look you! a man whose dart's drawn out am I,
Departed is my grief and I am cleansed.
I grieve not, weep not, heeding you, young man!
So in compassion work the very wise,
Turning us back from grief as you your sire."

The Teacher . . . assigned the Jataka: " Then Sujāta was just I."

THE KARANDIYA JATAKA

(Kārandiya-jātaka)

"YOU only in the forest."—This the Teacher told while living at the Jetavana about the "Soldier of the Mandate" (Sāriputta).[1] It is said that the Elder gave the moral code to anyone he saw come to him, men of poor morals such as deer-hunters, fishermen and the like, bidding them accept the code. Reverence for the Elder prevented them from cutting short his speaking, and they accepted the code, but not warding it they just went on with their own business. The Elder commented thereon to his fellow-disciples: "Reverend sir (said they), you give them the moral code without their approval; they accept it unable to interrupt your speaking; do you henceforth not give the moral code to that sort of folk." The Elder was unhappy. When the matter was known a discussion was started in the temple: "The reverend Sāriputta is said to give the moral code to just anyone he sees." The Teacher, coming and inquiring as to the talking, said: "Not now only, monks, but also in days of yore, to any he saw who were not asking for it would he give the moral code." And he brought up the past.

In the past, when Brahmadatta was reigning at Benares, the Bodhisat was reborn in a brahman family. When come of age he became the senior border-pupil of a world-famed teacher. That teacher was then giving the moral code to anyone he saw,

---

[1] A title by which he is in later documents often referred to is more usually rendered by Captain or General of the Law.

fishermen and the like, saying, " Accept the moral
code! Accept the moral code! " They, having
accepted, did not ward it. The teacher told the
matter to his pupils. The pupils: " Reverend sir,
you are giving to them without their approval;
therefore they break it; now henceforth you should
give only to those who ask (for it), not to those who
do not ask." He became regretful, howbeit he still
gave the moral code to anyone he saw.

Now one day people who had come from a certain
village invited the teacher for the purpose of (giving)
a brahman " word-fee." And he sent for the young
brahman Kārandiya and deputed him, saying,
" Dear one, I am not going; do you take these five
hundred youths and go to receive the word-fees,
bringing with you the portion given to us." He went,
and on the return journey he saw by the road a cave.
Thinking " Our teacher gives the moral code to
anyone he sees even if unasked; I will so act that
from now henceforth he'll give only to those who
ask," he rose up amid the young brahmans seated
at ease and lifting up a big piece of rock threw it
into the cave; and again he threw and yet again and
again. Then those youths rose up and said: " Teacher,
what are you doing?" He said never a word. They went
quickly and told this to the (chief) teacher. The teacher
came and conversing with him said the first verse:

" (You) only in the forest mountain-cave
  Consign the rocks you seize again, again,
  Seizing as one in haste to effect:
  Kārandiya, what now is 't here you seek? "

He, hearing his word and wishing to enlighten
the teacher, said the second verse:

" Sooth I this (thing) of borders girt by seas
  Will make as even as is palm of hand,

Distributing both dunes and rocky hills.
Hence am I throwing rocks within the cave."

Hearing him, the brahman said the third verse:

" No man is fitted by his lone to make
This broad earth even as the palm of 's hand.
Methinks in aiming at this cave alone,
Kārandiya, you'll forfeit world of life."

Hearing him, the young brahman said the fourth verse:

" If I am by my lone incapable,
A man, of levelling all-bearer earth,
So you, too, brahman, will not make these men
Of divers views to follow your behest."

Hearing him, the teacher made a fitting reply:
" Kārandiya, I will now not act in that way "; and discerning his own contrasted state, he said the fifth verse:

" Sir, in a form concise the weal of me,
Kārandiya, you've stated, even this:
Just as the earth cannot be made to win
A level surface by a man, so men."

So did the teacher speak praise of the young brahman. And he, after enlightening him, brought him to his house.

The Teacher . . . assigned the Jataka: " Then the brahman was Sāriputta, but the young brahman Kārandiya was just I."[1]

[1] The " moral code " = *sīla*, in its lowest (basic) terms, consisted of five injunctions (against taking life, taking the " not-given," sex-offences, evil speech, and strong drink. Now less could hardly be taught if morals were to be taught at all; even parent-child morals are omitted! Hence it is possible that the worthier, more *positive* moral teaching, said to be the Founder's own way of wording (*Dialogues*, i), may conceivably be here meant.

THE GREAT APE JATAKA

(Mahākapi-jātaka)[1]

"YOURSELF you made the way to pass."—
This the Teacher told when living at the
Jetavana about conduct for the weal of one's kin.
The occasion will be explained in the " Jataka of
the Auspicious Hall."[2] But just now discussion arose
in the temple on the way in which the Very Enlightened One acted for the weal of his kin (the
Sakyas), and the Teacher, coming and hearing what
was the talk, said: " Not now only, monks, but even
long ago, the Tathâgata acted for the welfare of his
kin." And he brought up the past.

In the past, when Brahmadatta was reigning at
Benares, the Bodhisat was reborn among the apes,
and growing up strong and vigorous, he dwelt with
a following of eighty thousand monkeys in the region
of Himavant. There, by the bank of the Ganges,
stood a mighty full-foliaged mango tree (some say
it was a banyan), soaring up like a mountain-peak.
Its sweet fruits of divine flavour were as large as
waterjars, and from one branch the fruits fell on
dry ground, from another they fell into the Ganges,
and the fruits of two other branches fell plumb to

[1] There is another Jataka so entitled in the 5th vol., No. 516,
which is quite different; one of the " Devadatta " group.

[2] This is No. 465 (misquoted in the edition as 444). The story
of the present is of considerable interest, giving episodes, quite
possibly new, in the relations, during the lifetime of the Founder,
between Kosala, the Sakyans, the Licchavis and the Mallas, but
it is too long for this volume. It may also be read in Burlingame's
Buddhist Legends, vol. 2, p. 30 ff.

the roots of the tree. The Bodhisat, eating the fruit with his herd, thought: " A time will come when the fruit which falls into the water will be a source of peril to us." So he made his herd eat or throw away the fruit which was growing over the water, in blossom-time while it was yet no bigger than *kalaya* peas. Though this was so, one ripe fruit, unseen by the monkeys, because hidden by a nest of ants, fell into the river and hung in the upper net where the king of Benares used to sport in the water with a net both above and below him. To the king, after he had been thus sporting during the day and had gone away in the evening, the fishermen, raising the net, showed the fruit, not knowing what it was. " Who will know what it is? " " The woodmen, sire." The woodmen said it was a mango, and the king, cutting it with a knife and making the woodmen taste it first, ate it himself, sharing it with his women and courtiers. The mango essence pervaded, persisting, the king's whole body. He, craving more, ascertained from which tree the fruit came, made the woodmen take him by a train of boats up the river, and encamping under the tree, he feasted on mangoes and there spent the night, his men guarding him with lighted fire.

When all were asleep, at midnight the Great Being came with his herd, and eighty thousand monkeys, leaping from branch to branch, ate mangoes. The king woke and, seeing them, made his men get up and sent for archers, saying, " So that the monkeys don't run away, surround them and shoot them. To-morrow we will eat mangoes and monkey-flesh." So they surrounded the tree and stood with arrows fixed. The monkeys, seeing this, came to the Great Being trembling, and asked what they should do. The Bodhisat said, " Fear not; I will save your lives," and, comforting the herd, he climbed a vertical branch and, going along a bough grown towards the river, he leapt from the end of it a hundred bow-lengths and alighted on the (further) bank of Ganges in a bush. Getting down, he calculated the length of his leap, broke a bamboo shoot at the root, stripped it, and reckoning " So much will be joined to the tree, so much will be fixed in air," he bound one end to the bush and the other to his waist, and then, with the speed of a wind-torn cloud, he sprang back home. Failing (owing to the short length) to alight on the great tree, he clutched a branch (as he fell) with both hands and gave the sign to the monkeys: " Swiftly treading on my back go to safety over the bamboo shoot." The eighty thousand monkeys, saluting and asking forgiveness, went so. Devadatta was then one of that herd. Saying " Now is the time to see my enemy's back! " he got up a high branch and, rallying speed, fell on to the chief's back. The Great Being's heart cracked and mighty pain arose. The other forthwith got away. The Great Being was alone. The king not falling asleep had seen everything, and thought: " That is but an animal, yet he has got his herd away safely not counting his own life." And when day broke he said: " It is not seemly to destroy the royal ape. I will contrive to get him down and take care of him." So he had the boat-train turned down-stream, and there built a platform and had the Bodhisat gently brought down. He then had him bathed, rubbed with refined oil, clothed in yellow gear and put to rest on an oiled hide. He sat down on a low seat by him and said the first verse:

" Yourself you made the way to pass, so that they
        safely crossed.

Now what are you to them, great ape, and what
    are they to you? "

The Bodhisat admonished the king in the remaining
verses:

" I, king, am lord of all those apes, conductor of the
    flock,
With grief oppressed and terrified at thee, tamer
    of foes.

I hurled myself a hundred times the length of
    bow detached,
With a strong shaft of bamboo to the middle of
    me bound.

Thrust like a cloud wind-torn I leapt across to
    reach the tree,
Failing t' alight I caught a bough and gripped it
    with both hands.

On me thus strung and taut between the creeper
    and the bough
The bough-beasts in unbroken line afoot went
    safely o'er.

Me can no bondage worry bring, nor will death
    worry me,
Weal have I brought to those o'er whom the
    governance was mine.

This parable for you, O king, is made to show
    you clear.
Of kingdom and of transport-world, of army and
    of town:
Of all the weal is to be sought by king who under-
    stands."

152

Thus admonishing and instructing the king the Great Being died. The king then bade his courtiers perform the obsequies of the ape-king as for a king, and he ordered his women to go to the funeral as the ape-king's retinue with red garments, dishevelled hair and with lamps[1] on staves in hand. At the crematorium the king erected a shrine, where lamps were burnt and flowers and incense offered. And the skull he had inlaid with gold, placed in front of it on the point of a spear and honoured as above; then taking it to Benares, he there honoured it for seven days, the city being decorated; then had it placed in a shrine. And, established in the Bodhisat's exhortation, he reigned righteously, working merit, and became a farer to the Bright World.

The Teacher . . . assigned the Jataka: " Then the king was Ānanda, the ape-king was just I."

---

[1] ? Or lanterns.

THE CHANDA-FAIRY JATAKA
(*Canda-kinnara-jātaka*)

" 'TIS passing away, methinks."—This the Teacher told while living in the Banyan Park near Kapilapura, about Rāhula's mother. But this Jataka must be told beginning at the Distant Epoch. And that beginning has been told in the (introductory) Nidāna-kathā as far as Kassapa of Uruvelā's confession at the Bamboo Wood . . . and there will be more about the visit to Kapilavatthu in the (last, the) Vessantăra Jataka.

Seated in his father's house (the Teacher), the meal being over, told the great story of Dhammapāla,[1] and then visited the house of Rāhula's mother and said, praising her virtue: " I will tell the story of the fairy Chanda." . . . His father began to speak of her virtues: " Reverend sir, when my daughter-in-law heard that you had adopted the yellow robe she robed in yellow gear; when she heard that garlands and the like were abandoned she gave up all such and became a floor-sitter; when you left the world she became a widow and refused gifts from other rajas. Thus constant in heart is she to you." The Teacher said: " It is not wonderful, majesty, that she should now in my last personal life be fond of me, constant, not another's; even when she was reborn in the non-human world she was so." And he brought up the past.

In the past, when Brahmadatta was reigning at Benares, the Great Being was reborn in the Himavant

[1] Jataka, No. 447; " great " as not the " little " Dhammapāla Jataka, 358.

region in the " Is-it-man "[1] world. His wife was
named Chandā. Both dwelt on a silver mountain
named Chanda (Moon-mountain). At that time the
king of Benares had handed over the realm to his
ministers, and putting on two yellow suits and
taking the five weapons, went alone to Himavant.
As he was eating venison he bethought him of a little
river and climbed up. The kinnaras who dwell on
Moon Mountain stay up during the rains and come
down when it is dry. Just then the Moon kinnara had
come down with his wife to this and that spot, pre-
fuming himself, eating pollen, donning and bedeck-
ing himself with flowery gear, sporting on creeper-
swings and singing with a sweet voice. Coming to
the little river, they went down at a halting-place,
played in the water, scattering flowers, then donned
again their flower-gear, prepared a flower-couch in
the sand, picked up a bamboo reed, and both seated
themselves. Then he played on the reed and sang in
a sweet voice; the kinnarī Chandā bending about
her flexible hands, danced and sang near him.

The king, hearing the sound, crept noiselessly
near, and, keeping hidden, saw the two, fell in love
with the kinnarī, and shot the kinnara that he might
carry her off. He, wailing in pain, said the four verses:

" 'Tis passing away, methinks, Chandā, I drown in a
    welter of blood.
'Tis life I abandon, the living breaths of me, O my
    Chandā, are ceasing.

Downsinking is mine, ill is mine, my heart is a-
    burning, I am come to the darkness.
And this is because thou, Chandā, art grieving;
    for this, naught else am I grieving.

[1] *Kin-năra*, usually rendered " fairy."

155

As grass, as the woodland I perish, as stream un-
    replenished I dry up,
And this is because thou, Chandā . . .
As rain on the lake at foot of the mountains the
    tears of me keep ever flowing,
And this is because thou, Chandā . . ."

Thus lamenting as he lay on his flowery couch
he lost consciousness and collapsed. The king stood
still. The other, intoxicated in her own enjoyment,
was unaware he was wounded. But then, seeing him
as he lay, she considered: " What now? Is my husband ill? " Then she saw blood dripping from the
wound, and unable to bear the mighty grief that
arose in her for the dear husband, she wailed loudly.
The king, judging the kinnara dead, showed himself. Chandā, thinking " This will be the bandit
who has shot my dear husband," fled away trembling,
and standing on the hillside reviling the king, she
said five verses:

" The wicked prince who shot the chosen mate
of wretched me, that (mate) lies wounded on the
ground. This my heart's grief may thy mother,
prince, repay, the heart's grief of me longing for
(my) fairyman. Yea, may thy wife repay it! . . .
May thy mother not see her children nor her lord
prince, who hast murdered my blameless fairyman
from desire for me."

The king, to comfort her, said:

" Weep not, Chandā, grieve not, thou with eyes
    like the wood-timira!
Do thou become my wife, the honoured lady in
    the royal house."

Chandā, thereat crying like lion, " You! what is this you say to me? " said the next verse:

" Nay, now I will die or ever thine, prince, I become; who hast murdered my fairyman from desire for me! "

Hearing her word he became void of desire and passion and said another verse:

" O fairy woman, both timid and lifeloving, go to Himavant! Thou feeder on *talisa* and *tagara*, in the forest deer will give thee joy."

So he went away. She, ware of it, came down, and clasping the Great Being took him up on the hill, placed him on level ground and laid his head on her lap, mightily lamenting in twelve verses:

" Those mountains and those caves and those crags
    and grots: there thee not seeing, O fairyman,
    what shall I do?

Those lovely spots flower-bespread, haunt of
    wild beast: there . . .

Clear flow the rivers coming from the crags,
    streams bestrewn with blossoms: there . . .

Blue are the tops of hills in Himavant and fair to
    see: there . . .

Yellow . . . tawny . . . sharp . . . white . . .
    varied in hue are the tops of hills in Himavant
    and fair to see: there . . .

In Gandhamādana whither troops of Yakkhas
    and of kinnaras resort, where grow the heal-
    ing plants, there . . ."

Ceasing her lament she laid her hand on his breast and was ware that it was yet warm. " Chandā lives yet," she thought, " I will set up a complaining and give him life." And she made complaint to the devas[1]: " What now? Are there no world-warders, or are they gone abroad, or dead, that they guard not my dear husband?" By the keenness of her grief Sakka's throne showed heat. He marking it and discerning the reason came in the form of a brahman and with a waterpot sprinkled the Great Being. Thereupon the poison vanished, colour arose, the very place of the wound was not manifest and he got up well. Chandā, seeing the dear husband in health, fell at Sakka's feet and said the next verse:

" I worship thee, venerable brahman, who hast besprinkled with ambrosial (drops) the chosen mate of wretched me, in reunion with the dearest."

Sakka gave them advice: " Hereafter climb the Hill of the Moon, and go not into the way of men; dwell just there." And he went to his own place. And Chandā, saying " What, husband, do we want with this place of peril? Come, go we to the hill of Chanda?" said the final verse:

" Let us now wander among the better rivers of the crags, the stream bestrewn with blossoms, the manifold tree-haunts, telling our love one to the other."

The Teacher then assigned the Jataka: " Then the king was Anuruddha, Chandā was Rāhula's mother, but the Kinnara was just I."

[1] Cf. p. 95.

THE UMMADANTI JATAKA

(*Ummadantī-jātaka*)

"**D**WELLING of whom, Sunanda, may this be?"—This the Teacher told while living at the Jetavana about a hankering monk. They say that one day when he was going about Sāvatthi for alms he saw a woman of exceeding beauty, gaily attired; falling in love with her and unable to turn away his mind, he just returned to the Vihara, and from that time, as if pierced by a dart, sick with passion, resembling a maddened deer, lean, his limbs as if covered with a network, his complexion ever sallower, caring for nought, getting no mental pleasure from any one posture, abandoning the duty to his teacher and so forth, absenting himself from studies through teaching, catechism and exercise:— so he lived. To his monk-comrades commenting on the change in him he said: " I don't care! " And they: " But you should care! It is hard to win rebirth in a Buddha's day; rebirth too when the right religion can be heard; rebirth too as a man. This you have won, and aspiring to make an end of ill, you put away your weeping kinsfolk and left the world in faith. Wherefore do you go under the influence of the passions bringing bane on you? " And they brought him before the Teacher in the temple. " Why, monks, have you brought a monk against his wish? " " We learn he is hankering." " Is this true? " " It is, reverend sir." " Sages of old, monk, even though in command of a kingdom, when this and that passion had arisen and they were come under its influence, restrained their mind and did

not do that which was unseemly." And he brought
up the past.

In the past in the kingdom of the Sivis, at the
city of Aritthapura, a Sivi king was reigning, and
the Bodhisat, born to his chief lady, was also named
Sivi. To the army captain also a son was born, and
they called him Ahipāraka.[1] They grew up as companions, and when sixteen years of age went to
Takkasilā, and when they had learnt the arts they
came back. The king made over his kingdom to
him, and he, making Ahipāraka his captain, ruled
righteously. Now in that city a citizen rich to the
amount of eighty crores of money, named Tirita-
vaccha, had a daughter of exceeding beauty and
loveliness, bearing auspicious features, and called
on her name-day Ummadantī. She at sixteen years
being of superhuman complexion, like a most fair
deva-nymph, all who beheld her were unable to
contain themselves, but became mad with passion
as if mad with strong drink, losing their presence
of mind. Then her father went to the king and said:
" Sire, in my house a woman-jewel has risen, fit
for a king. Send for the feature-augurs and have her
examined and act as you see fit." The king approved
and sent brahmans, who were well entertained in
the citizen's house and regaled with rice-milk. In a
moment Ummadantī in all her bravery of attire
came to them. They seeing her lost their presence
of mind, becoming as if passion-mad, forgot that
they were at an interrupted meal, and some, with
the idea they were eating, put the mouthful on their
head, some placed it beneath their arm, some smote
on the wall, all were crazy. She seeing them (said):
" They said these are to examine my features. Take

[1] One Burmese version reads Abhipāraka.

them by the neck and turn them out "; and she had this done. Confused and vexed with her they went to the king's dwelling and declared: " Sire, that woman is a witch, she is not suitable for you." The king—" A witch is she? "—did not bid her to him. She hearing of what had passed, said: " I, it seems, being a ' witch,' have not been chosen[1] by the king. So this is what witches are like! " And she plotted harm to him, thinking " So be it! When I shall see the king I shall know." Then her father gave her to Ahipāraka, and to him she was dear and charming. . . . (*The cause in a previous birth of her beauty is told.*)

Now at Aritthapura at the end of the rains a festival was proclaimed, and on full moon day the city was decorated. Ahipāraka, on going to his office of warding, advised her: " Lady dear, to-day is rains-end festival; the king making the luck-tour of the city will come first past the door of this house; do not show yourself to him; for if he sees you he will lose his presence of mind." She as he went[2] thought: " (Now) I shall know! " And when he was gone she bade a woman-slave: " When the king is coming past this house door, let me know." Then at sunset, when the city was adorned like a deva-city, lanterns burning everywhere, the king in brave attire driving in his best chariot and thoroughbreds, surrounded by officials . . . came past Ahipāraka's house door. Now that house was surrounded by a red wall, decorated, having gate and key, beautiful and attractive. At that moment the slave told Umma-dantī, and she, making her take a basket of flowers, stood near the window with fairy-grace and threw

[1] Lit. " taken." Cf. p. 42 *n.*
[2] Sā gacchantam . . . Burmese MSS. read: " Do you go, husband."

flowers to the king. He looking up at her, intoxicated with passion and unable to keep his presence of mind, was incapable of recognising the house as Ahipāraka's. And inquiring of the charioteer he said the two verses:

" Dwelling of whom, Sunanda, may this be?
Protected by this wall of colour bright?
Who is't I see like crest of fire afar,
Aloft in air like flame on peak of hill?

Daughter of whom, Sunanda, may she be,
Daughter-in-law of whom, or is she wife?
Quickly declare to me the thing I ask,
Is she yet unsecured or is there mate? "

Then he in telling him uttered two verses:

" I verily do know her, lord of men,
Both on the mother's and the father's side,
Likewise the man, O guardian of the land,
Successful he, and prosperous and rich.

By day and night full zealous for your weal,
One of your ministers, O lord of men,
Of Ahipāraka she is the wife,
And, by the name of her, Ummadantī."

Hearing him, the king, celebrating her name, straightway spoke a verse:

" O master, master, this the name of her
Full well by mother and by father given!
For sooth she'd but to cast her eye on me
And ' madman ' Ummadantī's made of me!"

She seeing his agitation closed up the window and went to her bower. For the king, from the time of his seeing her, there was no mind to carry out the luck-tour of the city. He bade the charioteer turn the chariot, saying, " This festival is not suitable for us; for the captain Ahipāraka it is suitable "; and driving home he went up to his chamber and lay down talking to himself:

" Of Ummadantī's charms . . ." (*Many verses of rambling talk follow.*)

Those officials told Ahipāraka of how the king had turned back at his house door, and he going home asked Ummadantī: " Lady dear, did you let the king see you? " " Husband, there was a man came by standing in a chariot, a big-paunched, big-toothed person; I know not whether he was king or belonging to the king—someone in authority, it was said—standing at the window I was throwing flowers, and at that he turned and went away." He hearing her said: " You have destroyed me! " Next day he went early to the king's dwelling, and standing at the door of his chamber heard him talking to himself about Ummadantī and thought: " He has fallen in love with Ummadantī; not getting her he will die. Letting neither the king nor myself in for anything unseemly, it is for me to save his life." Going home he summoned a strong attendant and said: " Tāta, by such and such a shrine there stands a hollow tree. Do you, letting no one know, go there at sunset and sit inside the tree. I shall go there to make an offering, and invoking the tree-deva I will pray: ' O deva-king, our king will not take part in the festival, but lies in his chamber talking to himself; we don't know why; the king has for years been a benefactor of devas spending a

163

thousand on sacrifice; because of this tell us why
he is talking and grant him life!' Do you at that
moment, having kept this going in memory, say:
' Captain, your king is not ill, but he has fallen in
love with your wife Ummadantī; if he will get her
he will live; if not he will die; if you wish him to live
give Ummadantī to him.'" So teaching him he sent
him off. They carried this into effect, and then the
captain went and, letting the officials know, ascended
the king's dwelling and knocked at the royal chamber
door. The king, collecting himself, said: "Who is
it?" "It is I, sire, Ahipāraka." Then to him the
king's door opened. And entering, he saluted the
king and said the verse:

> "To me the spirits worshipping their lord,
> A yakkha came and this is what he said:
> The king's mind is on Ummadantī set,
> I give you her; make of her your handmaid."

Then the king asked him: "Good Ahipāraka,
do even the Yakkhas know of my talking wildly
because of my having lost my heart to her?" "Yes,
sire." He was ashamed, saying, "By all the world
my shameful state is known!" And established in
the right he forthwith said the verse:

> "Fallen from merit, immortal am I not!
> The people this our evil (deed) may know!
> And mighty too in you the mind's upset
> Were your dear wife so given seen no more."

Then they two in many verses argued affection-
ately, Ahipāraka urging his gift: . . .

> "To me a mother and a father thou,
> Husband and master, fosterer and god.

I am thy slave with children and with wives,
As it may please thee, Sivi, take thy wish."

The king protesting:

" Who by his woe lays for another woe,
Or by his weal takes other's weal away:
Not so! as this for me, so in another's case:
Herein he knows he's understood the Right.

Not by the wrong e'en immortality
Would I desire, nor the whole earth to win.
Not for all that would I unjustly walk,
I who 'mong Sivis am become the Bull.

Leader, father, sovran, the kingdom's guard,
The standard (*dhamma*) of the Sivis cherishing,
He thus upon the Right (*dhamma*) in thought intent
Fares therefore not by hest of his own heart."

And Ahipāraka finally admonishing:

" Sure thou, my king, in whom such wisdom is,
Wilt reign long, luckily and ever safe.
We hail thee one not heedless in the Right;
The noble heedless in the right is lost.
Choose thou the right with parents, noble king!
Here choosing Right to Bright World wilt thou go.
Choose thou the Right with children and with
wife!
Here choosing Right to Bright World wilt thou
go,

and so with ' friends and ministers,' with ' bearers
(horse and man),' with ' villages, towns,' ' kingdom,' ' holy men,' ' wild things and birds,'
choose the Right, your majesty; Right practised
brings happiness along; choosing here the Right,

devas with Inda and with Brahma, by good practice,
have won devahood. Be not heedless of the Right."[1]

The Right being thus taught the king by Captain
Ahipāraka, the king brought his infatuated heart
into subjection.

The Teacher having brought up this lesson
assigned the Jataka: " Then Sunanda the charioteer
was Ānanda, Ahipāraka was Sāriputta, Ummadantī
was Uppalavannā, King Sivi was just I."

[1] The " many verses " are in all 157 lines.

THE SIX(-RAYED) TUSKER JATAKA
(*Chaddanta-jātaka*)

"WHY dost thou grieve."—This the Teacher told while living at the Jetavana about a young nun. She, it is said, daughter of the Sāvatthi families, seeing danger in domestic life, left the world. And going with the nuns to hear the Right, and contemplating the person of the Ten-Powered seated in his decorated pulpit, his supreme beauty outcome of infinite merit, she thought: "Was I ever, wayfaring in Becoming, the handmaiden of this man, cherishing him in the ages gone by?" Then in her at that moment memory of a former birth arose: "I was that at the time of the Six-Tusker elephant." And a glad rapture arose in her, and she laughed a great laugh in her rapture. Next she thought: "Handmaidens who are well disposed to their masters are few, they who are not well disposed are more in number; now was I the one or the other?" And remembering, she saw that she, laying up in her heart a trifling ill will, had sent the hunter Sonuttara after the Six Tusker, great lord of elephants, one hundred and twenty cubits high, and he had wounded him with a poisoned arrow and slain him. Then grief arose in her. She was unable to bear it, and gasping and panting she wept loudly. Seeing her, the Teacher broke into a smile, and when asked by the monks why he smiled, "Monks, that young nun has wept, remembering a misdeed she once did in bygone days concerning myself," and he brought up the past.

In the past, in Himâlaya near the Six Tusker Lake dwelt eight thousand elephants of magic power, fliers in air. Then the Bodhisat took birth as the son of the chief elephant, and he was all white with red feet and mouth. Later, when fully grown, he stood eighty-eight hands high, one hundred and twenty cubits in length; his trunk was fifty-eight hands long like a silver rope; his tusks fifteen hands round, thirty hands in length and having six-coloured rays. He was the chief of the eight thousand, and did homage to the lonely Buddhas. He had two chief consorts, Subhaddā Minor and Subhaddā Major, and they all dwelt in the Kañcana (golden) Cave.

Now that Six Tusker Lake at its heart is solely of gem-clear water, around which are zones of, first, lotuses, then of various fruit trees, of paddy fields, of other trees, then of a bamboo wood, then of seven mountain ranges, all of which is described in the Samyutta Commentary. On the north-east side of the lake was a huge banyan tree; on the west side the Golden Cave.

Then one day they announced that the great Sal Wood was in blossom. He with his following, minded to " play the sal-game," went to that wood and with his forehead smote a full-blossomed sal-tree. Subhaddā Minor was standing to windward, and on her body fell a mixture of dry twigs, old leaves and red ants. But Subhaddā Major stood to leeward, and on her body fell blossoms, pollen, stamens and (young) leaves. Subhaddā Minor thought: " These things have fallen upon his dear wife, those on my body; let be! I shall know! " And she nursed wrath against the Great Being. Again, another day the elephant king went down with his following to bathe in the Six Tusker Lake, and two

young elephants taking bunches of usīra-root washed
him down as if scrubbing Kelāsa's peak. When he
had come out they washed down the queen-elephants,
and they coming out stood beside the Great Being.
Then all the elephants going down into the water
played the water-game, and adorned the king and
queens with flowers; one elephant, going about in
the lake, found a great seven-headed lotus, and
brought it to the Great Being. Taking it with his
trunk he sprinkled pollen on his forehead and gave
it to Subhaddā Major. The other saw it and again
laid up wrath. Then one day, when the Bodhisat
was entertaining five hundred lonely Buddhas with
fruits and lotus-stalks and essences, she handed the
fruits she had received to the Buddhas and put up
the prayer: " When I go hence at death, may I be
reborn in the family of the Madda king as a king's
maiden, named Subhaddā, and when I am of age
may I become the chief lady of the Benares king;
may I be dear and attractive to him, able to get my
way; and may I send out a hunter who may kill this
elephant with poisoned arrow; and may I be able
to have brought me his twin tusks sending out rays
of six colours." From that time she took no food
and wasted away and soon died.

She was reborn according to her prayer, becoming chief lady of sixteen thousand women, and
she acquired knowledge of birth-memory. She
thought: " My prayer has availed; now I will have
the twin tusks of that elephant brought to me."
Thereupon smearing her body with (common) oil
and clothing herself in soiled garments, she mani-
fested symptoms of illness and took to her bed. The
king said " Where is Subhaddā? " and hearing she
was sick, entered the bedroom, and sitting on the
bed stroked her back saying the first verse:

" Why dost thou weep, (my) graceful one? Pale is
        (my) choicest lady grown;
(My) wide-eyed woman wilts away, like garland
        crumpled (in the hand)."

Hearing him, she said the second verse:

" Sick longing, majesty, is mine, o'erwhelming me
        in dream.
No easy thing it were to win; for such it is I long."

Hearing that, the king said a verse:

" Whatever men desire to have in this world's
        pleasant things:
All these are mine galore; to you your longed-for
        thing give I."

Hearing this, the queen, speaking of it, " Majesty,
my longed-for thing is hard to get. I will not tell it
now, but do you assemble all the hunters in your
kingdom, I will tell it before them," said the next
verse:

" Let trappers, sire, together come, as many as your
        kingdom owns;
To these I will declare what 'tis that I so greatly
        long to have."

The king consented and bade his officers summon
hunters by drum. Soon after, the trappers dwelling
in Kāsi kingdom, taking what offerings they could
afford, had their arrival announced to the king, and
there were sixty thousand of them. The king heard
and standing at the window pointed them out to
the queen:

" Here are those trappers, lady, well trained and
       stout of heart,
In woodcraft wise, in gamecraft wise, their lives
       at my behest."

Hearing that, the queen addressed them in another
verse:

" Men of the hunt, attend to me as many as are here!
White and six-tusked an elephant beheld I in a
       dream.
His tusks I need; not getting them no life is there
       (for me)."

Hearing that, the trappers spoke:

" Ne'er have our fathers nor our grandsires seen
Or heard there was a six-tusked elephant.
What 'twas in dream, king's daughter, you did see,
The sort of beast it was declare to us."

They said yet the next verse:

" Four quarters are there, four between;
Above, below: ten quarters these.
In which is found this elephant-king,
Whom in a dream you saw six-tusked? "

This said, Subhaddā contemplated all the trappers,
and among them she saw one, broad-footed, legs like
a leaf-basket, big-kneed, big-ribbed, thick-bearded,
brown-whiskered, scarred, unsightly, repellent,
noticeable among all as such, a hunter hostile in
former days to the Great Being, Sonuttara by name.
Thinking " That one will be able to carry out my
word," she got the king's permission and took him

up to the top floor of the seven-storied terrace, and opening the north casement, she pointed to the Himâlaya of the North and said four verses:

" Straight hence to quarter lying North
  When he has passed seven ridges vast,
  Stands the grand ridge hight Golden Brae,
  The flowery haunt of woodmen wild.

  Climbing the crest where fairies dwell,
  And looking down on mountain base,
  Thou'lt see in colour like a cloud,
  King Banyan-tree, eight-thousand-stemmed.

  There dwells the six-tusked elephant,
  All white, for others hard t' o'ercome.
  Eight thousand elephants him ward,
  With plough-pole tusks, wind-swift to strike.

  With trumpeting and snort they stand;
  The wind in moving them disturbs,
  But if a man they there observe,
  They'd blast him, leave not even dust! "

Hearing that, Sonuttara was mortally dismayed and said:

" Many in sooth are these in royal house,
  The ornaments wrought in fine gold, lady,
  The pearls, the jewels and the cat's eye gems.
  What will you make of ivory ornaments?
  Or is it hunter-folk you would destroy? "

Then the queen said the verse:

" A grudger and a griever, look! am I;
  And sorely do I wilt, remembering.
  Work you for me this good thing, hunter-man,
  And I'll give five choice villages to you."

Thus saying she reassured him thus: " Good hunter-man, I have given a gift to lonely Buddhas putting up the prayer, ' May I, having had this six-tusked elephant killed, be able to have brought me the twin tusks.' This is no matter of something seen in dream; but the prayer I offered will succeed. Do you go and fear not." He consented, and asking " Well, then, tell me clearly where 'tis he lives," he said:

" Where sits he, then? Where does he stand?
By which path does he go to bathe?
How does the king of elephants bathe?
How may we know the trumpeter's track? "

Thereon she by knowledge of birth-memory visualised the place of him she had seen and declared it:

" Just there's the lotus pool not far,
Lovely and fordable and full,
A-blossom and the haunt of many bees.
'Tis here that the king elephant does bathe.

Head of him bathed bearing the lotus-wreath,
And white all over as the lotus-stem,
Right joyously to his abode he goes,
Preceding his chief spouse ' All-lucky One.' "

Hearing that, Sonuttara consented, saying, " Very good, lady, I will kill the elephant and bring you the tusks." Then she, well pleased, gave him a thousand, and dismissed him: " Go first to your home and start thither after a week." And she sent for the smiths and ordered them to make quickly an axe, a spade, a chisel, a hammer, a bamboo-cutter, a sickle, an iron staff, stanchions, and a three-pronged grappling-iron. She sent for the saddlers and ordered them to " make us quickly a leather sack capable of containing a kumbha, also a leather rope, straps, gloves and shoes, and a leather umbrella." This they did. And she had provisions prepared, and all other requisites for his journey—fire-drills and so on. And when she had stowed everything into the leather sack, both tools and provisions—namely, a bag of barleymeal and so forth—the whole weighed about a kumbha.

Sonuttara, after making his own preparations, went on the seventh day and waited on the queen. And she said: " All that you will require on the journey has been got ready. Take this knapsack." And he being as strong as five elephants lifted it up as if it were a bag of sweets, and adjusting it on his loins, left his hands free. She bestowed a maintenance fund on his children, informed the king and dismissed him. Saluting king and queen the hunter descended from the palace, mounted a chariot and with a great escort departed from the city. Passing through towns and villages he came to the frontier, and there turned back his people of the country, and escorted by borderfolk entered the forest. When he had reached the end of men's pathways he turned back the borderfolk and went on alone.

For thirty yojanas (? 210½ miles) he worked through seventeen sorts of jungle, reaping and chopping a path, felling trees and digging out roots. In a bamboo jungle he fashioned a ladder, mounted a bamboo cluster, and swung himself along from stem to stem. In a marsh jungle he took two planks and laid them down one after the other as he went; and to cross a watery jungle he made a canoe. Finally he came to the foot of a mountain precipice. Here he tied his grappling-iron to his rope, and throwing it aloft hooked the rock with it, and climbed up. He then drove his brazen staff shod with diamond into the rock, and into the cleft hammered a stanchion. Getting on to this, he hauled up his grappling-iron, and again hooked it aloft. (Going up and driving in the second stanchion), the rope hanging down, he descended by it, and making fast the lower stanchion to the rope, he clutched the latter in his left hand, and taking his mallet in the right he struck at the rope till the stanchion was extracted. Then he climbed up again. On this wise he ascended to the summit, and traversing descended by similar method. Hammering in a stanchion at the top of the first ridge, he wound his rope on to it, and fastening his knapsack to the rope, and sitting in the sack he went down, like a spider paying out its web. Some say that he caught the wind as well with his umbrella, descending like a bird.[1]

Thence he proceeded to cross six more mountain ranges, the last and greatest being the glorious peak Golden Brae. Finally from the Fairies' Rock he looked down on the base of the mountains, and saw afar the great Banyan Wood, with its thousands of pillared stems, in colour cloud.

Having reached the abode of the Great Being, it is said in more than seven months, in seven years and seven days, and marked that abode, he determined to dig a pit, stand in it and so wound and kill the lord of elephants. He entered the forest and cut down trees for props and strewed a heap of grass. And when the elephants were gone to bathe, where he (the king) would stand he dug a square pit with his great spade, and the soil dug out he sprinkled

[1] Cf. my article, " The Earliest Rock-climb," *Jl. P.T.S.*, 1897-1901, p. 80.

with water as if he were sowing seed, and having
set up props on mortar-stones and giving them
weights and ropes, he spread planks over them. He
made a slit the size of an arrow, and scattering soil
and rubbish above, he made an entrance for himself
at one side, and so the pit being finished, at day-
break he tied on a false topknot, donned yellow robes,
and taking his bow with a poisoned arrow he went
down and stood in the pit.

Showing the matter the Teacher said:

" Making a pit, with planks the trapper hid
The same, himself crept down with bow.
Marking the coming elephant he shot
With arrow broad, doer of ill! he said.[1]

The wounded elephant loud trumpeted,
The elephants all roared like roar (again),
Crushing to powder grasses and brushwood,
They ran all round about the quarters eight.

Minded to slay the man, accosting him,
He saw the yellow robe, banner of seers!
Smitten with pain the thought arose in him
' The saintly banner, for the good inviolate.' "

And he said the pair of verses:

" Who suffers vice yet dons the saffron robe,
Keeping apart from self-control and truth,
Unworthy he to wear the saffron hue.

Who vice rejects, steadfast in virtuous ways,
And yokes himself to self-control and truth,
Worthy is he to wear the saffron hue."[2]

[1] *Vatvā*, referring presumably to the teller.
[2] *Psalms of the Brethren* (Theragāthā), ver. 969 f.

176

So saying, the Great Being extinguished the thought concerning the hunter, and asked: " My man, for what purpose have you wounded me, for your own purposes, or are you employed by another? "

Then informing him the trapper said the verse:

" The king of Kāsi's queen, my lord,
  Honoured at court, Subhaddā she,
  She saw you and directed me:
' I need his tusks,' to me she said."

Hearing that, and discerning " This is the work of Subhaddā Minor," the Great Being, enduring the pain, explained, " She has no need of my tusks; it was to kill me that she sent you," and said the pair of verses:

" Splendid tusk-yokes are mine galore,
  Those of my sires and my grandsires;
  Knows that the angry king's daughter,
  Wanting to kill, the fool made feud.

  Get you up, trapper, take the file,
  Cut off these teeth before I die;
  Say to that angry king's daughter,
' Slain is the beast. Lo! here his tusks.' "

He hearing his word rose from where he sat and, taking a saw to saw the tusks, approached him. But he being eighty-eight hands high was remote as a mountain, and his tusks unreachable. Then the Great Being stooped and lay down, lowering his head; and the hunter, climbing up on that silver rope of a trunk, stood on the forehead as if on Kelāsa's peak and pushed his knee into the mouth, and descending from the forehead inserted the saw into the mouth. Great pain arose in the Great Being and the mouth was filled with blood. The hunter shifting hither and thither was unable to cut with the saw. Then the Great Being clearing his mouth of blood endured the pain and asked, " What, my man, are you not able to cut? " " No, master." Then the Great Being summoning presence of mind said, " Well, then, lift up my trunk and make it catch the end of the saw; I have no strength to lift it up myself," and the hunter did so. The Great Being taking the saw with his trunk worked it to and fro and cut off the tusks as they were sprouts. Then handing them over he said: " Good trapper-man, in giving you these tusks I give them not as something I care not for, nor as one praying for Sakka-ship or Māraship or to be Brahmā, but because the tusks of the knowledge of everything-known are a hundred thousand degrees dearer to me than these tusks, and may this merit be for me the cause of the knowledge of everything-known! " And asking " My man, how long did it take you to come here?" and the other saying " More than seven months, seven days, seven years," he said, " Go: by the power of these tusks you will reach Benares within seven days." And dismissing him with a warding-rune, he died before the elephants and Subhaddā had yet come to him.

The hunter having departed, the elephants, not seeing the enemy, came back.

With them came Subhaddā, and they all weeping and wailing went to the lonely Buddhas, neighbours of the Great Being, and told them saying, " Reverend sirs, your requisite-provider is dead, wounded by a poisoned arrow; come to his cemetery-show." And the five hundred lonely Buddhas coming through the air descended into the funeral-circle. At that

moment two young elephants lifting up the body of
the elephant-king on their tusks placed it on the
pyre, the lonely Buddhas saluting, and cremated it.
The lonely Buddhas all night long made recitation
in the crematory. The eight thousand elephants,
having put out the fire and bathed, went back with
Subhaddā at their head to their abode.

And Sonuttara, the seventh day not yet come,
entered Benares with the tusks.

Presenting himself he said: " Lady, he for whom
you made such illwill in your heart, that elephant
has been slain by me and is dead." " That he is
dead is what you say." " Learn (for yourself) that
he is dead; here are the tusks." With a jewelled fan
she took the tusks variegated with the rays of six
colours and placed them on her knees. Contemplating the tusks of him who was her husband in a
former becoming, she remembered him: " Having
put an end to the life of so beautiful a elephant with
poisoned arrow and sawn off his tusks has he come!"
Grief unbearable arose in her; there, even there her
heart broke; that very day she died.

Showing the matter the Teacher said:

" The Enlightened One, the Mighty One
    Smiled in midst of the company.
    Asked him the monks with minds set free:
    So Buddhas show not without cause?
    The young maid you have seen abroad,
    The homeless one in saffron robe,
    She then was daughter of the king,

    I then was the king-elephant.
    The trapper-man who took the tusks
    Of trumpeter incomp'rable,

Fair lovely things unmatched on earth,
And to the Kāsi city came,
He then was Devadatta('s self).

This world-old faring, high and low,
This long procession of the nights
On which the sun yet doth not set:
He from whom pain and grief had fled
And (hunter's) dart, he of the things
Himself knew well, the Buddha told.

I for you at that time was there, ye monks,
Elephant-king was I then: thus do ye
The story of a former lifetime learn."

These verses were placed (on record) by the Elders reciting Dhamma praising the virtues of the Ten-Powered One.

NOTE. Comy:—The ancestral tusks mentioned were treasured in a secret place. Let him not despoil! let him take mine!

THE KUSA JATAKA

(Kusa-jātaka)

"THIS realm of yours."—This the Teacher
told while living at the Jetavana about a
hankering monk . . . (the "present" episode is in
effect identical with that in the Ummadantī Jataka, but
the Teacher introduces his "past" on a different note,
curiously in conflict with the story's conclusion) . . .
The Teacher said: "Abide not in passion, monk;
as to woman, she is evil; repress your enamoured
thoughts of her; take pleasure in the religion; verily
because of enamoured thoughts of a woman wise
men of old, though ardent, lost their ardour, and
came to confusion and ruin." And he brought up
the past.

In the past in the realm of the Mallas, at the raja-
residence of Kusavati a king named Okkāka was
reigning righteously. The chief lady of his eighteen
thousand women was named Sīlavatī (Virtuous).
She had neither son nor daughter . . . but by the
power of her virtue Sakka perceiving her desire
thought: "To this one it behoves me to grant a
son; is there now in deva-world a son suitable for
her?" Then he beheld the Bodhisat, who, it is said,
having passed a life in the Thirty-three's realm, was
desirous of being reborn in a higher deva-world.
Sakka going to the door of his mansion called him
forth, saying, "My lord, it behoves you to go to the
world of men and take rebirth in the chief consort
of king Okkāka." And causing him to consent he
said to yet another son of devas: "You too will

become a son of hers." And he brought the lady herself in a trance to his realm. And she, become conscious there, rose up and approached Sakka seated beneath the Paricchattaka tree surrounded by divine dancers, saluted him and sat down at the side. Then Sakka said to her: " A choice I give you, lady, choose."[1] " Why, then, deva, give me a son." " Lady, let alone one, I will give you two sons. But of these one will be wise not handsome; one will be handsome not wise. Which do you desire first? " " The wise one, sire." "Very well," said he, and giving her a blade of kusa grass, and a divine robe, divine sandalwood and a Kokanada lute, he took her back to the king's bedchamber, laid her on a bed, touched her navel with his thumb and went to his own place. And the wise lady knew she had conceived . . . and showed the king Sakka's gifts to convince him of the good news. When the son born to her began to walk they called him by no other name but just Kusa. Then when he began to walk the other deva-son was born and him they called Jayampăti (conquering lord).

The Bodhisat learnt nothing from any teacher, but being wise attained all arts by his own wisdom. When he was sixteen years old the king desiring to give him the kingdom informed his consort: " Lady dear, in giving our son the kingdom we will arrange a dancing-festival; living we will see him established in the kingdom. The king's daughter in all Jambudīpa whom you desire we will bring here and make her his chief lady. Learn his mind as to which king's daughter he prefers." She agreed, and sent a lady-in-waiting to the prince to tell him. Hearing her, the Great Being thought: " I am not handsome; if they bring me a handsome princess, she will say

[1] Lit. " take." Cf. pp. 6, 42.

' What have I to do with this ugly one?' and will run away. Hence there will arise a shameful matter for us. What have I to do with the domestic life? While they live I will wait on the parents; when they are gone I will go away and leave the world." And he said: " I have no need of kingdom or festivities; when the parents are gone I will leave the world." The king was displeased and asked him again after some days and yet again. The fourth time he thought: " It is not seemly to be entirely opposed to the parents; I will make a plan." And he sent for the head smith and giving him much gold bade him make an image of a woman. When he had gone the prince took more gold and himself made a woman's image.

The plans of Bodhisats succeed.

No tongue could tell the beauty of that image. The Great Being had it robed in linen and placed in the royal chamber. When he saw the image brought by the chief smith he found fault with it and said: " Go and fetch the image standing in our chamber." He entered it and seeing that said, " It will be a deva-nymph come to take her pleasure with the prince," and not daring to lay hands on it he went out saying, " Sire, in the chamber there stands a lady alone, a deva-daughter; I cannot approach." " Tāta, go, it's of gold; fetch it." And he did so. The prince had the statue made by the smith laid in the golden chamber, the one made by himself adorned and placed in a chariot and sent it to his mother thus: " Winning one like this I choose[1] (her)." She sent for the ministers and said: " Dear sirs, my son is full of merit and is Sakka-given; he will win a suitable maiden; do you, placing this statue in a covered car, tour over all Jambudīpa,

[1] Lit. " take." Cf. p. 42.

and to the king who has a daughter like the statue give it, saying ' King Okkāka will arrange a marriage with you,' and fixing the date come back." They, consenting, took it, and, departing with a great retinue, made a tour from one raja's residence to another, exhibiting the statue much adorned and bewreathed on a golden litter at eventide to concourses of people by the landing-path, standing aside themselves to hear the talk of the passers-by. The people seeing it did not recognise it as a statue, but said, " She's so beautiful that, though human, she's like a divine nymph. Now why is she there? Whence did she come? There's no one like her in our city! " and passed on. The ministers, concluding that had there been such a maiden they would have said, " Like the raja's or the minister's daughter," took the statue to another city. So touring they came to Sāgala, in the kingdom of the Maddas. There the king had seven daughters exceedingly beautiful like divine nymphs, the eldest of them being named Pabhāvatī. From her body rays streamed as from the risen sun; though it were dark in her four-cubit bower, there was no need of a lamp. Now she had a humpbacked nurse. Giving Pabhāvatī food, she took eight pretty slaves with jars, and went in the evening to the ghat to get water wherewith to wash her lady's head. There she saw the statue set up, and thinking it was Pabhāvatī, she was vexed and said: " That ill-conducted one has thought ' I will wash my head,' and sending us to get water she comes ahead of us and stands there at the landing road." And she spoke to the statue, " Fie, family-shaming-bazaar-girl! there you stand, getting ahead of us! If the king comes to know, he will do for us! " and she smote it on the cheek with her hand, making a crack as big as her palm.

Then seeing it was a statue she laughed, and going to the slaves said: "Look at my work! I thought that was my daughter, I gave it a slap. What's its worth compared with my daughter? I've only earned a hurt hand." Then the king's messengers took her and said: "You were saying ' My daughter is more beautiful than this '; of whom were you speaking?" "Of the Madda-king's daughter Pabhāvatī; this figure isn't worth the sixteenth part of her." They were pleased, and going to the king's door with " The messengers of the king Okkāka stand at the door," caused him to be brought. Interviewed by the king they said, " Sire, our king asks after your health," and explained their tour. He, thinking " With such a king a daughter's marriage will be lucky," consented and entertained them with honour. They, pleading that they could not delay, went back, and king Sivi set out for Sāgala.

The lady Sīlavatī, through her wisdom thinking " Who knows what will happen? " after one or two days said to the Madda-king, " Sire, we are desirous of seeing our daughter-in-law," and accordingly Pabhāvatī, in brave attire with her nurse-retinue, came and saluted her mother-in-law. The latter seeing her thought: " This princess is very beautiful; my son is ugly; if she sees him, that same day she will leave and run away. I will devise a plan." And she said to the Madda-king: " Your majesty, the daughter-in-law is suitable for my son; but there happens to be a traditional custom for comers into our family. If she will conform to this custom we will bring her." " Why, what is your custom? " " In our line till they have conceived, (brides) do not get sight of their husbands by day. Will she do thus? " The king asked his daughter and she said "Yes, tāta." Then king Okkāka, giving much dowry to the Madda-king, departed, the king's daughter being sent along with a great following. Okkāka proclaimed his son king and Pabhāvatī his chief lady; all prisoners were released, the city decorated and all were bidden to obey Kusa. In all Jambudīpa kings with daughters sent them to Kusa, and they who had sons sent these as pages desiring his friendship. The Bodhisat's dancing retinue was very large and he reigned with great glory.

But he never got to see Pabhāvatī by day nor she him, only by night. The radiance of her body was by day only, and he left his chamber while it was yet night. After some days he told his mother he wished to see her by day. She refused, saying," Only wait till she has a child." But he asked her again and again, and she said: "Well, then, go to the elephant stables and stand there dressed like a groom; I will bring her there, then you may fill your gaze with her, but don't make yourself known." This was done, and the queen said to Pabhāvatī: " Come and see your husband's elephants." And she showed her each by name. She walking behind the mother, the king hit her on the back with a lump of elephant-dung, and she being angry said, " I will get the king to cut off your hand," annoying the queen, who appeased her by stroking her back. The same thing happened at the horse stables, the king being again anxious to get a sight of her. Again, Pabhāvatī being anxious to see the Great Being, repeatedly asking her mother-in-law, was told, " Well, then, to-morrow my son will make a luck-tour of the city; you may see him if you stand at the casement," and she had this brought about, but got prince Jayampati to act the part of the king; then taking Pabhāvatī to the casement she said: " See the auspicious beauty of your husband!" She was pleased, saying, "I have won a husband suitable for me."

But on that occasion the Great Being, dressed as a groom, was seated behind Jayampati; and he looking his fill on Pabhāvatī showed the enjoyment in his heart's choice by gestures. The elephant gone by, the queen-mother asked her, " Did you see your husband?" " Yes, lady, but behind him there sat a groom, a very ill-conducted (fellow), who made gestures and the like to me; why do they make one so ill-favoured sit behind the king?" " My child, it is desirable to have a guard in rear of the king." She thought: " That groom is over-bold; he doesn't look upon the king as king; is it possible he is king Kusa? Can it be that he is ugly and that is why they will not let me see him?" So she said in the ear of the humpback (nurse): " Mother, go and learn whether the king sat on the front seat or behind." " How shall I learn?" " By this sign, of course: the king is he who will alight first." She went and saw the Great Being alight first, then Jayampati. The former, looking about and seeing the nurse, knew why she had come and strongly charged her: " Do not speak of what has just taken place to Pabhāvatī!" But she did tell, and Pabhāvatī believed her. Once more the king expressed his desire to see her, and his mother, unable to refuse him, said: " Well, then, go into the garden disguised." He going entered the lotus-pool up to his neck, and stood with a lotus-leaf over his head and a lotus spread before his face. The mother in the evening took Pabhāvatī to the garden, and stirring lust of looking in her by saying " Look at these trees . . . birds . . . deer . . ." sent her to the pool. A wish to bathe coming over her, she went down to it with her attendants and there disported herself. Seeing that very lotus, she stretched out her hand to pluck it, when the king, displacing the leaf, grasped her hand saying, " I am king Kusa! " Seeing his face she screamed, " A yakkha has seized me! " and fainted, the king letting go her hand. When she recovered she thought: " Surely it was king Kusa who seized my hand, treated me as he did at the stables and on the elephant! What have I to do with such an ugly, ill-faced lord? I live yet and will get another husband." And summoning the courtiers with whom she had come, she bade them: " Make ready my car. I will go this very day."

They told the king. He thought: " If she is not let go it will break her heart; let her go. I will bring her back again by my own power." So he suffered her to go. She went to her father's city. The Great Being also left the garden, entered the city and ascended the decorated terrace.

The truth is, it was through a prayer in the past that she would not have him, and it was through an act of his in the past that he was ugly. He was her brother-in-law, and was vexed because she gave cakes she had baked for him to a saint, and she then prayed for future beauty and to be apart from him. He then confirmed the gift, praying to the saint that he might become fit to fetch her from any distance to be his wife.

He, sorely grieved at her going, would not look on another woman, however well he waited on; without Pabhāvatī the whole dwelling shrank as if empty. Thinking " Now she will have reached Sāgala," he told his mother next morning: " Mother, I shall go to bring Pabhāvatī; do you command the kingdom." And he said the first verse:

" This realm of yours, all rich and armed,
The home of kings and all that men desire,
This is your realm, mother, give you the word.
I go where is the dear Pabhāvatī."

She hearing him say thus said, " Well, then, dear
one, you should be careful, for woman's habits are[1]
not pure," and filling a gilt ewer with the choicest
food she gave it him for provisions and sent him
forth. He took it and, saluting his mother and making
thrice the luck-circle, said: " If I live I will see
(her) again." Entering his chamber he donned the
five weapons, and taking ewer and a thousand (coins)
in a bag, and his Kokanada lute, he departed from
the city and set out a-wayfaring.

By noonday, being very strong and sturdy, he
travelled fifty leagues, then broke his fast and went
another fifty leagues. And thus by eventide having
bathed he entered the city of Sāgala. Now his ardour
was such that his mere entering made it impossible
for Pabhāvatī to endure lying longer in bed, and
getting down she lay on the floor. And a certain
woman, seeing the Bodhisat walking wearily along
the street, invited him in, made him sit and bathed
his feet, and gave him a bed; while he slept she
prepared a meal and woke him and he supped.
Pleased with her he gave her his ewer and a
thousand coins. Leaving his weapons there and
saying " There's a place I have to go to," he took
his lute, and going to the (royal) elephant stables, he
got the elephant-keepers to let him stay and play to
them. After he had rested and got over his fatigue,
he played and sang so that all the city might hear
him. Pabhāvatī as she lay heard, and knew the lute
could be none else than his, and thought: "Without

[1] Burmese MS.: " heart is . . . "

189

doubt the Kusa king has come for my sake." The king, also hearing, thought: " He is playing most sweetly; to-morrow I will send for him and make him my minstrel." The Bodhisat thought: " I cannot see her by staying here; it's not the right place." And next morning he breakfasted in an eating-house, and putting aside his lute, he went to the royal potter and apprenticed himself. One day, getting the house full of clay, he said: " Master, I will make vessels." " Ay, make away." And placing a lump of clay on the wheel, turned this with such a turn that it went on till noon, and he made divers vessels large and small, and he made one for Pabhāvatī, and raised divers shapes on it.

The intents of Bodhisats succeed.

He resolved that Pabhāvatī should see those shapes. He dried and baked all the vessels, a very houseful. The potter taking divers vessels went to the royal family, and the king asked who had made them? " By me, sire." " I know they were not made by you; tell me who made them." " My apprentice, sire." " Not your apprentice, the man is your master; do you learn your craft from him. Henceforth let him make vessels for my daughters, and give him this thousand (coins). Give my daughters those little vessels." The potter took them to the daughters who were all come (to see), saying " These are to play with," and gave Pabhāvatī the vessel made expressly for her. She took it, and seeing on it the shapes of herself and her humpbacked nurse, knew who had made it, and was angry, saying, " I have no use for this; give it to them who want it." Then her sisters seeing she was cross, laughed at her: " You fancy that's made by the king Kusa; it wasn't; the potter made it; accept it." About his coming and making it she said to them nothing.

The potter gave the thousand to the Bodhisat, with the king's message, adding, " I will take your vessels to them." He thinking " Then though I live here I shall not be able to see Pabhāvatī," and giving back the money, he went and became apprentice to a rushmaker in the king's service. As such he made a palm-leaf fan for Pabhāvatī, and on it depicted divers figures: a white umbrella and banqueting floor and Pabhāvatī standing holding her robe. The rushmaker took this and other wares and went to the royal family. A similar talk with the king took place, and with Pabhāvatī, who threw the fan on the floor, the others laughing.

The Bodhisat again gave back the money, thinking " This is not the place for me to live in," and apprenticed himself to the king's garland-maker. Making up divers styles of garlands he made one for Pabhāvatī like a cushion, of varied shapes and colours. The garlands were taken to the royal family and a similar talk took place, Pabhāvatī throwing the garland also on the floor.

The Bodhisat, returning the fee again, apprenticed himself to the king's cook. One day the cook, bringing a variety of viands for the king, gave bone-meat to the Bodhisat that he might cook it for himself. He so prepared it that the odour spread over the whole city. The king smelling it asked: " Is there any other flesh in our kitchen? " "No, sire, save only some bonemeat I gave my apprentice to cook; the odour will be of that." The king had it brought him, and placing a morsel on the tip of his tongue, it suffused and agitated the seven thousand nerves of taste. The king, succumbing to taste-craving, gave a thousand and said: " Henceforth let your apprentice prepare my food and my daughters' food; you bring me mine, and let him bring them theirs." The

cook went and told him, and he, pleased, thought:
" Now has my mind's desire won to the top; now
shall I get to see Pabhāvatī! " And giving him the
thousand on the next day he prepared food, and
sending in dishes to the king, he himself took a food-
yoke and mounted to Pabhāvatī's terrace.

She seeing him carrying and climbing thought:
" He is doing what is unsuitable for him and should
be done by slaves, but if I shall keep silence, he will
get the idea I approve of him, and not going elsewhere he will stay here gazing on me; I will now
upbraid and berate him and not let him stay a
minute, and then I'll run away." So half opening
the door, letting one hand hang from the panel and
the other pushing the crossbar, she said the second
verse:

> " Bearing the heavy load with crooked mind,
> Devoted[1] both by day and dead of night,
> Swift hie back, Kusa, to Kusavati.
> I want not with an ugly one to live."

He, pleased to think " With Pabhāvatī have I
gotten speech! " said the third verse:

> " Not will I go hence to Kusavati!
> Craving thy beauty, O Pabhāvatī,
> My joy I find in Madda's happy home,
> Forsaking kingdom, fain to look on thee.
>
> Craving thy beauty, O Pabhāvatī,
> As one distraught I fare about the earth.
> Where am I, that I know and whence I've come.
> For you I'm mad with your soft eyes of deer."

---

[1] *Ratto*, which may mean either as above or " by night."

This said she thought: " I berate him thinking to make him regret, but he speaks as if delighted; if he were to seize my hand and say ' I am king Kusa! ' who could prevent him? Someone may hear this talk! " And she shut and bolted herself in. And he taking his yoke gave the daughters their food. Pabhāvatī sent her humpback, saying, " Go bring the food at the king's dinner." She did so and said " Eat." " I don't eat what that man has cooked; do you eat it and prepare me a meal from your own rations, but tell no one of king Kusa's coming." This arrangement went on, and Kusa could no more see her. So he thought, " I will examine whether Pabhāvatī is at all fond of me or not," and taking their dinner to the daughters, as he passed he struck his feet against the floor at the door of her bower, and clattering the dishes and moaning fell headlong as if fainting. At the sound of his moan she opened the door, and seeing him stretched out she thought: " This king is the king paramount in Jambudīpa; on my account he suffers hardships day and night; being delicately made he has fallen laid out by a food-yoke. Is he alive? " And coming out of her bower she bent over him and watched his face to find out if he breathed. Filling his mouth with spittle he let it fall on her body. Berating him she entered her room, and standing in the half-open door said:

" No progress, sir, he makes who the unwanting wants.
The unwilling, king, by will[1] you want, unlovely, the lovely one."

He through his devoted heart, though upbraided and berated, felt no regret and said the next verse:

[1] Kāmehi, lit. " by (sense) desires."

193

" Will she or will she not, the man who wins his
love,
Winning 'tis here we praise, loser is shamed."

She, too, thereupon not giving way, speaking in a
firm voice, wishing to make him run away, said another verse:

" You dig a rocky bed with *kanikara* wood,
The wind with net you bind who the unwanting
want."

Hearing her, the king said three verses:

" A rock sure in your heart is laid, you of the gentle
face,
I do not find you pleasant though 'cross the lands
I've gone.

When you with beetling brow, king's daughter,
look on me,
Food-bearer am I then in Madda-king's harem,

When you with smiling face, king's daughter,
look on me,
No more food-bearer I, then am I Kusa king."

She, hearing his word, thought: " He talks sticking
overmuch. By lying tactics must I drive him away."
And she said a verse:

" If word of augurs has been spoken true, let me
In seven be hewn or ever you my husband be! "

Hearing that, the king contradicted her, saying,
" Lady dear, by me too in my own land were augurs
asked, and they answered: ' Save the lion-voiced
king Kusa there's no husband for you.' " And he
said the next verse:

" If word of others or of mine be true,
  Save Kusa of the lion-voice no husband is for you."

She, hearing his word, thought: " It is impossible
to make him ashamed. Let him run away or not,
what is he to me? " And shutting her door she did
not let him see her. He took the yoke and went down.

From that time he did not get to see her; food-
maker's work tired him excessively; after breakfast-
ing he split wood, washed dishes, fetched water on
a yoke, sleeping he slept on sacks, then rising early
he cooked, fetched and served food, suffering much
hardship because of his passionate love. One day
he saw the humpback passing the cookhouse door
and summoned her. Not daring to go near him for
fear of Pabhāvatī, she went the quicker. But swiftly
overtaking her he said: " Humpback! " She turned
and stopped, saying, " Who is it? I'm not listening
to you." Then he said: " Humpback, your mistress
and you also are too stiff. So long time are we living
near you and never even a report of her health do
we get. Is it a gift you want? Let that be till you
have succeeded in making Pabhāvatī gentle to me."
She said: " Very well." Then he inciting her said:
" If you will manage to let me see her, I will have
your crookedness made straight and will give you a
necklace." And this he said in five verses.

Hearing his word she said, " Do you go, sire, I
will bring her to heel to you in a few days. Watch
my energy," and planning what she had to do, she
went to Pabhāvatī and, as if cleaning her living-room
leaving no bit of dirt fit to hit with, even taking off
her slippers, she swept the whole room, then at the
door, keeping outside the threshold, she prepared
a high seat and for Pabhāvatī a low seat, and made
her sit down, saying, " Come, child, I will hunt

your head for lice," and placing her head on her own lap, and tickling her a little, " O my! lots of 'em on her head! " she took some from her own head and placing them on her said, " See how many lice on your head! " then crooning she talked of the virtues of the Great Being:

" Surely e'en yet this daughter of a king
No pleasure finds in Kusa, though he work
As cook, as wage-earner, needing no fee."

She was wrath with the humpback. Then the humpback, seizing her by the neck, flung her into the room and standing outside pulled on to the cord hung to close the door. Pabhāvatī, unable to seize her, stood at the door upbraiding her in another verse:

" Doth not for sure that humpback get her tongue
cut out
With well-honed sword for such ill-spoken
speech? "

Then the humpback, clutching the hanging cord, said: " O naughty ill-conducted one, what purpose will your fine looks serve? Shall we maintain ourselves by eating them? " And in many verses her humpback's shout spoke of the Bodhisat's qualities, estimating his position, power, voice and talents as outweighing his lack of height and comeliness.

Pabhāvatī (tried to) scare her: " Humpback, you shout too loud. Getting at you with my hand I will let you know you've got a mistress." She too tried to frighten her, saying in a loud voice: " Shielding you I'm not telling your father of king Kusa's coming. Let be! To-day I'll tell him." She thinking " No one must hear this," appeased the humpback.

And the Bodhisat, not getting to see her for seven
months, wearying of poor food and sorry lodging,
thought: " What good is she to me? Seven months
I cannot see her for all my living here; she is too
harsh and brutal; I will go and see my parents."
At the moment Sakka, noticing how he hankered,
thought he would create for him an opportunity,
and he sent messengers, as if they were envoys, one
to each to seven kings from king Madda, saying
that since Pabhāvatī had put aside king Kusa they
could come and claim her. They came largely attended, the one not knowing of the other's coming.
When they asked the one the other " Why are you
come? " and learnt why, they were vexed, saying,
" Will he give one daughter forsooth to seven?
look at his misbehaviour! He mocks us with his
' Take her.' Either he's to give Pabhāvatī to the
seven of us, or he's to give us battle! " And dispatching their ultimata they surrounded the city.
The Madda-king, affrighted, consulted his ministers.
They declared that if he did not give Pabhāvatī,
they would make a breach in the wall, enter the
city and slay them all. Let Pabhāvatī be sent while
the wall was yet intact, saying the verse:

" These champions stiff-necked stand there all clad
        in mail;
    Before they crush the wall bring out to us
        Pabhāvatī."

The king, declaring " If I send Pabhāvatī to one
of them, the rest will fight; she has put aside the
king paramount in the whole of Jambudīpa; let her
get the fruit of her (home-)coming. I will kill her
and send her to the seven in seven pieces," said the
next verse:

" Seven portions of her making, I this Pabhāvatī
Will offer to the nobles who come here me to slay."

What he said spread over the whole dwelling and
the attendants told Pabhāvatī. She in mortal fear
rose from her seat and went to her mother's bower.
Saluting her she bewailed in many verses the ruth-
less destruction of so beautiful a body. And the
Madda-king ordered the executioner to come bringing axe and block. His coming was made known
over the whole palace, and Pabhāvatī's mother
hearing of it rose from her seat and went in woe to
the king:

" And can it be that Madda with this blade
His modest slender-waisted daughter slays
And to the nobles offers? "

Then the king quieted her, saying, " Lady, what
are you saying? Your daughter has put aside the
king paramount in all Jambudīpa as ugly; and when
her outgoing traces had not vanished from the road
comes back with death bound to her brow. Now let
her win the fruit of the jealousy won by her looks."[1]
Hearing his word she went to her daughter bewail-
ing:

" You did not heed my word, my child, who willed
     your good;
To-day you go to Yama's realm covered with
     blood.
Such doth befall the man, and e'en to worse he
     fares,
Who heeds not word of well-wishers intent on good.

[1] Jealousy = issā; the word here is issāsa, archery. A pun is conceivably meant, viz. that she had not had " good shooting " with
her beauty.

If thou to-day hadst chosen the prince of gallant
    mien,
The jewel-belted prince born by the Kusa blade,
Honoured by kin you had not gone to Yama-doom.
Where drums galore are beat and trumpets ele-
    phant,
In princely house, dear, what were happier than
    this?
Where neighs the horse, and whines the minstrel
    at the gate,
In princely house, dear, what were happier than
    this?
With peacocks' call and herons' and cuckoos'
    carolling, etc."

And after these verses she thinking " If Kusa,
lord of men, were here to-day, he would put these
seven kings to flight, release my daughter from ill,
take her and go! " she said the verse:

" Where's now foe-tamer, crusher of others' realms,
    Wise splendid Kusa, everyone he'll slay for us!"

" My mother's mouth in speaking praise of Kusa
is inadequate. I will tell her of his living here doing
cook's work," thought Pabhāvatī, and she said the
verse:

" He's here, foe-tamer, crusher of others' realms,
    Wise, splendid Kusa, everyone he'll slay for us."

Then her mother, thinking " She is talking awry
in her mortal fear," said the verse:

" Talk you like lunatic or speak you like a fool?
    If Kusa be now here, why keep it hid from us? "

She hereon thinking " My mother does not believe it; she does not know he has been living here for seven months; I will show her," and taking her by the hand, she opened the casement and pointing said:

" That cooking man in the apartments of your girls,
    His loins firmly begirt who's stooping washing
        pots."

He then, they say, fetched water and began to wash the dishes, thinking, " To-day my mind's desire reaches the top; Pabhāvatī in mortal fear is sure to tell of my being here; I'll wash the dishes and put them away." Then the mother berating her said the verse:

" Are you a bamboo-worker or of Chandāla-folk,
    Or are you blighter of our house? How could you
        make,
    Born in the Maddas' house, a slave your para-
        mour? "

Thereon Pabhāvatī, thinking " My mother does not know, methinks it is for my sake he is living thus," said another verse:

" I'm not a bamboo-worker, nor of Chandāla-folk.
    God save you! 'tis Okkāka's son you deem a slave."

And then in many verses she expanded the contrast.
Then her mother, thinking " She speaks fearlessly. It is surely he! " believed her and went and told the king. Swiftly he came and asked: " Is it true, dear child, that king Kusa is here? " " To-day

it is seven months that he has been doing the cooking for your daughters." Not believing her he asked
the humpback, and she confirming, he scolded his
daughter:

> " Quite wrongly have you done, you child,[1]
> That mighty noble being here,
> An elephant in guise of frog,
> This you did not declare to us! "

Thus scolding his daughter, he went swiftly to
him, greeted him with courteous deference, and
confessed his offence in the verse:

> " Our misdeed, majesty, will you condone, bull of
>   desire,[2]
> That in this unknown guise your coming here we
>   did not know? "

Hearing him, the Great Being thought, " If I
shall speak harshly to him his heart will break. I
will comfort him," and he said another verse:

> " For one like me 'twas ill that I became a cook.
> 'Tis you must be appeased; nay, sir, you've done
>   no wrong."

The king, thus receiving welcome, ascended the
terrace and sent for Pabhāvatī to dispatch her to
apologise:

> " Go, fool, apologise to Kusa mighty king.
> With your apology Kusa will give you life."

[1] *Bālă* means " young " and " foolish "; it is scarcely as brutal
as " fool."
[2] Why should not *ratha* here mean " desire "? See *n.* Cambr.
Translation.

Hearing her father's word she went to him, attended by her sisters and attendants. And he, having heard she was coming to him, waited in the guise of a smith, and thinking " To-day breaking Pabhāvatī's pride I will make her fall at my feet in the mud," he poured out the water he had brought and churned up a space as big as a threshing-floor, making it just mud. She going there fell at his feet and lay in the mud apologising:

" The nights without thee, sire, have passèd by—
　I greet thee head to feet; be not wrath with me,
　　　bull of desire!
Truly I promise thee, majesty, list to me:
That what's not dear to thee I'll do no more.
If word of me thus begging thou wilt not do,
He'll now me slay and to the princes give."

Hearing her, the king thought: " If I shall say ' See you to that!' her heart will break; I will comfort her ":

" When it is you[1] who beg, should I not do your
　　　word?
　I am not wrath with you, fair one; fear not, Pabhā-
　　　vatī!
Truly I promise thee, king's daughter, list to me:
That what's not dear to thee I'll do no more.
Do you forgive, fair woman. Much hardship have
　　　I borne,
Many for Madda's house I'll slay to wed Pabhā-
　　　vatī."

In him, seeing her as waiting on himself, like a handmaid of deva-king Sakka, rose up the warrior's

[1] The emphasis *te yācamānāya* should not be overlooked in translation.

pride: " While I forsooth yet live, shall others go
taking my wife? " Like a lion pacing the king's
court, striding, roaring, snapping fingers, " Let the
whole city know that I am here. Now will I take
them alive! Let chariot and horse be made ready,"
he said the next verse:

" Let horses and well-painted chariot be together
      brought.
   Then shall ye see the swiftness of me scattering
      the foe."

He dismissed her, saying, " The capture of the
foes is my charge. Do you go and bathe and adorn
yourself and ascend the terrace." And the Madda-
king sent his courtiers to act as retinue to him.
They put up a tent round him at the kitchen door
and made barbers wait upon him. He shaved and
bathed, and bravely adorned and surrounded by courtiers said, " I will ascend the terrace," looked over
the country and snapped his fingers, and wherever
he looked there was a trembling (of earth). " Now
watch my advance," he said.

Then the Madda-king sent him a caparisoned
elephant trained to be steady (under attack). He
mounted on its back, with white umbrella reared,
said " Bring here Pabhāvatī! " and seating her
behind him, he left the city by the east gate, attended
by a fourfold army, and looking on the opposed
army he thrice roared his lion's roar: " I am king
Kusa! Let those who seek their lives fall on their
bellies! " and churned up the foe.

   Alive he took and bound the warriors his foes,
   And to his wife's sire brought them near: " Lo,
      sire, your foes

203

All now are in your power; destroyed your foes.
Do what you will; they're yours to free or slay."

The king said:

" Yours are these foes, sooth foes of mine they're
      not.
'Tis you are now our king. Or set them free or
      slay."

This said, the Great Being thought: " What to
us are these men dead? Let not their coming be of
no use. Pabhāvatī has juniors; the Madda-king has
seven daughters; I will bestow these on them."

" Those thy seven daughters fair as deva-maids,
    Give one to each; make them your sons-in-law."

Then the king said:

" Of us and eke of them you are lord of us all.
    You are of us the king; give to them as you will."

He had them all adorned and given one to each
king.
The Teacher, explaining the matter, spoke five
verses:

" Joying in their gains, pleased with the lion-
voiced Kusa, the seven thereupon set forth to their
kingdoms. Taking Pabhāvatī, the mighty king Kusa
went to Kusāvatī. They in one chariot together
rode, neither outshining the other in their appearance. The mother went forth to meet the son; then
the pair were in harmony, dwelling prosperous and
fertile."

The Teacher assigned the Jataka: " Then the mother and father were (of our) king's family; the younger (son) was Ānanda; the humpback was Khujjuttarā: Pabhāvatī was Rāhula's mother; her retinue was the Buddha-retinue; king Kusa was just I."

THE SAMA JATAKA

"WHO is't with dart has wounded me?"—
This the Teacher told while living at the
Jetavana about a monk who supported his mother.
One of the very rich Sāvatthi families, 'tis said, had
an only son, dear and attractive. Seeing the multitude going along the street below his casement with
offerings in hand to hear the Right taught at the
Jetavana, he was minded to go too, taking his offerings. He listened, was induced thereby to leave the
world, was bidden seek his parents' permission,
extracted it by fasting for a week, and was ordained.
After studying dhamma for five years, he felt the
need of undistracted seclusion to complete the task
of insight, and retired to the forest. And there he strove
for twelve years without evolving anything remarkable.

Meanwhile his parents fell into great poverty, for
want of a man to protect the estate and the staff.
The house had to be sold and they in rags went
about begging. Then a monk came to the son's
retreat from Sāvatthi, and the son, next after news
of the Jetavana, asked after the health of such and
such a family, namely his own. He was bidden not
to, since it appeared their only son had left them as
monk and they were then in great poverty. The son
began to weep, and to the questioning monk said:
"These are my parents, I am their son." He was
bidden go and tend them, since their distress was
his fault. Thinking that for twelve years he had
reaped no good result, and that to him incapable the
holy life was no good, that he would return to house-

life, keep his parents, give gifts and then go to the Bright World, he handed over his forest quarters to the elder, and the next day set out, arriving in due course at the back of Jetavana which is near Sāvatthi. There two ways were, one to Jetavana, one to Sāvatthi. Standing and considering which should he do first, see parents or the Ten-Powered, he thought: " I shall not often be able to see him, I will go to see him to-day, and to-morrow my parents." And leaving the road to Sāvatthi he arrived in the evening at the Jetavana.

Now early that morning the Teacher, contemplating the world, had seen the ripening conditions in this man, and when he came was praising parental qualities as in the Parent-tending Sutta. He listening at the edge of the congregation thought: " I can support my parents once I'm in the house-life again; but the Teacher has said that a son in orders is a help. I went away without seeing the Teacher; for such a religious life I proved no good. But now, without becoming a houseman, still a monk, I will support them." And he took his ticket and by it got food and gruel, but feeling as if after twelve years of forest life he really deserved expulsion. Going next morning to Sāvatthi he . . . took gruel and went to the wall of the home now another's and saw the parents sitting after their alms-round. His eyes filled, but they did not know him, and the mother said: " He will be standing there for alms. . . . Pass on, reverend sir, there's nothing fit to give you." At length they knew him as he wept, and fell at his feet and there was a mighty pitying.

Then he said, " Do not be thinking about it; I will support you . . ." and from that time he shared with them all the alms he got. But the monks noticed he grew white and thin, and they brought him, when they heard of his sharing alms with laymen, before the Teacher. The Teacher asked him, " Is it true that you are supporting laymen with the gifts of faith?" He admitting it was, the Teacher, desiring to praise his well-doing and to publish his own past conduct, asked, " Supporting laymen, monk, whom is it you are supporting? " " My parents, reverend sir." Then the Teacher, desirous of stirring up zeal in him, applauded him with " Well done!" three times, adding, " You are standing in the way I have gone; I once went about supporting my parents." And that monk acquired zeal. The monks asked about this and the Teacher brought up the past.

In the past, not far from Benares, on the hither side of Ganges, was a hunter's village, and on the further side another. In each dwelt five hundred families, and the two hunter-headmen were friends and in their youth had made a compact that if the one had a son the other a daughter there should be a sending and welcoming of a bride. And this did happen; the boy of this side was called Dukūlaka, the girl of the further side, Pārikā. Both were beautiful, and though born in a hunter-family they hurt no living thing. At sixteen years of age, against the wish of both, their parents married them, but they lived celibate, and at length got leave to renounce the lay life. They went up Ganges, entering the Himâlaya region where the Migasammatā emerges to join the Ganges.

Now Sakka's throne showed heat, and he discerning the cause said to Vissakamma: " Tāta, two great beings have left home and entered Himavant; it behoves that they find a dwelling; come, build them leaf-huts not far from the river and put monk-requisites there." He did so, making a footpath to it and driving away wild beasts and unpleasant noises. Here they dwelt, Dukūlaka as a rishi, Pārikā as a nun, practising goodwill in the range of sense-experience. By the power of their goodwill all beasts and birds there acquired mutual goodwill, none did injury to the other. Pārī fetched water and things to eat, swept out the hermitage and did all necessary chores; both gathered fruits, and ate, then entered each his own leaf-hut for religious duties. Sakka ministering to them, and foreseeing they would lose their sight, admonished Dukūlaka he should get a son to tend him. He was shocked, nevertheless he promised to touch his wife with his hand, and so, said Sakka, would Pārī obtain a son. The Bodhisat deceasing in deva-world was born to her, and named Suvanna-Sāma. Fairy nymphs of the hills came and served as nurses.

When he was sixteen, and his parents were coming home with gathered fruits, a great storm-cloud arose. They stood under a tree on an anthill, within which lived a serpent. The sweat from their bodies dripped and the serpent, smelling it, got angry and blasted their eyes and blinded them. And this happened because they in a former life had been unfair to a physician and harmful to his sight.

Sāma went out looking for them and led them home. And as he looked at them he both wept and laughed, saying " I was weeping because while you are yet young you have lost your eyes; I laughed because I shall now take care of you. Do not be thinking about it. I will take care of you." And he brought them in, and did everything for them, also fixing cords to guide them to this and that room.

Now at that time the king of Benares was named Piliyakkha, and he, lusting after venison, made over the government to his mother, and came to Hima-

vant to shoot deer. Coming to where Sāma used to
go to draw water, he put up an ambush, and laid in
wait with a poisoned arrow fitted to his bow. And
Sāma came. Never had he before seen a man in that
region, and he wondered was he a deva or a sprite?
Unwilling to return to his courtiers unable to tell,
he decided to wound him and so weaken him and
then ask him. For the Great Being was surrounded
by a herd of deer, and on the backs of two of them
he had placed his water-jars, leading them with his
hand. The deer went down first and drank; then
Sāma, in bark-garment and deerskin, went with
jar on shoulder and dignity down to the river. Then
the king shot him through the side so that the arrow
came out at the other side. The deer seeing this fled
affrighted, but the wise Golden Sāma, though
wounded, adjusted his jar, and keeping his head
came slowly up the bank. Scooping out sand he laid
down, facing the direction of his parents' abode, like
a golden image on a silver plate, with lucid mind
thinking, " In this Himavant region there are no
enemies of mine, nor am I at enmity with anyone."
So saying he wiped the blood from his mouth and
as if not seeing the king said the verse:

" Who is't with dart hath wounded me zestful and
water-fetching?
Noble, Brahman, trader, who, me wounding, liest
low? "

So saying he went on to show the worthlessness
of his body for food:

" Not eatable my flesh, there is no profit in my skin,
What vantage didst thou deem to get that I should
wounded be? "

And asking name, etc.:

" Who art thou or whose son art thou? How may
    we come to know?
I ask thee, good man, tell me why, me wounding,
    liest low? "

Hearing that, the king thinking " I have felled and
wounded him with poisoned arrow, yet he neither
upbraids nor berates me; he speaks kindly as if to
comfort my heart, I will go up to him," and going
he said:

" I am king of the Kāsians, as Piliyakkha known;
    From lust I left my kingdom and wander seeking
        deer.
In archery am I skilled, famous in use of bow
        am I;
No elephant could 'scape from me were he in
        my shaft's range.

But thou, whose son art thou, and thee how may
    we come to know?
Reveal to me thy father and what thy name and
    clan."

The Great Being thought, " If I were to say I was
deva, or cobra-man, or fairy, or else a noble or the
like, he would believe me, but I ought to say the
true," and he said:

" A hunter-man—with compliments—Sāma the
    name my folk
Called me while living, but to-day I lie and pass
        away.
Wounded am I with arrow broad, poisoned, as
        were I deer.

With my own blood bedabbled, king, behold me
    outstretched here.
By dart gone through, my skin transfixed, behold
    me spitting blood.
Sick am I; once again I ask: why wounding me
    li'st low?"

      .   .   .   .

The king then lied to him:

" The deer that present was had come within my
    arrow's range,
And seeing thee it fled, Sāma; I was not wrath
    with thee."

      .   .   .   .

And Sāma said:

" Since I myself remember, since I have come to
    know,
No deer has been afraid of me, nor forest thing
    with legs.
Since I in bark-gear go about, since adolescent I,
No deer has been afraid of me, nor forest thing
    with legs.
Grim beings, king, in mountain and in the scented
    wood:
We hail each other pleasantly on hillside or in
    glade.
What, then, the reason that a deer should betray
    fear at me?"

And the king:

" Not thee the deer beheld, Sāma—why should I
    tell a lie?
By wrath and lust bemastered I did aim the shot
    at thee."

Then, thinking " He will not be all by himself, he will have folk here," he asked:

" Whence, good man, didst thou come, or who is it
     did send thee here
As water-bearer to the river Migasammatā? "

He in pain and with flowing blood said:

"Blind are my mother and my sire, my charge in
     the great wood;
Their water-bearer I am come to Migasammatā.

And wailing over them he added:

" Scanty the food their life to keep; but six days
     will it last;
And in that they no water get, methinks they,
     blind, will die.
To me this (fate) is not so ill, all men must come
     to this,
But not to see my mother is for me the greater ill.
And not to see my father is for me the greater ill.
They verily now many days will weep in misery.
For me to rise and tend them and chafe their feet
     for them
They'll wail aloud Sāma! Tāta! and wander through
     the wood.
This is a second arrow that tears the heart of me,
That I my blind ones no more see, that I lay down
     my life."

The king, smitten with remorse at his sin in harming one so holy, formed a resolution:

" Weep not so sorely, Sāma who art so fair to see!
I'll be their worker, I'll maintain them in the
     mighty wood.

In archery am I skilled, famous in use of bow
am I,
I'll be their worker," etc.
" The track of deer pursuing and forest roots and
fruits,
I'll be their worker . . .
Which is the wood where are, Sāma, mother and
father thine?
I will support them in such ways as thou'st sup-
ported them.

.   .   .   .

That is the footpath, king, the one which goes
where lies my head;
Go down it half a kosa, to their cottage you will
come.
There are the mother, father, mine; hence go and
bring them aid."

So showing him and having borne great suffering
from his affection and because of their maintenance,
he prayed, saluting with outstretched hands:

" Hail to thee, Kāsi king, all hail the luck of Kāsi-
land!
Blind are my mother, father: nourish them in
mighty wood.
I stretch my hands out to thee, Kāsi-king, all hail
to thee!
Tell what I said to parents mine, bid them render
salute."

. . . Then he lost consciousness. . . .

Now a deva-daughter named Bahusodarī, dwelling
on Gandhamadana, and who had been mother to

the Great Being in his seventh previous life, had always watched the Bodhisat with mother-love, but for a time had been in her deva-bliss unmindful. But at this moment she remembered him, and foreseeing much misery to parents and king, she decided to rescue them and restore her son by making before them an Act of the True. She first went and upbraided the king, bidding him go to the parents, that, in supporting them, he might go to the Bright World. The king, restraining his sorrow, and deeming Sāma dead, paid honour to the body with flowers, sprinkling and luck-tour,[1] then took the jar and sadly went. Finding them he gradually broke the news to them, and offered his services. They in such misery treated him gently and with respect.

" This were not right, your majesty, it would not
    us befit.
A king for us thou art, and at thy feet we thee
    salute."

The king in pleased amazement thought, " Oh, but this is marvellous: to me working them such ill-will there is not one harsh word! " and he said:

" The Right ye utter, hunter-folk. Honoured am I
    by you.
Father art thou to me, and thou my mother
    Pārikā! "

They asked him only to lead them to their son. He could not face the scene but gave way to their entreaties. They took Sāma's head and feet to their bosoms and uttered their dirge. Then the mother, placing his hand in her breast and finding it warm, thought: " My son's (life-)warmth persists; he will

[1] See above, p. 161.

have become senseless by the swiftness of the poison;
to get him disempoisoned I will make an Act of the
True for him ":

" The truth that in the past Sāma was man of righteous life,
By this true word for Sāma let the poison be destroyed.

The truth that in the past Sāma was man of
godly life,
By this true word . . .

The truth that in the past Sāma was man of truth-
ful speech,
By this true word . . .

The truth that in the past Sāma was parent-
fosterer,
By this true word . . .

The truth that in the past Sāma honoured the
head of house,
By this true word . . .

The truth that in the past Sāma better I loved
than life,
By this true word . . .

Whate'er of merit he hath wrought for father and
for me,
By all that good for Sāma let the poison be destroyed! "

When the mother had thus made the Act, Sāma
turned over as he lay. Then said the father: " My

son lives! I too will make for him an Act of Truth!"
And he spoke as she had done. Then Sāma turned
over on the other side as he lay. Then that deva-
daughter made her Act of Truth:

" A mountain woman I have long in Gandhamadana
>   dwelt.
Dearer than Sāma is to me no one hath ever been.
By this true word for Sāma let the poison be
>   destroyed.

All woods are sweet with odours in Gandhama-
>   dana's hill,
By this true word . . .

To them thus babbling many runes their pity to
>   express
Swiftly there rose up Sāma, young and lovely for
>   to see."

Thus, that Sāma was restored, that the parents
were able to see this, and the dawn of day and the
manifestation to all four at the hermitage by the
deva-daughter's power took place at the same
moment. The parents were exceeding glad, and then
Sāma the wise uttered verses:

" Sāma am I, and I will you well; safe have I risen up.
Weep not so sore, to me your happy salutation
>   give.
And be thou welcome, majesty, not far is't thine
>   to go,
For with thee rests authority and what thou needst
>   make known.
Fruits have we here of many kinds; thou mayst
>   not know the names,

Taste for thyself and eat, sir king, the best of this and that.
And sweet cold water have I brought, drawn from the mountain's womb,
From that drink, majesty, if thee desire thereto doth move."

The king, seeing the miracle, said:

" I am confused, bewildered I, the world's all in a maze!
I saw thee one gone hence, Sāma; how art thou now alive? "

Sāma, to explain his " undead-state," said:

" Although a man be living, sire, be his sensation strong,
Suspended is his work of mind, men deem the living dead.

Although a man be living, sire, be his sensation strong,
He to a state of stoppage come, men deem the living dead."

Then to apply this to the king's welfare he taught him the Right and said:

" Who righteously his mother and his father doth maintain,
Even the devas watch him well as bearing filial load,
E'en here him they commend, hereafter welcome him."

Then the king: " Marvellous, sir, is this! Of one supporting his parents even devas heal the sickness. Exceedingly beautiful is Sāma! "

" Lo! more bewildered yet am I, the world is all a
       maze,
   To thee, Sāma, I come, do thou a refuge be to
       me! "

Then said Sāma: " If, majesty, you are fain to go
to deva-world, fain to enjoy divine bliss, walk in
these ten right farings:

" Fare in the Right with parents, sire,
   So thou'lt to Bright World go.
   Fare in the Right to wife and child,
   So . . .
   Fare in the Right with friends and staff,
   So . . .
   Fare in the Right with world of war,
   So . . .
   Fare in the Right with towns and villages,
   So . . .
   Fare in the Right with realm and countryfolk,
   So . . .
   Fare in the Right with holy men,
   So . . .
   Fare in the Right with beast and bird,
   So . . .
   Fare in the Right, for, sire, the Right
   Practised brings happiness along.
   Fare in the Right, for, sire, devas and gods
   By practice right win thing divine.
   Never be heedless as to Right! "

The king, accepting the admonition with his head
and having done homage, went to Benares and
working merit became one bound for the Bright
World. The Bodhisat with his parents became goers
to Brahmā-world.

The Teacher, saying " This is the lineage of the wise who tend their parents, added: " Then the king was Ānanda, the deva-daughter was Uppalavannā, the parents were Kassapa and Bhaddā of the Kapĭlas, but the wise Golden Sāma was just I."

THE NIMI JATAKA

(*Nimi-jātaka*)

" A WONDROUS thing in sooth it was when
in the world."—This the Teacher told,
when staying in the Makhadeva Mango Wood near
Mithilā, about his smiling. One day namely, when
the Teacher with many monks was walking about
that wood, he saw a pleasant spot, and being wish-
ful to talk of his conduct in the past, and the venerable Ānanda having asked the reason why he was
smiling, he said: " Ānanda, in days of old this spot
is where I used to stay, when, in king Makhadeva's
time, I was playing the Musing-game."[1] And asked
by the former he sat down on the seat prepared and
brought up the past.

In[2] the past, in the kingdom of Videha, in the city
of Mithilā, there was a king named Makhadeva.
For eighty-four thousand years he played the games
of young noblemen, for eighty-four thousand years
he was viceroy, for eighty-four thousand years he
was king. Having said " Good barber, when you
may see on my head grey hairs, then you should tell
me," the barber later on having seen them, drawing
them out with pincers, placing them on his hand,
the king looking at them, and seeing death drawing
nigh and as it were hanging to his brow, said, " Now
'tis time for me to leave the world," and giving the
barber the boon of a village, and sending for his

---

[1] *Jhāna-kīlam kīlanto.*
[2] This Jataka I have condensed by omitting lists of names in
verses.

eldest son, he said: " Tāta, take over the kingdom,
I will leave the world." " For what reason, sire? "
He said:

"These growths in my extremities for me,
These life-removers are made manifest:
Envoys divine; world-leaving time for me! "

Anointing him as king, and exhorting " Do you
carry on in this way and that," he departed from the
city, and being ordained a monk, and for eighty-four
thousand years exercising the four Divine Moods,
he was reborn in the Brahmā-world. His son also,
by just that method leaving the world, became one
questing the Brahmā-world; and so too his son. So
at length eighty-four thousand nobles less two had
seen grey hairs on their heads, had left the world in
this very wood, had practised the Divine Moods and
been reborn in the Brahmā-world. King Makhadeva, the first of all these to be so reborn, stood in
Brahmā-world, watching the way of his descendants,
and thrilled in mind watched, " Will there be henceforth more in the series? " and learning that there
would not, he thought, " It is I who will round off
my descendants," and deceasing thence he took
birth in the chief queen of the king in Mithilā city.
On his naming-day the augurs, watching his marks,
declared: " Your majesty, this child has come to
round off your line; after him it will not go on, for
your line is one of world-leaving." Hearing that, the
king gave him the name " Tyre-prince," saying,
" He is born to round off my line, like the tyre of a
chariot-wheel."

From his childhood the boy delighted in giving,
in morals, and in keeping holy days. And his father,
in the aforesaid way when he saw grey hair, gave the

barber boon of a village, handed over the kingdom
to his son, left the world in the Mango Wood and
became one questing the Brahmā-world. King Nimi,
from his giving-disposition, had five gift-halls built,
one in the city centre, four at the four gates, and
set afoot a great charity, in each hall a donation of
one hundred thousand; giving away daily five
hundred thousand " kahāpana's "; ever he warded
the five moral precepts; he kept holy day on the
moon-days; he encouraged the people in deeds of
merit—giving and the like—and taught the Right,
declaring the Way to the Bright World and warning
them against hell. Firm in his admonition and working merit, men as they deceased were reborn in
deva-world; the deva-world waxed full; hell became as if empty.

Then in the realm of the Three-and-Thirty (the
next world), when devas were assembled in the deva-
hall Sudhammā, they said, " Ha! our teacher, king
Nimi. Through him it is that we enjoy this unin-
termittent divine achievement—and also by Buddha-
knowledge! "—so praised they the virtues of the
Great Being. And in the world of humans also talk
of his virtues spread like blazing oil on the surface
of the sea.

The Teacher, making the matter clear, spoke to
the monk-company thus:

" O wondrous in the world it is when men of vision
      rise!
As when king Nimi lived, the wise man, seeking
      good.
The king victorious to all Videhans gave his gifts.
In him his gifts thus giving uprose a pondering:
The giving or the holy life: which will more fruit-
      ful be? "

At that moment the region where Sakka was felt
hot, and Sakka, minding the reason thereof and
seeing him thus considering, said, " I will cut short
his doubt." By himself swiftly coming he made the
whole dwelling one radiant sheen, and entering the
private chamber and diffusing radiance he stood in
the air and made reply to the question.

Explaining the matter the Teacher said:

" Ware of his pondering, divine bull-elephant,
The Maghavant, the thousand-eyed, stood manifest,
In beauty slayer of the dark.

With stiffened hair to Vāsava spake Nimi king:
' Art deva or Gandharva or Sakka giver to men?
Ne'er have I seen such beauty, nor ever heard of
    such! '

Ware that his hair had stiffened this word spake
    Vāsava:
' Sakka I am, the deva-lord; near you I'm come;
Be calm, man-lord, and ask the question you are
    fain.'
The chance to him thus given, to Vāsava Nimi
    spake:
' This ask I, O thou strong-armed, of every crea-
    ture lord,
The giving or the holy life: which will more fruit-
    ful be? '

By the man-deva asked, to Nimi Vāsava spake,—
Of holy life's results knower to one who knew
    not:—

' By lower holy life a man's reborn a nobleman,
By middle (stage), to devaship; by highest, he is
    pure.

224

Not easy are the worlds to win by one who beggars
    tends—
The worlds wherein there come to be ascetics
    without home.' "

Having shown in these verses the great fruitfulness of living the holy life, he now showed kings
who in the past giving great gifts had been unable
to surpass the worlds of sense-desire. . . .

" . . . They won not past the Preta world."

He then referred to ascetics who by the holy life
had won past the Pretas to the Brahmā-world. . . .
He then brought up what he had witnessed in the
past : . . . and then said : " Although, your majesty,
the holy life is of greater fruitfulness than giving,
both of these are of a great man's ideas. Therefore
be earnest about both; give gifts; ward the moral
code." So admonishing he went to his own place.
Then the company of devas said to him : " Your
majesty, you have not been visible; where have you
been?" " My lords, a certain doubt had arisen in
king Nimi of Mithilā; I have been to discuss the
question and resolve his doubt," and he thereupon
declared the affair in verse :

" This, sirs, heed well, as many as here are met :—
Much praise of righteous men, high praise and low,"

telling them of king Nimi's doubt.
Thus he spoke praise of the king, diminishing
naught. Hearing that the devas, wishing to see the
king, said, " Your majesty, king Nimi is our teacher;
we owe our divine achievement to him; we would
see him; let him be sent for, your majesty," and he,

assenting, sent for Mātali: " Good Mātali, make
ready the ' Conqueror's chariot,' go to Mithilā,
place king Nimi in the deva-carriage and bring him
here." And he, assenting, made ready the chariot
and departed.

Now while Sakka was speaking with the devas,
ordering Mātali and dispatching the chariot, a month
by men's reckoning had gone by. And thus to king
Nimi, who had opened the eastern casement for
the holy day of full moon, and was seated on the
great terrace with his court, meditating on the Moral
Code, just as the moon's disc rose from the eastern
horizon, this chariot appeared. The people, who
had supped and were seated at their house-doors
engaged in pleasant talk, said: " To-day two moons
are risen! " Then as they were talking the chariot
became manifest and all the people said, " This is
no moon; a chariot! " and as gradually the thousand
Sindh horses, Mātali the driver and the " Conqueror's chariot " became manifest, they thought,
" To whom has this divine carriage come? " then,
" To whom else but our righteous king; to him the
' Conqueror's chariot ' will have been sent by Sakka;
that is meet for our king! " And thrilled and elated
they said the verse:

" A wonder, look! has risen in the world, hair-
    stiffening!
The car divine revealed for the Videhan (king)
    renowned! "

Now, as the people were talking, Mātali with the
swiftness of the wind turned the car and stopped it
at the western side at the windowsill, made ready
the mounting-step, and invited the king to mount.
Describing the matter the Teacher said:

" The son of devas, deva-charioteer,
  The mighty Mātali, Videha's king,
  Invited: ' Come, best king, lord of the world,
  And mount this car. The devas, with their king
  The Thirty-three, are fain to see you. Lo,
  The devas are remembering you and they
  Within Sudhammā's hall together sit.' "

The king, thinking " I shall see the deva-world I
have not seen before, and I shall be showing a favour
to Mātali, I will go," and addressing the harem and
the people he said, " In no long time I shall return;
do you zealously give gifts and work merit," and he
mounted the chariot. Describing this the Teacher
said:

" Thereon with haste Videhan king, dweller at
        Mithilā,
  Rose from his seat, turning himself about, mounted
        the car.
  To him, thus mounted in the car divine, Mātali
        said:
  ' By which way would you (please to fare), O
        best king, lord of the world?
  By that where evildoers go, or that of merit-work?' "

Then the king, thinking " Both places have I not
seen before, I will see the two," said:

" Mātali, deva-charioteer, lead me along both ways:
  By that where evildoers go and that of merit-
        work."

Thereon Mātali: " I am not able to show the two
at one stroke; I will ask him "; and again asking he
said the verse:

" By which would you (fare) first, O best king, lord
of the world?
By that where evildoers go or that of merit-
work? "

Thereon the king, thinking " I shall certainly see
the deva-world (hereafter), I will first see hell,"
said the verse:

" I first (would) see the hell-abodes, them of the
evil deeds,
The places of the cruel deeds, bourne of immoral
men."

Then he first showed him the Vetaranī (river).
Describing the matter the Teacher said:
" Mātali showed the king the ill-flowing river
Vetaranī, foul and rocky, scalding like flames of fire."
Thus the king, affrighted at seeing beings suffering greatly in the Vetaranī, asked Mātali: " Now
what have those beings done that is evil? " And he
told him.
Describing the matter the Teacher said:
" Nimi verily addressed Mātali, saying, when he
saw the people falling in the evil place, ' Fear truly
besets me, driver; I ask you, Mātali, deva-charioteer,
these mortals, what evil have they done, that they
fall into Vetaranī? ' Asked, to him thus answered
Mātali deva-charioteer, the result of evil deeds the
knower declared to the not-knower: ' Whoso being
strong in the world of life harm the weak, molest
them, they being very evil, cruel in deed, engendering evil, these folk fall into Vetaranī.' "
Then Mātali having answered and the king having
seen the river, he caused that region to disappear,
and driving the chariot onward, he showed a place

of devouring by dogs and other (beasts). And when the affrighted king asked he answered.

Describing the matter the Teacher said:

" Dark dogs and speckled vultures and horrid flocks of ravens approach them: fear truly besets me, driver; I ask you . . . what evil have those mortals done through which the ravens approach them? "

Mātali (described as before) answered: " Whosoever has been grudging, hard of heart, despisers of holy men, harming, molesting, they being very evil, cruel in deed, engender evil: to these folk the ravens approach."

" But they who in a blaze fare over the ground smiting with redhot bars: fear truly besets me, driver . . . What evil have those mortals done that they lie pounded with bars?"

" They being very evil in the world of life harmed, molested the man and the woman who were not evil; they workers of cruelty have engendered evil; those folk it is who lie limb-pounded."

" Others, men weeping with charred limbs, plunge about in fiery pits . . . what evil have they done?"

" Whosoever in a matter of a company's property have suborned witnesses to forswear a debt, they having defaulted to the people, O lord of people, they workers of cruelty have engendered evil. . . ."

" Afire, ablaze, aflame a mighty iron cauldron now appears; fear truly besets me . . . what evil have those mortals done that into it they fall?"

" Whosoever has harmed, molested the virtuous man, recluse or brahman, they workers of cruelty. . . ."

" But (these) who drag those up twisting their necks and souse them in hot water . . . what have those mortals done of evil that hurled by the head they sink?"

" They being very evil in the world of life caught birds and hurt them . . . workers of cruelty. . . ."

" The river flowing there of ample stream and shelving banks well within depth men scorched with heat are drinking, and to them drinking the water becomes chaff . . . what have those mortals done of evil? . . ."

" Whoso (as sellers) gave, in deed impure, pure grain mixed with chaff to the buyer. . . ."

" With spikes, with spears and shafts these are thrusting at both flanks of those who wail aloud . . . what have those mortals done of evil that they sink spear-slain?"

" Whoso with wrongful act in world of life have taken things not given, maintained themselves thereby—grain, treasure, silver, gold, the goat, the sheep, the herd, the buffalo—they workers of cruelty. . . ."

" Yoked by the neck, lo! some, and others being sliced, and some again being cut in pieces . . . what have those mortals done of evil . . .?"

" Sheep-butchers, pig-killers and fishermen, who, slaying kine, the buffalo, goat and sheep, spread them in their slaughter-shops: they workers of cruelty. . . ."

" That pool of dung and muck so foully smelling wafting its stinking rottenness: men parched with thirst are going up to it: what have those mortals done of evil that they feed on that?"

" Whoso, while owing duties to others, have molested (them), living with them ever to harm them: they workers of cruelty. . . ."

" That pool (too) full of blood and pus so foully smelling, wafting its stinking rottenness: men scorched with heat are drinking there: what have those mortals done of evil that they feed on that?"

" Whoso have slain mother or father in the world, the excommunicate slayers of saints: they workers of cruelty. . . ."

" And see that tongue pierced with a spit like hide transfixed with many barbs, like fishes wriggling thrown upon the land, they dribble weeping: who are they? "

" Those men who in public places have haggled in their buying, value with value, fraud with fraud, out of their greed for wealth, like hidden (bait) for slaying fish. Verily no shelter is there for the fraud-worker who does but fare in front of his own deeds. Workers of cruelty they. . . ."

" Those women with their limbs all broken, (arms) outstretched, and weeping unsightly, bent, stained and smeared with blood and pus, like cattle dismembered in the slaughter-house, they ever buried in the earth up to their backs on fire . . . what have those women done of evil . . .?"

" They were of good family on earth, of deeds impure, unseemly; they were deceivers, leavers of their husbands, goers to another man, to sport in lust; they in the world of life have taken their pleasure. . . ."

" Who now are these whom, taking by the feet, they hurl into hell-fire . . . what have those mortals done of evil? . . ."

" They, wrongful doers in the world of life, did seduce the wives of another, in theft of his supreme commodity. . . . Many series of years they suffer ill in hell. Verily no shelter is there for the evildoer, who does but fare in front of his own deeds. Workers of cruelty they engender evil; these folk do they hurl into hell."

So saying, Mātali the driver, making hell also to disappear, drove the chariot onward and showed him the maturing hell for those of wrong views. When asked he answered him.

(The king) "Manifold proceedings, great and small, are these, shown in the hells so terrible to see. Fear truly besets me seeing them, driver. I ask you, Mātali, deva-charioteer, what have those mortals done of evil that they suffer sorely ills sharp, hard, and bitter?"

(Mātali) . . . "Whoso in world of life had very evil opinions doing deeds in relying on these dull (minds), causing others to adopt them: they in their evil opinions engendering evil suffer thus. . . ."

Now in deva-world the devas looking for the coming of the king were just seated in Sudhammā. Sakka, considering "Why does Mātali delay?", discerned the reason: "Mātali, to show eminence as envoy, is going around showing the hells, saying 'Your majesty, having done such deeds, they are maturing in such a hell'; but he may be wearing out king Nimi; he ought not to go to the limit in hell-showing." And he sent a very swift son-of-devas, saying, "Bid Mātali quickly take the king and come." Swiftly going he told Mātali, who, hearing, said, "Not able am I to delay," and at one stroke showing the king the many hells in the four quarters, he said the verse:

"You have seen, your majesty, the abode of evil-doers, the places for cruel deeds, the bourne of the immoral. Go forward now among the rajas of the deva-raja."

So saying he drove thither. Going to deva-world, the king saw in the sky the mansion of that daughter-of-devas Bīranī, twelve leagues long, on pillars of gold beset with jewels highly decorated, with lotus-ponds, and surrounded with kappa-trees, and the deva-daughter herself in her gable-chamber reclining on a couch surrounded by a thousand nymphs looking out at the opened casement. Seeing Mātali she asked, and he answered in verses:

" That five-pillared mansion that I see—there sits upon a couch a woman decked with wreaths, mighty she, and exercising potency both high and low. Felicity besets me, driver, in the sight. I ask you, Mātali, deva-charioteer, that woman, what has she done of good, that she, to Bright World won, rejoices in the mansion? "

(Mātali) . . ." Hast never heard in world of life of Bīranī? She was home-born slave of a brahman. Understanding hospitality to guests, delighting in them as a mother in her own son, virtuous and generous, she rejoices in the mansion."

So saying, Mātali drove the chariot onwards and showed the seven gilded mansions of the deva-son Sonadinna. Seeing their glory, he asked as to deeds done, and the other declared:

" Seven mansions created shine resplendent, where is a Yakkha of great potency profusely adorned, head of a troop of women everywhere attending. Felicity truly besets me . . . what has that mortal done of good . . .? "

(Mātali) . . . " He was Sonadinna householder, a prince of givers; he had seven viharas made for recluses. Zealously he waited on the monks there dwelling. Clothing and food and lodging and light he gave with upright believing heart. He kept all holy days, both usual and extra, kept them in all eight ways, ever in moral self-restraint, virtuous and general he rejoices in the mansion."

Further on he showed a mansion of crystal twenty-five leagues high, with some hundreds of seven-jewelled pillars, adorned with some hundreds of gables, enlaced with a network of bells, with floating banners of gold and silver (work), embellished with gardens and woods of varied blossoms, and delightful lotus-ponds, alive with nymphs skilled in music and song and the like; seeing which the king and charioteer conversed:

" This residence sheds splendour, well created with crystals, alive with troops of women, its gables in clear relief, supplied with food and drink, with dance and song . . . what have those women done of good . . .? "

(Mātali) . . . " Whatever women ' here ' in world of life were virtuous laywomen, their joy in giving, their mind in constant faith, persistent in truth, zealous in keeping holy day, self-controlled and generous, they rejoice in the mansion."

Then . . . further on he showed a mansion of gems, standing in a pleasant spot, lofty as a hill of gems, radiant, alive with many deva-sons, who made it resound with divine song and playing of music, seeing which the two conversed:

" This residence sheds splendour created in beryls, supplied with pleasant places, symmetrical, well planned, and sounds divine and lovely of drum and dance and song, well performed, issue forth and are heard. Sure never do I allow that I have seen before or heard the like, so very charming . . . what have those mortals done of good . . .? "

(Mātali) . . . " Whatsoever mortals ' here ' in world of life were moral lay-followers, (makers of) parks and wells and water-conduits, providing zealously for saints ' made cool ' the requisites of robe and alms and lodging, giving to upright folk with believing heart; keepers of holy days, both usual and extra, in all eight ways, ever in moral, self-restraint, virtuous and generous, they rejoice in the mansion."

Describing thus the deeds of those he drove on and showed yet another crystal mansion. This was adorned with several gables, was covered with divers flowers, adorned with fine trees, and on the bank of a river of stainless clear water, where various birds sang, the dwelling of one who had wrought merit, surrounded by a troop of nymphs; and thereon the two conversed:

(King) . . . " What has that mortal done . . .?"

(Mātali) . . . " He was a householder at Kimbilā, a prince of givers, maker of park and well and water-conduit, he supplied the saints ' made cool ' . . . and kept the holy day . . . (even as those other men). . . ."

. . . further on he showed yet another crystal mansion, which surpassed the former in its verdure of flower and tree. . . . Conversing in verses this was shown as the mansion of a householder of Mithilā.

. . . further on he showed yet another crystal mansion similar to the former, declared to be the reward of a householder of Benares.

. . . further on another, which was declared to be the mansion of a householder of Sāvatthi.

So while there was talk of these eight mansions, Sakka deva-raja, thinking " Mātali delays too long," sent yet another swift deva-son. And Mātali, hearing and saying " Not able are we to delay here," at one stroke showed many mansions and conversed about their owners thus:

(King) " Those many in the air made of gold, shining resplendent like lightning in a mass of cloud . . . what have those mortals done . . .?"

(Mātali) . . . " Because of their being well settled in faith, the right dhamma well understood, they did the Teacher's word, the teaching of the Very

235

Enlightened One, hence theirs those places which you see, raja."

Having shown him the airy mansions he set out to go to Sakka, saying:

" You've seen, your majesty, the abodes of evil-doers, then the places of the welldoers have you seen. Go forward now among the rajas to the deva-raja."

So saying, he drove the chariot onwards, making the tour of Sineru, and showing him the seven hills encircling it, whereon the Teacher, explaining the king's inquiry, said:

> " Standing in car divine by a thousand horses
>   drawn
>   The great king saw the mountains in the Sīda
>   Sea,
>   Seeing, to driver spake: 'What may these moun-
>   tains be?'"

Mātali gave the seven names. . . .

Thus showing him the deva-world of the Four (elemental) Kings, and making the tour of the Painted Gables, the portals of the realm of the Thirty-three, he showed him the statues of Inda, and thus the two conversed:

" What shines forth (here) of divers shapes, of varied colours charming, bestrown with Inda-like-nesses, well warded by tigers? Felicity besets me truly, driver, at the sight. I ask you, Mātali deva-charioteer, by what name do they call this gate? "

(Mātali) . . . " Painted Gable is what they call the portals of the deva-raja; here shines the gate-way of Mount Beautiful. . . . Enter this way, royal seer; approach the dustless plane! "

So saying, Mātali made the king enter the deva-city, wherefore it is said:

" Standing in car divine by a thousand horses
    drawn,
The king being conducted saw that deva-hall."

So going and standing in the divine car he saw
the deva-hall Sudhammā, about which the two conversed:
(The king) " As in the autumn the sky ever appears as blue, so is this building created of beryls . . .
by what name is it called? "
(Mātali) . . . " Sudhammā is it called; look on
the hall you see; of divers gems and precious miner-
als, well-planned octagonal pillars, well made, all
of beryl, support it; there the Three-and-thirty
devas, who all have Inda as their head, are seated together thinking on the weal of devas and men. Enter
it, royal seer, to the welcome of the devas! "
Now the devas were seated watching for his coming;
they hearing " The king is come! " went out to meet
him with perfumes and flowers in their hands as far
as the Painted Gables portals, saluting him therewith and, bringing him into Sudhammā hall after
he alighted from the chariot, the devas invited him
to a seat, Sakka also inviting him to both seat and
pleasures of sense.
Describing the matter the Teacher said:

" The devas at his coming gave him joy:
    ' Be welcome, majesty! You're come at last!
    Sit you now, royal seer, beside the deva-king.'
Sakka moreover to the king gave joy,
    The Vāsava bade him to pleasures and a seat;
    ' Well are you come to the Disposers' home,
    Taste 'mid the Thirty-three non-human sense.'"

Invited thus by Sakka to divine sense-pleasures
the king declining said:

" As chariot asked for, as wealth asked for, even such is the value of that which depends upon the giving by another. But I desire not that which depends upon the giving by another. My works of merit are wrought by myself; that is the wealth which is specially mine. I will go and do much good among men by giving, justice, order and self-restraint. Whoso does this is well, and has no aftermath of regret."

Thus did the Great Being in a sweet voice teach right to the devas, and, teaching that, he stayed seven days by men's reckoning, giving pleasure to the devas; then standing in their midst he said, speaking of the virtues of Mātali:

"Much-helper was to us sir Mātali deva-charioteer, who made me see of good deeds (the reward) and evil ones."

Then the king addressed Sakka, saying, " I wish, your majesty, to go to the world of men." Sakka said: " Well then, good Mātali, bring Nimi the king forthwith to Mithilā." And he assenting made ready the chariot: the king exchanged felicitations with the troop of devas, turned from the devas and mounted the chariot. Mātali, driving the chariot towards the east, reached Mithilā, and the people seeing the divine chariot were glad, saying, " The king is come to us! " And Mātali, going round Mithilā by the left, caused the Great Being to descend at that same casement, and taking leave with the words " We go, your majesty," went to his own place.

And the people, surrounding the king, asked: " What is the deva-world like? " The king, praising the happy achievement of the devas and of Sakka deva-king, taught them the right, saying, " Do you work merit, giving and the like, so will you be reborn in that world."

Afterwards, when his barber announced the appearance of grey hairs, he acted as once before he had done . . . and leaving the world, dwelt in this very Mango Wood, and practising the Divine Moods, he was reborn in the Brahmā-world.

Declaring his world-lorn state the Teacher said the last verse:

" Saying this king Nimi, the Vedehan, dweller at Mithilā, sacrificing ample sacrifices, attained to self-control."

But his son Kalāra-janaka, cutting off the line, left the world.

The Teacher . . . assigned the Jataka: " Then Sakka was Anuruddha, Mātali was Ānanda, the eighty-four thousand kings were the Buddha-congregation, king Nimi was just I."

INDEX OF SUBJECTS

(These do not include what is indicated enough by the titles of stories)

Alpinism, 175

Animal, rebirth as, xix f; *passim*

Astrology, 9

Augurs, 160, 222

Bandit (*chora, chorī*), 67, 71, 121, 125, 138 f

Becoming (*bhava*), 2, 6, 11, 18, 23, 159, cf. Reincarnation

Body censured, 15

Caravan, xxvii, 2, 119

Change and the unchangeable, xxi

Chaplain, 6

Charities, 223

Choice, 6 f., 42, 182

Civic action, 35

Clemency, 33, 204

Competitions, 101, 111

Covering (husband), 71

Cremation, 106, 143, 178

Crocodile, 58

Dancers, 140

Deer, tame, 212

Deer-drive, 18

Demon (*rakkhasa*), 7, 26

Deva, 24, 210, 223 ff.

—of the sea, 91

Devahood, 166

Deva-city (next world), 25, 34, 40, 49

Deva-maidens, 112 f.

Deva-realm, 96

Dhamma (right, duty, doctrine), 1, 21, 23, 25, 77, 114, 117, 165, 218 f.

Dicing, 61 f.

Divine (*deva, dibba*), 7

Driver, 79 f., 113, 226 ff.

Drum, 49, 106, 124, 162

Duty = dhamma, q.v.

Effort (*viriya*), 1 f., 31

Elephant, 101, 122, 167 f., 186 f.; morally sensitive, 29, 36

Everyman, xxiii

Farmer, landowner, 56, 71, 103, 121, 143

Festivals, 14, 108 f., 182

Fire-ordeal, 66

Gate of weal, 76

Gates, the three, 55

Goal, *see* weal

Good (men), 92

Great deep, lit. on the back of the sea, 39 f.

Hair, grey, 221

Hare in moon, 28, 135

Health (not-ill-ness), 77

Heat, of goodness, 95, 122, 208, 224

Hell = purgatory, 9, 25, 30, 223, 228 ff.

Jujubes, 129

Karma = deed(s), 4, *passim*; 23

Land-pilot, 3
Law Courts closed, 79
Left hand acceptance, 127
Low thing (*hīna*), 54
Lute, 64, 108 f., 182, 189 f.

Man, the, xvi, xix, xxv
Mandate, 26, 28
Memory, 73
Merchant, xxvii, 2, 14, 76, 83, 85, 98, 118 f.
Merit, 25, 227 (vicarious), 91
Monastic and human ideals, xxiv
Monkeys, 45, 149 f.
Morals, moral code (*sīla*), 21, 25, 33, 48, 50, 54, 62, 77, 80, 104, 119, 146 f.
Mourning rebuked, 143
Music, xv, 109 f.
Musing (*jhāna*)-game, 221

One-manster (*eka-purisikā*) 62

Parents neglected, 206; tended, 209 f.
Paternal range, 88 f.
Platform in tree, 29
Poetry and prose mixed, xv
Potter, 190
Precepts, five, *see* Morals
Purgatories comparable, xix

Quail, 88

Reincarnation, xx-xxii
Repeater (memorizer), 55
Ring, 12

Sacrifice condemned, 23
Science, lore, arts (*sippa*), 68, 79, 101
Seafaring, 98 f.
Sneezing, 82 f.
Spell (*vijjā*), 36
Sprite (*yakkha*), 9; (*nāga*), 210

Tablet-badge-sign, 22
Teaching, not esoteric, xxvii, 101, 110
Trappers, 170 f.
Truth, act of, 12, 66, 215 f.

Water, 26, 34, 67, 71
—, walking on, 90
Way, figure of, xxv, xxvii, 1, 167, 223
Wayfaring, xxvii, 4
Weal, welfare, xxiii, xxvii, 46, 47, 57, 76, 103, 152, 218
Widow, 71
Will and resolve, xviii f., 17 (There is no word for will; where used, it translates "wish" or "want")
Wish, 17, 53
Witch, 161
Woman, xxiv f., 37, 61, 67, 69, 71, 94, 97, 121, 126, 130, 158, 181
"Word-fee," 147
World, bright (or next), 21, 47, 78, 80, 84, 119, 165, 223, 232 f., *see* deva-city, Thirty-three
World-faring, 180
World-welfare, 47
World unseen, 47
Writing, xiv, 31

INDEX OF NAMES

(As a rule the accents are given, in the book, once only, as a guide to pronunciation. I have not tried to indicate consonantal peculiarities)

Ahipāraka, 160

Ānanda, cousin, and personal attendant of Gotama, 221 and *passim*

Anātha-pindĭka, merchant, great lay-supporter, and philanthropist, real name Sudatta, 16

Anuruddha, cousin, early disciple of Gotama, 158, 239

Aritthapura, 160

Asŭras, rivals to the Thirty-three; probably dethroned older Aryan deities, 38 f., 124

Bahusodărī, deva-daughter, 214

Bamboo Wood, near Rāja-gaha, first "church"-settlement, 58, 93, 101, 154

Bhaddā Kapilānī, a disciple, 220

Brahma-world, 222

Bodhĭsat, wisdom-being, name given to a Buddha-to-be. When first given unknown, 2 *passim*

Brahmadatta, mythical monarch, 2 *passim*

Ceylon, 98

Chanda (-Kumāra) Moon prince, 6

Chandālas, lowest class in community, 200

Devadatta, cousin of Gotămă, and dangerous schismatic, founded a rival Order, 15 *passim*

Ganges, 208

Gotămă, termed Buddha, Blessed One, Bodhisat, Tathâgata, Ten-powered, xviii f., 1 *passim*

Jambudīpa = India, 23 *passim*

Jetăvăna, second "church"-centre at Sāvatthi (q.v.), *passim*

Kapĭla-pura, -vatthu, home of Gotama, 154

Kassăpă (Mahā-) a disciple, 220

Kosălă, kingdom of N.E. India. Gotama was of it, 50 f., 71, 78, 80

Kosĭya, name of Sakka, 111

Kumāra-Kassăpa, 14, 17, 22

Kusāvăti, of the Mallas, 181f.

Khujjuttără, a disciple, 205

Madda's, a kingdom, 169, 184

Măgha, Maghavant, name for Sakka, 35, 224

243

Mahānāma, kinsman of Gotama, 11

Makhādeva, king, 221

Malla's, a kingdom, 181 f.

Mallika, a king of Kosala, 80

Mallikā, wife of Pasenǎdi, 128

Mātali, Sakka's charioteer, 39, 113, 226 f.

Mithilā, 221 f.

Moggallāna, early disciple, 81

Mūsila, a musician, 109

Nāga, cobras, snake-men, 91, 119

Nemi, Nimi (=tyre), 222 f.

Nurse, of Pabhāvatī, 184 f.

Okkāka, king of the Mallas, 181

Pabhāvatī, princess (= radiant one) of the Maddas, 184 f.

Pasēnǎdī, king of Kosala, 16, 78, 82, 128

Piliyakkha, a king of Kāsi, 211

Pretas, ghosts, form of rebirth, 225

Rāhula's mother, former wife of Gotama, 154, 205

Rājagaha, now Rājgir, mother " church " of early Budhism, 14, 35

Sāgala, of the Maddas, 184

Sāketa (= Ayodhya) in Oudh, 73

Sakka, i.e., Sakya, governor of next world's India, viz. Gotama's clan-name deified, 38 passim

Sakkan or Sakyan, Gotama's clan or sept of North Kosala, name by which his " church " was long known, 149

Sāma, courtesan of Benares, 138 f.

Sāriputta, early disciple and friend of Gotama, 146

Sāvatthi, capital of Kosala, apparently the residence of Gotama in his old age, 1 passim

Sīlavatī, queen, 185

Sindh, famous for horses, 31, 226

Sivi, 160

Six-setter monks, a schismatic clique, 125

Sonuttǎrǎ, trapper, 171 f.

Subhaddā, elephant, queen, 168 f.

Sujātā, 93

Sujātā, name of the Mallikā, queen, 128

Sunanda, charioteer, 162

Suriya (-kumāra), Sun prince, 6

Tāta, appellative of amity, masculine, 4, 7 passim

Tathâgata, name applied to Gotama in the after-time, origin unknown

Taxilā (Pali, Takkasilā), 47, 79, 160

Thirty-three (Tāva-timsa), next world so called from its council (cf. Sakka). Probably 30, not 33, and often called Ti-dasa (thrice ten). Cf. the 30, p. 35, 38

Ujjeni, 108
Ummadantī (=maddening, intoxicating), a beauty, 160 f.
Uppalavannā, a disciple, 166

Vāsava, name of Sakka, 224
Vessăvănă, governor of the Northern firmament, 7
Vetaranī, hell-river, 228

Vissakamma, Sakka's artificer, 208

Yakkha, a, is often used for any great mysterious person, 233
Yakkhas, probably aborigines, 52, 83, 97, 157, 164
Yama, judge of men arriving in next world, 107, 199

A CATALOG OF SELECTED
DOVER BOOKS
IN ALL FIELDS OF INTEREST

A CATALOG OF SELECTED DOVER
BOOKS IN ALL FIELDS OF INTEREST

CONCERNING THE SPIRITUAL IN ART, Wassily Kandinsky. Pioneering work by father of abstract art. Thoughts on color theory, nature of art. Analysis of earlier masters. 12 illustrations. 80pp. of text. 5⅜ x 8½.   23411-8 Pa. $4.95

ANIMALS: 1,419 Copyright-Free Illustrations of Mammals, Birds, Fish, Insects, etc., Jim Harter (ed.). Clear wood engravings present, in extremely lifelike poses, over 1,000 species of animals. One of the most extensive pictorial sourcebooks of its kind. Captions. Index. 284pp. 9 x 12.   23766-4 Pa. $14.95

CELTIC ART: The Methods of Construction, George Bain. Simple geometric techniques for making Celtic interlacements, spirals, Kells-type initials, animals, humans, etc. Over 500 illustrations. 160pp. 9 x 12. (USO)   22923-8 Pa. $9.95

AN ATLAS OF ANATOMY FOR ARTISTS, Fritz Schider. Most thorough reference work on art anatomy in the world. Hundreds of illustrations, including selections from works by Vesalius, Leonardo, Goya, Ingres, Michelangelo, others. 593 illustrations. 192pp. 7⅛ x 10¼.   20241-0 Pa. $9.95

CELTIC HAND STROKE-BY-STROKE (Irish Half-Uncial from "The Book of Kells"): An Arthur Baker Calligraphy Manual, Arthur Baker. Complete guide to creating each letter of the alphabet in distinctive Celtic manner. Covers hand position, strokes, pens, inks, paper, more. Illustrated. 48pp. 8¼ x 11.   24336-2 Pa. $3.95

EASY ORIGAMI, John Montroll. Charming collection of 32 projects (hat, cup, pelican, piano, swan, many more) specially designed for the novice origami hobbyist. Clearly illustrated easy-to-follow instructions insure that even beginning papercrafters will achieve successful results. 48pp. 8¼ x 11.   27298-2 Pa. $3.50

THE COMPLETE BOOK OF BIRDHOUSE CONSTRUCTION FOR WOODWORKERS, Scott D. Campbell. Detailed instructions, illustrations, tables. Also data on bird habitat and instinct patterns. Bibliography. 3 tables. 63 illustrations in 15 figures. 48pp. 5¼ x 8½.   24407-5 Pa. $2.50

BLOOMINGDALE'S ILLUSTRATED 1886 CATALOG: Fashions, Dry Goods and Housewares, Bloomingdale Brothers. Famed merchants' extremely rare catalog depicting about 1,700 products: clothing, housewares, firearms, dry goods, jewelry, more. Invaluable for dating, identifying vintage items. Also, copyright-free graphics for artists, designers. Co-published with Henry Ford Museum & Greenfield Village. 160pp. 8¼ x 11.   25780-0 Pa. $10.95

HISTORIC COSTUME IN PICTURES, Braun & Schneider. Over 1,450 costumed figures in clearly detailed engravings–from dawn of civilization to end of 19th century. Captions. Many folk costumes. 256pp. 8⅜ x 11¾.   23150-X Pa. $12.95

STICKLEY CRAFTSMAN FURNITURE CATALOGS, Gustav Stickley and L. & J. G. Stickley. Beautiful, functional furniture in two authentic catalogs from 1910. 594 illustrations, including 277 photos, show settles, rockers, armchairs, reclining chairs, bookcases, desks, tables. 183pp. 6½ x 9¼. 23838-5 Pa. $11.95

AMERICAN LOCOMOTIVES IN HISTORIC PHOTOGRAPHS: 1858 to 1949, Ron Ziel (ed.). A rare collection of 126 meticulously detailed official photographs, called "builder portraits," of American locomotives that majestically chronicle the rise of steam locomotive power in America. Introduction. Detailed captions. xi + 129pp. 9 x 12. 27393-8 Pa. $13.95

AMERICA'S LIGHTHOUSES: An Illustrated History, Francis Ross Holland, Jr. Delightfully written, profusely illustrated fact-filled survey of over 200 American lighthouses since 1716. History, anecdotes, technological advances, more. 240pp. 8 x 10¾. 25576-X Pa. $12.95

TOWARDS A NEW ARCHITECTURE, Le Corbusier. Pioneering manifesto by founder of "International School." Technical and aesthetic theories, views of industry, economics, relation of form to function, "mass-production split" and much more. Profusely illustrated. 320pp. 6⅛ x 9¼. (USO) 25023-7 Pa. $9.95

HOW THE OTHER HALF LIVES, Jacob Riis. Famous journalistic record, exposing poverty and degradation of New York slums around 1900, by major social reformer. 100 striking and influential photographs. 233pp. 10 x 7⅞. 22012-5 Pa. $11.95

FRUIT KEY AND TWIG KEY TO TREES AND SHRUBS, William M. Harlow. One of the handiest and most widely used identification aids. Fruit key covers 120 deciduous and evergreen species; twig key 160 deciduous species. Easily used. Over 300 photographs. 126pp. 5⅜ x 8½. 20511-8 Pa. $3.95

COMMON BIRD SONGS, Dr. Donald J. Borror. Songs of 60 most common U.S. birds: robins, sparrows, cardinals, bluejays, finches, more—arranged in order of increasing complexity. Up to 9 variations of songs of each species.
Cassette and manual 99911-4 $8.95

ORCHIDS AS HOUSE PLANTS, Rebecca Tyson Northen. Grow cattleyas and many other kinds of orchids—in a window, in a case, or under artificial light. 63 illustrations. 148pp. 5⅜ x 8½. 23261-1 Pa. $5.95

MONSTER MAZES, Dave Phillips. Masterful mazes at four levels of difficulty. Avoid deadly perils and evil creatures to find magical treasures. Solutions for all 32 exciting illustrated puzzles. 48pp. 8¼ x 11. 26005-4 Pa. $2.95

MOZART'S DON GIOVANNI (DOVER OPERA LIBRETTO SERIES), Wolfgang Amadeus Mozart. Introduced and translated by Ellen H. Bleiler. Standard Italian libretto, with complete English translation. Convenient and thoroughly portable—an ideal companion for reading along with a recording or the performance itself. Introduction. List of characters. Plot summary. 121pp. 5¼ x 8½. 24944-1 Pa. $3.95

TECHNICAL MANUAL AND DICTIONARY OF CLASSICAL BALLET, Gail Grant. Defines, explains, comments on steps, movements, poses and concepts. 15-page pictorial section. Basic book for student, viewer. 127pp. 5⅜ x 8½. 21843-0 Pa. $4.95

BRASS INSTRUMENTS: Their History and Development, Anthony Baines. Authoritative, updated survey of the evolution of trumpets, trombones, bugles, cornets, French horns, tubas and other brass wind instruments. Over 140 illustrations and 48 music examples. Corrected and updated by author. New preface. Bibliography. 320pp. 5⅜ x 8½. 27574-4 Pa. $9.95

HOLLYWOOD GLAMOR PORTRAITS, John Kobal (ed.). 145 photos from 1926-49. Harlow, Gable, Bogart, Bacall; 94 stars in all. Full background on photographers, technical aspects. 160pp. 8⅜ x 11¼. 23352-9 Pa. $12.95

MAX AND MORITZ, Wilhelm Busch. Great humor classic in both German and English. Also 10 other works: "Cat and Mouse," "Plisch and Plumm," etc. 216pp. 5⅜ x 8½. 20181-3 Pa. $6.95

THE RAVEN AND OTHER FAVORITE POEMS, Edgar Allan Poe. Over 40 of the author's most memorable poems: "The Bells," "Ulalume," "Israfel," "To Helen," "The Conqueror Worm," "Eldorado," "Annabel Lee," many more. Alphabetic lists of titles and first lines. 64pp. 5³⁄₁₆ x 8¼. 26685-0 Pa. $1.00

PERSONAL MEMOIRS OF U. S. GRANT, Ulysses Simpson Grant. Intelligent, deeply moving firsthand account of Civil War campaigns, considered by many the finest military memoirs ever written. Includes letters, historic photographs, maps and more. 528pp. 6⅛ x 9¼. 28587-1 Pa. $12.95

AMULETS AND SUPERSTITIONS, E. A. Wallis Budge. Comprehensive discourse on origin, powers of amulets in many ancient cultures: Arab, Persian Babylonian, Assyrian, Egyptian, Gnostic, Hebrew, Phoenician, Syriac, etc. Covers cross, swastika, crucifix, seals, rings, stones, etc. 584pp. 5⅜ x 8½. 23573-4 Pa. $15.95

RUSSIAN STORIES/PYCCKNE PACCKA3bl: A Dual-Language Book, edited by Gleb Struve. Twelve tales by such masters as Chekhov, Tolstoy, Dostoevsky, Pushkin, others. Excellent word-for-word English translations on facing pages, plus teaching and study aids, Russian/English vocabulary, biographical/critical introductions, more. 416pp. 5⅜ x 8½. 26244-8 Pa. $9.95

PHILADELPHIA THEN AND NOW: 60 Sites Photographed in the Past and Present, Kenneth Finkel and Susan Oyama. Rare photographs of City Hall, Logan Square, Independence Hall, Betsy Ross House, other landmarks juxtaposed with contemporary views. Captures changing face of historic city. Introduction. Captions. 128pp. 8¼ x 11. 25790-8 Pa. $9.95

AIA ARCHITECTURAL GUIDE TO NASSAU AND SUFFOLK COUNTIES, LONG ISLAND, The American Institute of Architects, Long Island Chapter, and the Society for the Preservation of Long Island Antiquities. Comprehensive, well-researched and generously illustrated volume brings to life over three centuries of Long Island's great architectural heritage. More than 240 photographs with authoritative, extensively detailed captions. 176pp. 8¼ x 11. 26946-9 Pa. $14.95

NORTH AMERICAN INDIAN LIFE: Customs and Traditions of 23 Tribes, Elsie Clews Parsons (ed.). 27 fictionalized essays by noted anthropologists examine religion, customs, government, additional facets of life among the Winnebago, Crow, Zuni, Eskimo, other tribes. 480pp. 6⅛ x 9¼. 27377-6 Pa. $10.95

FRANK LLOYD WRIGHT'S HOLLYHOCK HOUSE, Donald Hoffmann. Lavishly illustrated, carefully documented study of one of Wright's most controversial residential designs. Over 120 photographs, floor plans, elevations, etc. Detailed perceptive text by noted Wright scholar. Index. 128pp. 9¼ x 10¾. 27133-1 Pa. $11.95

THE MALE AND FEMALE FIGURE IN MOTION: 60 Classic Photographic Sequences, Eadweard Muybridge. 60 true-action photographs of men and women walking, running, climbing, bending, turning, etc., reproduced from rare 19th-century masterpiece. vi + 121pp. 9 x 12. 24745-7 Pa. $10.95

1001 QUESTIONS ANSWERED ABOUT THE SEASHORE, N. J. Berrill and Jacquelyn Berrill. Queries answered about dolphins, sea snails, sponges, starfish, fishes, shore birds, many others. Covers appearance, breeding, growth, feeding, much more. 305pp. 5¼ x 8¼. 23366-9 Pa. $9.95

GUIDE TO OWL WATCHING IN NORTH AMERICA, Donald S. Heintzelman. Superb guide offers complete data and descriptions of 19 species: barn owl, screech owl, snowy owl, many more. Expert coverage of owl-watching equipment, conservation, migrations and invasions, etc. Guide to observing sites. 84 illustrations. xiii + 193pp. 5⅜ x 8½. 27344-X Pa. $8.95

MEDICINAL AND OTHER USES OF NORTH AMERICAN PLANTS: A Historical Survey with Special Reference to the Eastern Indian Tribes, Charlotte Erichsen-Brown. Chronological historical citations document 500 years of usage of plants, trees, shrubs native to eastern Canada, northeastern U.S. Also complete identifying information. 343 illustrations. 544pp. 6½ x 9¼. 25951-X Pa. $12.95

STORYBOOK MAZES, Dave Phillips. 23 stories and mazes on two-page spreads: Wizard of Oz, Treasure Island, Robin Hood, etc. Solutions. 64pp. 8¼ x 11. 23628-5 Pa. $2.95

NEGRO FOLK MUSIC, U.S.A., Harold Courlander. Noted folklorist's scholarly yet readable analysis of rich and varied musical tradition. Includes authentic versions of over 40 folk songs. Valuable bibliography and discography. xi + 324pp. 5⅜ x 8½. 27350-4 Pa. $9.95

MOVIE-STAR PORTRAITS OF THE FORTIES, John Kobal (ed.). 163 glamor, studio photos of 106 stars of the 1940s: Rita Hayworth, Ava Gardner, Marlon Brando, Clark Gable, many more. 176pp. 8⅜ x 11¼. 23546-7 Pa. $14.95

BENCHLEY LOST AND FOUND, Robert Benchley. Finest humor from early 30s, about pet peeves, child psychologists, post office and others. Mostly unavailable elsewhere. 73 illustrations by Peter Arno and others. 183pp. 5⅜ x 8½. 22410-4 Pa. $6.95

YEKL and THE IMPORTED BRIDEGROOM AND OTHER STORIES OF YIDDISH NEW YORK, Abraham Cahan. Film Hester Street based on Yekl (1896). Novel, other stories among first about Jewish immigrants on N.Y.'s East Side. 240pp. 5⅜ x 8½. 22427-9 Pa. $6.95

SELECTED POEMS, Walt Whitman. Generous sampling from *Leaves of Grass*. Twenty-four poems include "I Hear America Singing," "Song of the Open Road," "I Sing the Body Electric," "When Lilacs Last in the Dooryard Bloom'd," "O Captain! My Captain!"–all reprinted from an authoritative edition. Lists of titles and first lines. 128pp. 5$\frac{3}{16}$ x 8¼. 26878-0 Pa. $1.00

THE BEST TALES OF HOFFMANN, E. T. A. Hoffmann. 10 of Hoffmann's most important stories: "Nutcracker and the King of Mice," "The Golden Flowerpot," etc. 458pp. 5⅜ x 8½.   21793-0 Pa. $9.95

FROM FETISH TO GOD IN ANCIENT EGYPT, E. A. Wallis Budge. Rich detailed survey of Egyptian conception of "God" and gods, magic, cult of animals, Osiris, more. Also, superb English translations of hymns and legends. 240 illustrations. 545pp. 5⅜ x 8½.   25803-3 Pa. $13.95

FRENCH STORIES/CONTES FRANÇAIS: A Dual-Language Book, Wallace Fowlie. Ten stories by French masters, Voltaire to Camus: "Micromegas" by Voltaire; "The Atheist's Mass" by Balzac; "Minuet" by de Maupassant; "The Guest" by Camus, six more. Excellent English translations on facing pages. Also French-English vocabulary list, exercises, more. 352pp. 5⅜ x 8½.   26443-2 Pa. $9.95

CHICAGO AT THE TURN OF THE CENTURY IN PHOTOGRAPHS: 122 Historic Views from the Collections of the Chicago Historical Society, Larry A. Viskochil. Rare large-format prints offer detailed views of City Hall, State Street, the Loop, Hull House, Union Station, many other landmarks, circa 1904-1913. Introduction. Captions. Maps. 144pp. 9⅜ x 12¼.   24656-6 Pa. $12.95

OLD BROOKLYN IN EARLY PHOTOGRAPHS, 1865-1929, William Lee Younger. Luna Park, Gravesend race track, construction of Grand Army Plaza, moving of Hotel Brighton, etc. 157 previously unpublished photographs. 165pp. 8⅞ x 11¾.   23587-4 Pa. $13.95

THE MYTHS OF THE NORTH AMERICAN INDIANS, Lewis Spence. Rich anthology of the myths and legends of the Algonquins, Iroquois, Pawnees and Sioux, prefaced by an extensive historical and ethnological commentary. 36 illustrations. 480pp. 5⅜ x 8½.   25967-6 Pa. $10.95

AN ENCYCLOPEDIA OF BATTLES: Accounts of Over 1,560 Battles from 1479 B.C. to the Present, David Eggenberger. Essential details of every major battle in recorded history from the first battle of Megiddo in 1479 B.C. to Grenada in 1984. List of Battle Maps. New Appendix covering the years 1967-1984. Index. 99 illustrations. 544pp. 6½ x 9¼.   24913-1 Pa. $16.95

SAILING ALONE AROUND THE WORLD, Captain Joshua Slocum. First man to sail around the world, alone, in small boat. One of great feats of seamanship told in delightful manner. 67 illustrations. 294pp. 5⅜ x 8½.   20326-3 Pa. $6.95

ANARCHISM AND OTHER ESSAYS, Emma Goldman. Powerful, penetrating, prophetic essays on direct action, role of minorities, prison reform, puritan hypocrisy, violence, etc. 271pp. 5⅜ x 8½.   22484-8 Pa. $7.95

MYTHS OF THE HINDUS AND BUDDHISTS, Ananda K. Coomaraswamy and Sister Nivedita. Great stories of the epics; deeds of Krishna, Shiva, taken from puranas, Vedas, folk tales; etc. 32 illustrations. 400pp. 5⅜ x 8½.   21759-0 Pa. $12.95

BEYOND PSYCHOLOGY, Otto Rank. Fear of death, desire of immortality, nature of sexuality, social organization, creativity, according to Rankian system. 291pp. 5⅜ x 8½.   20485-5 Pa. $8.95

A THEOLOGICO-POLITICAL TREATISE, Benedict Spinoza. Also contains unfinished Political Treatise. Great classic on religious liberty, theory of government on common consent. R. Elwes translation. Total of 421pp. 5⅜ x 8½. 20249-6 Pa. $9.95

MY BONDAGE AND MY FREEDOM, Frederick Douglass. Born a slave, Douglass became outspoken force in antislavery movement. The best of Douglass' autobiographies. Graphic description of slave life. 464pp. 5⅜ x 8½. 22457-0 Pa. $8.95

FOLLOWING THE EQUATOR: A Journey Around the World, Mark Twain. Fascinating humorous account of 1897 voyage to Hawaii, Australia, India, New Zealand, etc. Ironic, bemused reports on peoples, customs, climate, flora and fauna, politics, much more. 197 illustrations. 720pp. 5⅜ x 8½. 26113-1 Pa. $15.95

THE PEOPLE CALLED SHAKERS, Edward D. Andrews. Definitive study of Shakers: origins, beliefs, practices, dances, social organization, furniture and crafts, etc. 33 illustrations. 351pp. 5⅜ x 8½. 21081-2 Pa. $8.95

THE MYTHS OF GREECE AND ROME, H. A. Guerber. A classic of mythology, generously illustrated, long prized for its simple, graphic, accurate retelling of the principal myths of Greece and Rome, and for its commentary on their origins and significance. With 64 illustrations by Michelangelo, Raphael, Titian, Rubens, Canova, Bernini and others. 480pp. 5⅜ x 8½. 27584-1 Pa. $9.95

PSYCHOLOGY OF MUSIC, Carl E. Seashore. Classic work discusses music as a medium from psychological viewpoint. Clear treatment of physical acoustics, auditory apparatus, sound perception, development of musical skills, nature of musical feeling, host of other topics. 88 figures. 408pp. 5⅜ x 8½. 21851-1 Pa. $11.95

THE PHILOSOPHY OF HISTORY, Georg W. Hegel. Great classic of Western thought develops concept that history is not chance but rational process, the evolution of freedom. 457pp. 5⅜ x 8½. 20112-0 Pa. $9.95

THE BOOK OF TEA, Kakuzo Okakura. Minor classic of the Orient: entertaining, charming explanation, interpretation of traditional Japanese culture in terms of tea ceremony. 94pp. 5⅜ x 8½. 20070-1 Pa. $3.95

LIFE IN ANCIENT EGYPT, Adolf Erman. Fullest, most thorough, detailed older account with much not in more recent books, domestic life, religion, magic, medicine, commerce, much more. Many illustrations reproduce tomb paintings, carvings, hieroglyphs, etc. 597pp. 5⅜ x 8½. 22632-8 Pa. $12.95

SUNDIALS, Their Theory and Construction, Albert Waugh. Far and away the best, most thorough coverage of ideas, mathematics concerned, types, construction, adjusting anywhere. Simple, nontechnical treatment allows even children to build several of these dials. Over 100 illustrations. 230pp. 5⅜ x 8½. 22947-5 Pa. $8.95

DYNAMICS OF FLUIDS IN POROUS MEDIA, Jacob Bear. For advanced students of ground water hydrology, soil mechanics and physics, drainage and irrigation engineering, and more. 335 illustrations. Exercises, with answers. 784pp. 6⅛ x 9¼. 65675-6 Pa. $19.95

SONGS OF EXPERIENCE: Facsimile Reproduction with 26 Plates in Full Color, William Blake. 26 full-color plates from a rare 1826 edition. Includes "TheTyger," "London," "Holy Thursday," and other poems. Printed text of poems. 48pp. 5¼ x 7. 24636-1 Pa. $4.95

OLD-TIME VIGNETTES IN FULL COLOR, Carol Belanger Grafton (ed.). Over 390 charming, often sentimental illustrations, selected from archives of Victorian graphics–pretty women posing, children playing, food, flowers, kittens and puppies, smiling cherubs, birds and butterflies, much more. All copyright-free. 48pp. 9¼ x 12¼. 27269-9 Pa. $7.95

PIANO TUNING, J. Cree Fischer. Clearest, best book for beginner, amateur. Simple repairs, raising dropped notes, tuning by easy method of flattened fifths. No previous skills needed. 4 illustrations. 201pp. 5⅜ x 8½. 23267-0 Pa. $6.95

A SOURCE BOOK IN THEATRICAL HISTORY, A. M. Nagler. Contemporary observers on acting, directing, make-up, costuming, stage props, machinery, scene design, from Ancient Greece to Chekhov. 611pp. 5⅜ x 8½. 20515-0 Pa. $12.95

THE COMPLETE NONSENSE OF EDWARD LEAR, Edward Lear. All nonsense limericks, zany alphabets, Owl and Pussycat, songs, nonsense botany, etc., illustrated by Lear. Total of 320pp. 5⅜ x 8½. (USO) 20167-8 Pa. $7.95

VICTORIAN PARLOUR POETRY: An Annotated Anthology, Michael R. Turner. 117 gems by Longfellow, Tennyson, Browning, many lesser-known poets. "The Village Blacksmith," "Curfew Must Not Ring Tonight," "Only a Baby Small," dozens more, often difficult to find elsewhere. Index of poets, titles, first lines. xxiii + 325pp. 5⅜ x 8¼. 27044-0 Pa. $8.95

DUBLINERS, James Joyce. Fifteen stories offer vivid, tightly focused observations of the lives of Dublin's poorer classes. At least one, "The Dead," is considered a masterpiece. Reprinted complete and unabridged from standard edition. 160pp. 5³⁄₁₆ x 8¼. 26870-5 Pa. $1.00

THE HAUNTED MONASTERY and THE CHINESE MAZE MURDERS, Robert van Gulik. Two full novels by van Gulik, set in 7th-century China, continue adventures of Judge Dee and his companions. An evil Taoist monastery, seemingly supernatural events; overgrown topiary maze hides strange crimes. 27 illustrations. 328pp. 5⅜ x 8½. 23502-5 Pa. $8.95

THE BOOK OF THE SACRED MAGIC OF ABRAMELIN THE MAGE, translated by S. MacGregor Mathers. Medieval manuscript of ceremonial magic. Basic document in Aleister Crowley, Golden Dawn groups. 268pp. 5⅜ x 8½. 23211-5 Pa. $9.95

NEW RUSSIAN-ENGLISH AND ENGLISH-RUSSIAN DICTIONARY, M. A. O'Brien. This is a remarkably handy Russian dictionary, containing a surprising amount of information, including over 70,000 entries. 366pp. 4½ x 6⅛. 20208-9 Pa. $10.95

HISTORIC HOMES OF THE AMERICAN PRESIDENTS, Second, Revised Edition, Irvin Haas. A traveler's guide to American Presidential homes, most open to the public, depicting and describing homes occupied by every American President from George Washington to George Bush. With visiting hours, admission charges, travel routes. 175 photographs. Index. 160pp. 8¼ x 11. 26751-2 Pa. $11.95

NEW YORK IN THE FORTIES, Andreas Feininger. 162 brilliant photographs by the well-known photographer, formerly with *Life* magazine. Commuters, shoppers, Times Square at night, much else from city at its peak. Captions by John von Hartz. 181pp. 9¼ x 10¾. 23585-8 Pa. $13.95

INDIAN SIGN LANGUAGE, William Tomkins. Over 525 signs developed by Sioux and other tribes. Written instructions and diagrams. Also 290 pictographs. 111pp. 6⅛ x 9¼. 22029-X Pa. $3.95

ANATOMY: A Complete Guide for Artists, Joseph Sheppard. A master of figure drawing shows artists how to render human anatomy convincingly. Over 460 illustrations. 224pp. 8⅜ x 11¼. 27279-6 Pa. $11.95

MEDIEVAL CALLIGRAPHY: Its History and Technique, Marc Drogin. Spirited history, comprehensive instruction manual covers 13 styles (ca. 4th century thru 15th). Excellent photographs; directions for duplicating medieval techniques with modern tools. 224pp. 8⅜ x 11¼. 26142-5 Pa. $12.95

DRIED FLOWERS: How to Prepare Them, Sarah Whitlock and Martha Rankin. Complete instructions on how to use silica gel, meal and borax, perlite aggregate, sand and borax, glycerine and water to create attractive permanent flower arrangements. 12 illustrations. 32pp. 5⅜ x 8½. 21802-3 Pa. $1.00

EASY-TO-MAKE BIRD FEEDERS FOR WOODWORKERS, Scott D. Campbell. Detailed, simple-to-use guide for designing, constructing, caring for and using feeders. Text, illustrations for 12 classic and contemporary designs. 96pp. 5⅜ x 8½. 25847-5 Pa. $3.95

SCOTTISH WONDER TALES FROM MYTH AND LEGEND, Donald A. Mackenzie. 16 lively tales tell of giants rumbling down mountainsides, of a magic wand that turns stone pillars into warriors, of gods and goddesses, evil hags, powerful forces and more. 240pp. 5⅜ x 8½. 29677-6 Pa. $6.95

THE HISTORY OF UNDERCLOTHES, C. Willett Cunnington and Phyllis Cunnington. Fascinating, well-documented survey covering six centuries of English undergarments, enhanced with over 100 illustrations: 12th-century laced-up bodice, footed long drawers (1795), 19th-century bustles, 19th-century corsets for men, Victorian "bust improvers," much more. 272pp. 5⅜ x 8¼. 27124-2 Pa. $9.95

ARTS AND CRAFTS FURNITURE: The Complete Brooks Catalog of 1912, Brooks Manufacturing Co. Photos and detailed descriptions of more than 150 now very collectible furniture designs from the Arts and Crafts movement depict davenports, settees, buffets, desks, tables, chairs, bedsteads, dressers and more, all built of solid, quarter-sawed oak. Invaluable for students and enthusiasts of antiques, Americana and the decorative arts. 80pp. 6½ x 9¼. 27471-3 Pa. $8.95

HOW WE INVENTED THE AIRPLANE: An Illustrated History, Orville Wright. Fascinating firsthand account covers early experiments, construction of planes and motors, first flights, much more. Introduction and commentary by Fred C. Kelly. 76 photographs. 96pp. 8¼ x 11. 25662-6 Pa. $8.95

THE ARTS OF THE SAILOR: Knotting, Splicing and Ropework, Hervey Garrett Smith. Indispensable shipboard reference covers tools, basic knots and useful hitches; handsewing and canvas work, more. Over 100 illustrations. Delightful reading for sea lovers. 256pp. 5⅜ x 8½. 26440-8 Pa. $8.95

FRANK LLOYD WRIGHT'S FALLINGWATER: The House and Its History, Second, Revised Edition, Donald Hoffmann. A total revision—both in text and illustrations—of the standard document on Fallingwater, the boldest, most personal architectural statement of Wright's mature years, updated with valuable new material from the recently opened Frank Lloyd Wright Archives. "Fascinating"–*The New York Times.* 116 illustrations. 128pp. 9¼ x 10¾. 27430-6 Pa. $12.95

AUTOBIOGRAPHY: The Story of My Experiments with Truth, Mohandas K. Gandhi. Boyhood, legal studies, purification, the growth of the Satyagraha (nonviolent protest) movement. Critical, inspiring work of the man responsible for the freedom of India. 480pp. 5⅜ x 8½. (USO) 24593-4 Pa. $8.95

CELTIC MYTHS AND LEGENDS, T. W. Rolleston. Masterful retelling of Irish and Welsh stories and tales. Cuchulain, King Arthur, Deirdre, the Grail, many more. First paperback edition. 58 full-page illustrations. 512pp. 5⅜ x 8½. 26507-2 Pa. $9.95

THE PRINCIPLES OF PSYCHOLOGY, William James. Famous long course complete, unabridged. Stream of thought, time perception, memory, experimental methods; great work decades ahead of its time. 94 figures. 1,391pp. 5⅜ x 8½. 2-vol. set.
Vol. I: 20381-6 Pa. $13.95
Vol. II: 20382-4 Pa. $14.95

THE WORLD AS WILL AND REPRESENTATION, Arthur Schopenhauer. Definitive English translation of Schopenhauer's life work, correcting more than 1,000 errors, omissions in earlier translations. Translated by E. F. J. Payne. Total of 1,269pp. 5⅜ x 8½. 2-vol. set.
Vol. 1: 21761-2 Pa. $12.95
Vol. 2: 21762-0 Pa. $12.95

MAGIC AND MYSTERY IN TIBET, Madame Alexandra David-Neel. Experiences among lamas, magicians, sages, sorcerers, Bonpa wizards. A true psychic discovery. 32 illustrations. 321pp. 5⅜ x 8½. (USO) 22682-4 Pa. $9.95

THE EGYPTIAN BOOK OF THE DEAD, E. A. Wallis Budge. Complete reproduction of Ani's papyrus, finest ever found. Full hieroglyphic text, interlinear transliteration, word-for-word translation, smooth translation. 533pp. 6½ x 9¼.
21866-X Pa. $11.95

MATHEMATICS FOR THE NONMATHEMATICIAN, Morris Kline. Detailed, college-level treatment of mathematics in cultural and historical context, with numerous exercises. Recommended Reading Lists. Tables. Numerous figures. 641pp. 5⅜ x 8½.
24823-2 Pa. $11.95

THEORY OF WING SECTIONS: Including a Summary of Airfoil Data, Ira H. Abbott and A. E. von Doenhoff. Concise compilation of subsonic aerodynamic characteristics of NACA wing sections, plus description of theory. 350pp. of tables. 693pp. 5⅜ x 8½. 60586-8 Pa. $14.95

THE RIME OF THE ANCIENT MARINER, Gustave Doré, S. T. Coleridge. Doré's finest work; 34 plates capture moods, subtleties of poem. Flawless full-size reproductions printed on facing pages with authoritative text of poem. "Beautiful. Simply beautiful."–*Publisher's Weekly.* 77pp. 9¼ x 12. 22305-1 Pa. $7.95

NORTH AMERICAN INDIAN DESIGNS FOR ARTISTS AND CRAFTSPEOPLE, Eva Wilson. Over 360 authentic copyright-free designs adapted from Navajo blankets, Hopi pottery, Sioux buffalo hides, more. Geometrics, symbolic figures, plant and animal motifs, etc. 128pp. 8⅜ x 11. (EUK) 25341-4 Pa. $8.95

SCULPTURE: Principles and Practice, Louis Slobodkin. Step-by-step approach to clay, plaster, metals, stone; classical and modern. 253 drawings, photos. 255pp. 8⅛ x 11. 22960-2 Pa. $11.95

THE INFLUENCE OF SEA POWER UPON HISTORY, 1660–1783, A. T. Mahan. Influential classic of naval history and tactics still used as text in war colleges. First paperback edition. 4 maps. 24 battle plans. 640pp. 5⅜ x 8½. 25509-3 Pa. $14.95

THE STORY OF THE TITANIC AS TOLD BY ITS SURVIVORS, Jack Winocour (ed.). What it was really like. Panic, despair, shocking inefficiency, and a little heroism. More thrilling than any fictional account. 26 illustrations. 320pp. 5⅜ x 8½. 20610-6 Pa. $8.95

FAIRY AND FOLK TALES OF THE IRISH PEASANTRY, William Butler Yeats (ed.). Treasury of 64 tales from the twilight world of Celtic myth and legend: "The Soul Cages," "The Kildare Pooka," "King O'Toole and his Goose," many more. Introduction and Notes by W. B. Yeats. 352pp. 5⅜ x 8½. 26941-8 Pa. $8.95

BUDDHIST MAHAYANA TEXTS, E. B. Cowell and Others (eds.). Superb, accurate translations of basic documents in Mahayana Buddhism, highly important in history of religions. The Buddha-karita of Asvaghosha, Larger Sukhavativyuha, more. 448pp. 5⅜ x 8½. 25552-2 Pa. $12.95

ONE TWO THREE . . . INFINITY: Facts and Speculations of Science, George Gamow. Great physicist's fascinating, readable overview of contemporary science: number theory, relativity, fourth dimension, entropy, genes, atomic structure, much more. 128 illustrations. Index. 352pp. 5⅜ x 8½. 25664-2 Pa. $8.95

ENGINEERING IN HISTORY, Richard Shelton Kirby, et al. Broad, nontechnical survey of history's major technological advances: birth of Greek science, industrial revolution, electricity and applied science, 20th-century automation, much more. 181 illustrations. ". . . excellent . . ."–*Isis.* Bibliography. vii + 530pp. 5⅜ x 8¼. 26412-2 Pa. $14.95

DALÍ ON MODERN ART: The Cuckolds of Antiquated Modern Art, Salvador Dalí. Influential painter skewers modern art and its practitioners. Outrageous evaluations of Picasso, Cézanne, Turner, more. 15 renderings of paintings discussed. 44 calligraphic decorations by Dalí. 96pp. 5⅜ x 8½. (USO) 29220-7 Pa. $4.95

ANTIQUE PLAYING CARDS: A Pictorial History, Henry René D'Allemagne. Over 900 elaborate, decorative images from rare playing cards (14th–20th centuries): Bacchus, death, dancing dogs, hunting scenes, royal coats of arms, players cheating, much more. 96pp. 9¼ x 12¼. 29265-7 Pa. $12.95

MAKING FURNITURE MASTERPIECES: 30 Projects with Measured Drawings, Franklin H. Gottshall. Step-by-step instructions, illustrations for constructing handsome, useful pieces, among them a Sheraton desk, Chippendale chair, Spanish desk, Queen Anne table and a William and Mary dressing mirror. 224pp. 8⅛ x 11¼. 29338-6 Pa. $13.95

THE FOSSIL BOOK: A Record of Prehistoric Life, Patricia V. Rich et al. Profusely illustrated definitive guide covers everything from single-celled organisms and dinosaurs to birds and mammals and the interplay between climate and man. Over 1,500 illustrations. 760pp. 7½ x 10⅛. 29371-8 Pa. $29.95

Prices subject to change without notice.

Available at your book dealer or write for free catalog to Dept. GI, Dover Publications, Inc., 31 East 2nd St., Mineola, N.Y. 11501. Dover publishes more than 500 books each year on science, elementary and advanced mathematics, biology, music, art, literary history, social sciences and other areas.